The INSIDER'S GUIDE to Buying a New or Used Car

3RD EDITION

BURKE LEON *and* STEPHANIE LEON

BETTERWAY BOOKS
CINCINNATI, OHIO

04   03   02   01   00   5   4   3   2   1

Library of Congress Cataloging-in-Publication Data

Leon, Burke
   The insider's guide to buying a new or used car / by Burke Leon and Stephanie Leon.—3rd ed.
      p.   cm.
   Includes index.
   ISBN 1-55870-566-X (alk. paper)
      1. Automobiles—Purchasing. 2. Consumer education. I. Leon, Stephanie, 1941-II. Title

   TL162.L46   2000
   629.222'029'7—dc21   00-034308
                                                                            CIP

Edited by Don Prues and Meg Leder

The Insider's Guide to Buying a New or Used Car, 3rd Edition

Dedication

As our readers will find out, I (Burke) am the technical guru behind this book. Even though I know what to say, I need a lot of help in writing and organizing the material. My beautiful wife, Stephanie, is not an auto expert, but she knows how to take my thoughts and translate them into prose. Stephanie, once again, thanks for coming to my rescue for this third edition.

About the Authors

Burke Leon, a chemist by training, is actively engaged in the auto business and owns and operates BL Auto Enterprises in Fullerton California. Stephanie Leon is an English major, a special education teacher and the literary force behind this book. Burke and Stephanie live in Placentia, California and have three children: Jeff, Andrew and Steven.

Not Only Do You Get a Great Book, But You Get the Author, Too!

One of the nice things about buying this book is that you can talk with Burke Leon about your auto problems and experiences. When he is not writing books, Burke owns and operates BL Auto Enterprises, a unique California dealership in North Orange County, California, just east of Los Angeles. Burke buys and sells nearly new cars from dealers only auctions.

Readers living nearby can call and talk to him about the process. It is an adventure. Readers from more distant parts of the known universe such as Oregon, Washington, Texas, Oklahoma or even New Mexico can fly into Southern California and drive home in a great used car bought to their specifications (or maybe even participate in a buy).

If you live anywhere in the U.S.A. and want advice about new- or used-car buying, Burke will answer your questions free of charge if you are not too demanding. Even if you are a pain, he will answer your questions if you ship him a sample of some great local gastronomic delicacy. If he misses your call, he will try to call back *collect*.

Burke can be reached at

(714) 996-9955,

blauto@earthlink.net,

P.O. Box 483
Placentia, CA 92871-0483,

or

www.usedcarphd.com.

Table of Contents

Introduction: How This Book Was Born

The single question I'm asked most often is, "How did a nice, honest professional like you get into a grubby business like this?" While I have had a lifelong interest in games and human psychology and have developed an interest in the art of negotiation, I did not spend my life preparing to be an auto dealer, an auto salesman or a consumer auto expert.

I went to high school in a small town in upstate New York and breezed through college with a B.S. in chemistry, a M.S. in inorganic chemistry and eventually a Ph.D. in physical chemistry. My Ph.D. thesis was entitled "Magnetic Coupling and Phase Boundaries for Some C15 and C22 'Pseudo Binary' Alloys Containing Lanthanides."

When I was in school, I took one of the most difficult curricula available: calculus, physics, chemistry, etc. No basket weaving for me. Yet outside the classroom I had to give a 150 percent effort to achieve the most sought-after prizes that some of my "slippery" classmates achieved effortlessly. Somehow, things came more easily to them. They could talk their way into things I had to work hard for and still couldn't get. Even more important, they could talk their way out of things with equal ease. If one of them asked me for favors, I would almost always oblige. About the only things at which I could beat them (other than intellectual pursuits) were games for money, such as poker and bridge, that I really knew how to play.

It was later in life when I realized that, highly trained in our specialties as we might be, many intellectuals are grossly untrained in dealing with people and in negotiating situations—skills that can reap enormous monetary paybacks. We simply aren't trained to negotiate; in fact, we are trained NOT to negotiate (I will write more on this later). One of the advantages of being a reasonably well-paid scientific professional during the field's heyday was that I didn't have to worry about my finances. I could ignore that lower-level technicians were making hundreds or thousands of dollars on the side by buying, rehabbing and selling cars in their spare time. I was a scientist, not a technician—a big social and economic difference. I could just pay sticker price (get taken, that is) when buying a new car, and it didn't hurt my pocketbook too badly.

My interest in knowing how to negotiate for cars began when the company I worked for in New York went under. I hung around Huntington Station, Long Island, for a couple of months before I realized the job market wasn't going to recover anytime in the foreseeable future. So I called on some old friends and landed in Orange County, California, during its economic boom. I knew I was going to have to buy a new car once I moved there, and frankly, I still had bad vibes from my previous purchases. Now that money was a problem for me, I realized I had to be smarter when buying a car. So I went to my local bookstore, bought every book ever written on how to buy a car and read them all from cover-to-cover, taking notes the entire time. At the end of the reading sessions, I said to myself, "So that's how they do it" and "So that's what I did wrong" and "Boy, was I dumb." I decided that never again would I be out of control in a car-buying situation—never—and that car dealers would never trick me again. I knew then that I would get my "revenge" when I bought my car. Here's what I did.

My First Revenge

Picture the scene: I went to California first and was waiting for my wife to sell our home in New York. My company car allowance was about to run out, and now was the time to get a new car. I had to act quickly. At first, I didn't know what I wanted, but I finally narrowed my choices to a Ford Taurus and a Dodge Lancer. I liked the Taurus; my wife liked the Lancer. Guess who won? The conversation at the dealership went something like this:

> **Salesperson:** Why don't you just buy the Lancer?
> **Me:** I don't know if my wife would like it. She hasn't seen it.
> **Salesperson (insinuates):** Be a man. Make up your mind and just do it.
> **Me:** I really want some input from my wife.
> **Salesperson:** So why don't you call her and get her input?

So I did. I made a twenty-minute long-distance call from Orange

County, California, to Huntington Station, New York, for my wife's input—on the dealership's bill. Eventually I bought the Lancer, and we loved it.

The buy took place on the last day of the month, a Sunday, after a rainy holiday weekend. The negotiation started in a nearly empty showroom at 9:00 P.M.—one hour before closing—and ended at 1:00 A.M. with no one shaking my hand or telling me what a good deal I got. Sixty seconds after I drove out of the dealership with my new car, the place was deserted. The staff was tired and couldn't wait to get away.

During the course of the negotiation, the salesman switched from talking about price to payments to leasing to value to asking me "Don't we have to make a profit?" I brought a co-worker whose only job was to get in the way—and he did. The dealership sales staff (at the end, there were four people trying to wrap it up) couldn't figure out what he was doing there or how to handle me. By repeating "I really want to buy a car tonight" and "Why won't you let me buy a car tonight?" I kept them interested when it looked as if we had reached a deadlock.

I started off negotiating for a bare-bones Dodge Lancer and eventually got what I wanted: a year-old, brand-new, fully loaded Lancer ES with only twenty-five original miles and a very, very small dent in the fender. The price also dropped from an asked $15,200 to $9,995 with a special low-interest package. Ten days later, the dealer tried to force me to pay a higher interest rate by saying the bank wouldn't approve me. I told them to take back the car, and, amazingly, the bank approved me.

How I Became a Used Car Maven and Why I Wrote This Book

It wasn't easy to negotiate the first time, but I did it—and did it well. I did it so well that when others in my company heard about it, they asked me to negotiate for their new cars. Each time I bought cars for other people, I got better at it, and it's now a part of my business.

I found that it was not enough just to tell people how to buy a car. Soon I was organizing my thoughts, writing down my techniques and eventually teaching courses on the subject. As of this writing, I have taught over one hundred courses on "How to Buy a Car" and "How to Negotiate" at five different colleges. I have also appeared as a guest expert on television. After my television appearance, I started thinking about what all experts envision themselves doing: writing a book—so I did.

Most of the books written on how to buy a car deal primarily with buying new cars. The few people who do write about buying used cars never seem to have been substantially involved in the used-car business; they invariably are in some ancillary function of the new-car business. I, however, have been buying and selling used cars every week for the past ten years, and this book contains the techniques I use—and the techniques you will soon be using—during every stage of the car-buying process. You might dream of driving to a dealership in your old car, tossing the keys to a salesperson, pointing to a fully loaded dream car, paying the asking price with a roll of hundreds and driving out fifteen minutes later with all the paperwork done. Unfortunately, that happens only in your dreams. This book arms you with the "insider" information you need when you're under the pressure of buying a car in the real world.

New Information on Using the Internet to Buy and Sell Cars

I have always taken a good deal of pride in the first and second editions of *The Insider's Guide to Buying a New or Used Car*—I felt both were well written, informative and up-to-date. Imagine my surprise when I discovered Amazon.com customers gave my books a four-star (out of a possible five-star) rating. A reader from Bowie, Maryland, said the book was flawed because I wasn't Internet savvy, and he was right.

When I wrote the second edition, I didn't have Internet access and the impact of the Internet on buying cars was miniscule. My spell checker didn't even have the word *Internet* in its dictionary. No one had any indication that the Internet would have such a major effect on the auto industry in just three short years. Though E-commerce has blossomed in many fields, it has dramatically affected the way cars are bought and sold. This edition reflects these significant changes, providing Web site addresses of the best Internet sources for buying and selling cars. However, despite the Internet's impact and other recent changes in automobile marketing, the steps you must take to buy and sell a car remain largely unchanged. The Internet can make these steps easier (especially the research step), but it doesn't eliminate your need to possess strong planning, strategizing and negotiation skills when buying your car. Please note that Web sites come and go. Every effort has been made to confirm that the Internet information is current at the time of publication.

A Quick Note on the Organization of This Book

In the first two sections of the book, you'll find the steps you can take before the visit to the dealership and steps to take while you're there to ensure you'll get the best price on your purchase. Section three presents special advice and strategies that apply specifically to buying and selling a used car, and in the last section, you'll find additional buying tips, including a new section on buying cars over the Internet.

Setting the Stage for the Car-Buying Process

CHAPTER 1

What Type of Car Buyer Are You?

Before you try to determine what type of car you're going to buy, you should first figure out what type of car buyer you are. Fortunately for you, lots of research has been done by the auto industry on consumer habits and customer "types." One such marketing and information research firm is J.D. Power and Associates, which since 1968 has received numerous kudos from consumers and retailers alike. The firm publishes market reports, predicts trends and analyzes its research, all of which help determine what auto makers will do in the future.

Now you can access this wealth of information at the J.D. Power and Associates Web site (http://www.jdpower.com). It's a good place for you to visit if you're not yet sure what type of consumer you are, because it will prompt you to examine your car-buying self. Below, for example, is a summary of a June 24, 1999, report that delineates car buyers and classifies them into four groups, or "types."

1. Armed Unfriendlies
The youngest and most educated of the four groups, these car buyers are "a relatively antagonistic group of shoppers." Such folks perceive themselves as "precise and systematic, well equipped with information and ready to do battle with sales personnel."

2. Relationship Seekers
Power and Associates deems these buyers as "outgoing and loyal to brands and dealerships." They also approach shopping for a vehicle with enthusiasm and tend to look at the process as a rewarding challenge, not just a chore."

3. Low-Involved Pragmatists

If you fall into this category, you are "private and reserved." You are also rather indifferent when it comes to finding the ideal car at the ideal price. You view car buying as a laborious waste of time.

4. Highly Involved Deal Seekers

Car dealers don't like this type of buyer. Power says that 73 percent of those in this group are young men who gather lots of information and do not hesitate to shop around. Such consumers "consider themselves to be strong willed and direct."

So ... where do you fall? Really think about this, because before you can formulate a plan for buying a car, you must know which car-buying category you fit into. (I, for instance, know I'm a Highly Involved Deal Seeker with a little bit of Armed Unfriendly in my soul.) Why is realizing what type of buyer you are important? Because once you know the type of buyer you are, you are also likely to guess what type of buyer the dealer perceives you to be (dealers quickly put a tag on each customer who walks in the door). The more you know what the dealer thinks, the better off you'll be. Now let's explore a few more peculiarities of car-buying that'll give you an edge when purchasing a new or used car.

Car-Selling Rationale

As I get older, the philosophy behind car buying and selling—and the game-playing that goes along with it—intrigues me more and more. Most consumers, especially first-time buyers, often feel so overwhelmed by the complexity of the car-buying process, they simply throw up their hands and follow the suggestions of the salesperson. Not a good idea. Although dealers profess to make car buying simple, the system actually is engineered to make purchasing a car confusing, painful and protracted for you (the buyer), and profitable for the car company. By confusing you, tempting you and wearing you out, the system (and thus a dealer) hopes to extract the maximum amount of money from you. Dealers make buying a car complex so they will get more face-to-face time with you, and thus more time to convince you to buy the car—before you leave the lot. Salespeople are forced into this hard-sell mode.

During the transaction numerous items must be decided upon, and steps are mandated by consumer agencies to ensure the buyer gets a fair deal. However, you have to remember the most important part of the transaction for dealers is to make money. Therefore, assisting you with making critical car-buying decisions is not too high on the dealer's list of priorities (well, at least not as high as maximizing profits at each step of the transaction). You must be aware that dealers know and use lots of seductive—and undisclosed—strategies to add to their profits at the moment of the sale. Remember that buying a car is unlike purchasing most retail items, in which there is a marked price and only tax can be added. Be on guard, because the cost of your new purchase can keep escalating and escalating if you're not careful. Adequate planning is your best protection against paying for more than you bargained for.

Be Prepared to Spend a Lot of Time Shopping For Your Car

Although the dealer does intentionally make buying a car time-consuming for you, there are four other reasons purchasing a car these days takes such a long time:

1. The number of models has proliferated over the years. Today over five hundred makes and models exist for the consumer, and most buyers initially don't know what type of vehicles and features they need or want. Because the buyer is so undecided about the car, model, accessories, etc., sifting through all the available information and evaluating the options takes time.

2. Both salesperson and customer are determined to take whatever time and trouble are necessary to get what they individually want. The salesperson can wait the customer out, eventually putting the buyer in a car she will like and pay for. The customer will wait and wait to get the best price, always wondering if she could get a better deal elsewhere.

3. Getting financing is not always easy. Working out the details of financing can be very time-consuming, especially if the buyer doesn't have good credit, or if a cosigner is involved. Calculating the

amount of down payments, monthly payments, cash back, interest, etc., takes time even under the best circumstances.

4. Paperwork, paperwork, paperwork. In addition to figuring out financing, you'll spend a lot of time sifting through all the paperwork and legal matters. The dealer should explain—and you should understand—all (or most) legalities. This can be quite time-consuming and frustrating, especially when some of the legalities are unrelated to car buying. In California, for instance, the selling dealer has to take the buyer's drivers license number and enter it at registration time so the state can detect delinquent parents with outstanding child-support payments. Sometimes such data might also be used to catch those who don't report all their income. (If you report you made only $10,000, how can you buy a $30,000 car?)

If all the above sounds like a pain, well . . . it can be. One positive aspect of this you should keep in mind, however, is that neither the buyer nor the dealer feels happy about a car deal unless it takes a good long time to negotiate. If the deal goes through too fast, it will seem hurried and unsatisfactory for both parties. The customer may suffer more buyer's remorse from a quick sale than if she negotiated for days (even if the fast sale got her a better deal than the longer one ever could have). Likewise, the salesperson might regret he didn't "work the customer" a little harder to make the sale more lucrative.

Three Successful Steps to Buying a Car

Assuming you now know what type of car buyer you are, let's consider what you should do when you're ready to actively start looking and buying.

Step One: Research the Market

A determined "armed and dangerous" consumer can be much more informed than any one person in a dealership. If you think about it, who precisely in a dealership is actually an expert on all facets of the vehicles they sell? The repair force probably has an adequate knowledge of auto mechanics but has limited knowledge about prices, packages and availability. The dealership business office knows about Division of Motor Vehicles (DMV) work and other paperwork functions. The used-car sales force knows little about the new-car inventory. The new-car salespeople, many of whom are "green," know more about their previous occupations and may know about cars only what they have been told by someone else who may not know much. Probably the general manager or the owner is the closest to being a solid in-house generalist with an overview of most facets of the automobile business.

Fortunately, because you are buying a car in the information age, you are now privy to formerly protected information, thanks mostly to the Internet (more about the pluses and minuses of using the Internet later). Yes, you can cheaply, readily and routinely tap into Web sites to find out the status of your potential car. One Web site I recommend if you are in the market for a used car is Carfax at http://www.carfax.com, which lists a car's "lemon law" status, its actual recorded mileage, its salvage title status and other important information. Right now, Carfax has a free lemon law-checker, and the cost of the complete service is reasonable. (Nice job, Carfax!) Despite whether you're looking for a new or used car, the rule of thumb before you progress to step two is that you have finished researching when you "know what is a good deal."

Step Two: Find the Car You Want at the Price You Want

After doing enough research to know what is a good deal, you need to get to your goal of buying the car you want at a price you think is fair. If you're really new to car buying and don't have much confidence in yourself or your research, you might actually want to hire someone to get you access to used cars that you can't have access to yourself, such as those at dealers-only auctions. If you've done a good deal of research but don't know what to do with it, you might need someone to tell you how to utilize the knowledge you have gained. You also might want to read a "how to buy a car" book written, hopefully, by someone who has had the life experience and developed the street smarts to show you how to get the best results. (Good job—you're already reading this one!) Many consumers with lots of facts but no real understanding of how to use their knowledge unfortunately allow themselves to blunder through a buying situation without a plan. This is the way it was done in the 1950s, 60s, 70s and even later when there was no easy access to information. You learned at the dealership under pressure from a sales maestro. Not so anymore, as we'll see in the next chapter.

Step Three: Accomplish What You Have Researched

As a former New Yorker, I think the word that best describes this is *chutzpah*, a Yiddish word that basically means to have courage. Many buyers (Relationship Seekers and Low-Involved Pragmatists) find it painful to make the leap from researching a car to actually going to the dealer to get the best deal on it. These nice people just do not like confrontation (or even the prospect of confrontation). "How do I find the courage to fight off these tough sales guys time after time and not get beaten down into giving up all I have researched?" such buyers ask themselves. If this is you, at this point you either need a "champion" to help you along (an assertive, knowledgeable friend or dealer), which is what I do for people who buy cars through me, or you need to develop enough inner strength to stand up to a pushy salesperson and get the deal you want.

Current Trends in Auto Shopping

Today, many new marketing innovations are being touted as ways of making the car-buying process better, easier and "friendlier for consumers." While I don't always agree with such innovations, I do think you need to know the current trends in the auto industry and how they might affect your car-buying decisions.

Large Auto Malls

One new trend is the large auto malls dotting California, the state that traditionally has led the way in trends and fads. These huge auto malls feature competing dealerships, sometimes as many as two dozen, sharing one huge area, usually adjacent to a freeway. This is the wave of the future for California and may also be so for some other parts of the country. I don't envision this happening in sparsely populated areas. The economics of car buying seem to dictate this kind of coalescing. The psychology behind it is similar to that of neighborhoods and districts in all large cities that feature clusters of businesses, such as a jewelry section, an antique section or a furniture area.

No-Dicker Stickers

This was supposed to be the wave of the future with people coming in, picking out a car using a computer (nonconfrontational) and then buying a car with no haggling. In California, the biggest dealership, which had at least eight different franchises, did this and they recently went out of business. AutoNation USA, a superstore in the used car arena, recently pulled the rip cord on its no-dicker used cars.

The no-dicker sticker works only for Saturn because Saturns are in high demand, there are not enough of them and they have a great reputation. As soon as General Motors (GM) makes too many Saturns, as they do Oldsmobiles, Buicks, etc., the price of Saturns will become negotiable. In reality though, Saturns are sold "no dicker" because they are being sold at full retail price, a concept that horrifies me. You can only sell at full retail if the supply is limited and there is high demand. I predict it will never spread to other dealerships.

Large Department Store Chains Selling New and Used Cars

I see in the papers and the auto dealers' trade magazines that you will have nontraditional dealers selling new cars like they sell toasters or electronic equipment. This I would like to see. These "hardware stores" (Circuit City Stores, Inc., is one name that is bandied about) will still have to deal with trade-ins (and who really knows what they are worth?), financing, insurance and all the things that make buying a new car or a nearly new car a chore. And to you, my readers, don't you believe you can't fight for a great deal with a clerk from Kmart (or whoever else gets into this business) as well as with a veteran salesperson or sales manager? Of course you can. Fear these things not; they will not be much different from what is going on right now.

Large Superstores of Nearly New Cars

Just recently I saw in *Used Car Week* the following headline: "New-Car Dealers Rush to Build Glitzy Showrooms for Used Cars." The magazine indicates that some groups of investors are going into the used-car business in a big way. They are planning to set up superstores of nearly new (up to five years old) used cars with literally hundreds and hundreds of cars. This is nothing new, but the scale of it might be interesting. These dealerships are threatening to sell more cars at less profit per car, to have better and more salespeople and friendly management and, in general, to make car buying more attractive. Once again, I don't see anything unusual here, except that the financing through these types of dealerships will be remote and unforgiving if you have to miss a payment or if something goes wrong with the vehicle.

One question to ask at these superstores is, "What percent of your cars are repossessed in the first six months after sale?" My gut feeling is that these and the current nationally advertised used-car lots have a high rate of repossession (my unofficial sources indicate it may exceed 50 percent) and that they make their money by buying and reselling these cars again and again. Be aware of this.

The Continued Increase of Leasing

Leasing came on with a bang not too long ago and now accounts for a large portion of the retail market. I expect it to peak and to remain a viable and useful tool to get a new car. The only thing that will change this trend is if federal tax laws change, making it less advantageous to lease cars.

Now, if you want to look at getting a new car or a great used car, or if you want to sell your used car yourself, read the following chapters and see how it's done. It is easy, exhilarating and profitable. Even if you don't think you want a used car, I strongly suggest you consider a low-mileage used car for the right price and from the right sources.

"Highly Certified" Used Cars

The quality of modern cars is much better than cars of fifteen years ago. Car buyers want quality used cars these days and are often willing to pay a relatively higher "used-car price" for them. If you have the money and think the money's worth spending, you might consider this option. "Highly certified" used cars are those that receive a seal of approval after a certified mechanic, usually at a dealership, performs an extensive examination of the car to ensure everything is in good condition. The only problem, as mentioned, is that dealerships charge exorbitant prices for this certification. From my experience, though, "armed and dangerous" buyers who can afford nice cars are willing to pay to have a car certified. They think it's worth their money to have their car gone over with a fine-tooth comb. One good place to find highly certified used cars is at dealers-only auctions. Bank and franchise lines (which have a reputation for selling nice, quality cars) get absolutely top wholesale dollar for their vehicles at such auctions. Again, if the price is right, this might be a good idea for you.

Online Inventories for Retail Used-Car Buyers

This concept makes good sense and might be a used-car-buying norm in the next few years. The process sounds simple: A retail customer can tap into a huge multi-state inventory, read all about a vehicle, try to see it (on the screen) and eventually buy it. The trouble here is twofold: (1) There's the no-dicker problem (no negotiating and no face-to-face retail dealing once you find the car); (2) Each vehicle is unique and you should be able to test drive the car you want to buy, not just look at it on a screen.

Live Internet Auctions for Dealers Only

An Internet auction is one fun way to buy a car. I bring up dealers-only auctions here because if an idea is good enough on the wholesale level, it may reach the retail level a few years later. Electronic auctions like eBay (http://www.ebay.com) are the rage now, with all sorts of items for bid, including cars. I don't think it is too far-fetched to predict we will have live online auctions open to the general public in the next few years. However, it is my observation that currently cars don't sell well on eBay.

The first interactive live online auction was held in May 1999.

Just to let you know how important dealers-only online auctions are to me, I've been participating in one every week (and I buy cars through them every week) since that first auction. The bidding is fast; sometimes an average of two cars a minute (yes, that is right, over one hundred cars an hour) get sold. Not surprisingly, the pace requires a high degree of concentration. One problem that has occurred, however, is that online dealers seem to be getting beaten to a bid by the live dealers (those who are actually present at the deal site). If experienced dealers are having trouble buying cars in a live Internet auction, I suspect the average buyer is really going to find it difficult. My prediction is that this live online auction trend will continue to work wholesale but probably won't work so well for retail buyers trying to buy into a dealer's auction. We'll see.

✦✦✦

As you probably expect, the Internet is having a major impact on the way autos are bought and sold in both wholesale and retail markets. Unfortunately, there are limits to what the Internet can and cannot do for you, all of which we'll cover in the next chapter. What's most important is knowing you're accessing accurate information from the best sites for you. Often, the Web site you need may not be among the top ones pulled up by a search engine. You might have to try other search engines and dig a bit on your own. The manipulation of commercial directories such as HotBot or Yahoo in order to gain a favorably high placement is a key element in advertising jockeying. Businesses have been doing this for years in traditional directories like the yellow pages (lots of A or AA or AAA business names, so they can come first in the phone listings). Just remember that although shopping for cars on the Web is a new and useful trend, anybody can set up a Web site on the Internet and buy and sell cars. So know you're dealing with a reputable company.

CHAPTER 2

What the Internet Can and Can't Do for You When Buying a Car

The Internet strongly increases your strength as a buyer, providing you with the means to acquire lots of information before you meet face-to-face with a car salesperson. It does not give any advantages to the seller. My job in this chapter is not to provide a list of Web addresses but to tell you how the Internet can and cannot help you buy a car. Since the Internet is in a constant state of flux with Web sites appearing and disappearing daily, it doesn't make sense for this book to include an extensive list of transient Web sites. Magazines, newspapers, electronic literature and even advertising do a much better job recording these changes. That said, I will integrate what I think are noteworthy and credible Web sites (they're useful now and should continue to be great assets in the future). But the list of sites I refer to is short and by no means comprehensive.

What the Internet Offers You
The Privilege to Conduct Your Own Research at Your Own Pace
One of the major advantages to using the Internet is that you can research lots of material on your own, digesting it at a speed and in a quantity comfortable for you. You can access loads of information about cars—from raw data to predigested data to interpretations of data by experts—all at your own pace. The Internet allows you to do this easily (and abundantly). I can't emphasize enough how working at your own pace and not feeling pressure to buy are privileges you should absolutely embrace. Most of us need time to absorb the

material, evaluate the options and discuss buying possibilities with spouses, family and friends. The Internet finally allows us to do this, 'bout time.

Think about it: Historically, buyers could collect information only while at the dealership, on a test drive or "casually" talking to a salesperson. Thus the buyer's knowledge was at the mercy of the dealer's willingness to dispense accurate information at the rate he wanted to dispense it. Buyers had to absorb a lot fast. Add to this the close proximity of the salesperson (and his eagerness to make a sale), and it's easy to see that this was not a relaxed process. Talk about pressure! Now, however, the Internet allows you to make a well-informed decision, when you want to make it. Be grateful and use it to your advantage.

Now let's take a look at some important information the Internet offers to help you get the deal you want.

Data for You to Work and Play With

Some Web sites are merely brochures; others are splendid resources with loads of useful material. The "brochure sites" simply wave the company flag, offer phone, fax and E-mail information, and try to impress you with a graphic display. Such sites don't offer much research information and don't allow you to do anything other than look at the Web site. Unfortunately, many auto sites are still "brochure sites," but competition and technological improvements will likely push such sites to be more interactive and useful in the future.

The best sites are interactive playgrounds containing lots of valuable data. Such sites allow you to put together packages for your potential car, check list prices for it, figure out your own financing rate, inquire about leasing and generally control many if not all of the components of a complete car transaction. You might even see your vehicle in some sort of a streaming video and be able to check all the functions associated with an educated purchase (crash test data, fuel economy and other pertinent information). The GM Web site (http://www.gmbuypower.com), for example, is both useful and fun for conducting research, sporting many of the above features.

(Most manufacturers are loading their sites with such attributes; GM is just one fine example.) If consumers show a dealer they like to buy from a Web site, no doubt dealer sites will soon make it possible for you to avoid going to a dealership altogether (except to pick up the car and maybe they'll eventually deliver!). One caveat about buying a car through Web sites: you are not likely to get a good or better deal than when visiting a dealership, because Web pricing seems to be no dicker, which is a real no-no for me (see the no-dicker section in chapter one). Another drawback right now is that most sites conveniently ignore how to handle your trade-in.

Bulletin Boards and News Groups

Bulletin boards and news groups are cyber meeting places for small communities of like-minded people. Many of the big auto sites have bulletin boards; Edmunds even calls theirs the "town hall." Essentially, bulletin boards and news groups are personal postings (not corporate ad space) where people exchange ideas. Anyone can read and post a message, and older messages are replaced by newer messages so the discussion is always fresh and current. A lot of helpful advice is given to those who ask questions. Bulletin boards are also good for obtaining hard-to-find information, and they're an equally popular place for complaining about a manufacturer, dealership, law or any other car-related problem. (In fact, there was an interesting extortion case involving one manufacturer in 1999, in which an unhappy car owner threatened to post a lot of negative comments on bulletin boards if the manufacturer did not compensate him for his grievances.)

Good bulletin boards are those like alt.auto.mercedes or alt.autos .ford (if you want information on a Mercedes or Ford, respectively). The best way to find a bulletin board for the type of car you're looking for is to simply type into your search engine *alt.auto.***** or *alt.autos.***** with **** being the name of the car you're interested in. You should have no problem finding helpful pointers and information about that car. Typical discussion topics might be "Do you really know your 1997 Mazda?" or "Why did Toyota go to digital odometers?"

Dealer's Cost for New Cars

Obtaining a dealer's cost for a new car and its accessories is one of the best tools for knowing if you're getting a good deal. Thanks to the Web, such information is readily available. Two particularly great resources for locating dealer's cost are Edmunds (http://www.edmunds.com) and AutoTrader (http://www.autotrader.com), which recently merged with AutoConnect.

Inventories

You can check inventories on the Internet. Wearing my other hat as a dealer who sells used cars and trucks, knowing what is available at the dealers-only auctions in terms of inventories is crucial. Inventories are not as important for new cars as they are for used cars. This is because an unsold new car in Alabama is identical to that same unsold new car in Oregon. The two cars are owned by the same manufacturer and in the same condition and thus are essentially interchangeable.

For used cars, the situation is different. A used car in New York is not interchangeable with a similar used car in California. Used cars are never similar. Then there is the transportation cost to consider. Equal transportation costs are built into the cost structure of all new cars. There is no transportation component in used-car pricing—somebody's got to pay for it. The trend now is for used-car dealerships to put their entire inventory on the Net, either on their own Web site or in "cyber" car lots, and hope to pull in customers this way. It is a nice idea, but you don't know about the car's condition.

Dealer's Cost for Used Cars

Unfortunately the Internet can't do as much for you in terms of dealer's cost if you want to buy a used car. The problem is that determining the worth of a used car is difficult, even for dealers, because of the relative condition of used cars. Unlike new cars, in which there's a great deal of consistency regarding the condition of each car, no two used cars are alike. A new car typically has a fixed cost anywhere in the U.S., and it has no wear-and-tear problems, no mileage, no history, no accident and repair record, no missed oil change, etc. Used cars have these liabilities, and each set of problems for each car is different because each car has a unique history.

Complicating matters more is that even the dealer (who is an alleged expert) has a difficult time knowing and setting a reasonable price. Some online dealers, of course, can adjust a fixed base price from the *Kelley Blue Book Auto Market Report* (often called simply "the *Blue Book*"), but the *Blue Book* is only a guide of what things have sold for in the past and may sell for in the future (based on mathematical algorithms). Cars can sell for more or less than *Blue Book* wholesale. Moreover, not all dealers use the *Blue Book*. Some evaluate cars with the National Automobile Drivers Association (NADA) handbook and still others use the *National Auto Research Black Book Official Residual Value Guide for New and Used Vehicles in Percentage and Dollar Format* used car market guide.

One final problem is that it's very difficult to know what a dealer paid for a particular used car. There just aren't any reliable sources available to the retail customer that contain specific information about used-car transactions. There's good news, however, if you want to sell your car to a used-car dealer. Some dealers have "orders" (requests) for vehicles from customers who ask for a certain car. If you go to the dealer fortuitously trying to sell a clean, close fit to one of those sought-after cars, you just might get more money than you had hoped for (or than you could get from a typical dealership).

Most dealers who specialize in wholesale transactions usually try to buy a vehicle below the local dealers-only auction price, so they can get a "quick turn" of the vehicle for a fast profit. They would love to get an in-demand vehicle for as low as the *Blue Book* consumer edition "trade-in price." Most used-car professionals use a combination of a dealers-only auction market reports and the *Blue Book* to determine the price of a used car.

New Car Quality Reviews

Lots of sites, including GM's http://www.gmbuypower.com and J.D. Power and Associates' http://www.jdpower.com, offer performance reviews and statistical defect analyses of new cars. For recent defects reported by consumers and credible professional tests, my online

starting point would be *Consumer Reports* (http://www.consumerrepo
rts.org). Its quality product reviews of how new models are likely to
behave in their first ninety days of retail life are very useful. However,
cars this new are still well within the original bumper-to-bumper
factory warranty period and will be repaired free by the franchise
dealership. A good site for performance reviews of new cars is *Road
& Track* magazine (http://www.roadandtrack.com).

Used-Car Quality Reviews

Ascertaining reviews of used cars can be found online but relying on
them is pretty risky. One problem is that when buying an older used
car you usually don't get any repair history on a specific vehicle.
Because you're only offered reviews of the general make and model,
trying to assess the individual quality of a car over the Internet can
be fruitless. In addition, problems reported in the past could now be
fixed, making the review useless.

Look at the following scenario to get an idea of how finding
general reviews of older cars can be helpful but also problematic.
Suppose *Consumer Reports* indicates a certain year and model of car
has had persistent problems with the air conditioning system. That's
good to know, but what's your next step? It will probably be more
trouble than it's worth to find out if there was a recall on the car
or if the previous owner actually replaced the troublesome AC
compressor two years ago. I think it makes a lot more sense to base
your used-car buying at least partially on a mechanics inspection of
an individual car rather than on a review of a whole class of cars. My
recommendation is to use the reviews but use them judiciously, and
make your assessment based on the particular car you are considering.

Ownership Costs for New and Used Vehicles

Several organizations publish online the expected ownership costs for
vehicles. Potential expenses for gas, repairs, depreciation, insurance
and interest are all there for the surfing. Three good sites to start with
are J.D. Power and Associates, AutoTrader (http://www.autotrader
.com) and Intellichoice CarCenter (http://www.intellichoice.com).
Finding such information will likely scare you (it scares me!), especially

when you see how much we spend on cars over the long haul. When you visit these sites, notice how much of the spending is for depreciation, interest on the loan and insurance and then compare those numbers to the actual worth of the vehicle. You'll be shocked.

Crash History Reports

Twenty years ago the big three auto companies (General Motors, Ford and Chrysler) would not even talk about safety because they were certain it would adversely impact sales. Now people avoid some makes and models because the passenger-side crash test results were not good enough. Virtually any of the big auto-related Web sites can put you in touch with government crash test results. Safety data is certainly important. I would start with consumer advocate Ralph Nader and his Center for Auto Safety (http://www.autosafety.org). Not surprisingly, bigger and heavier cars are typically safer.

Rebates and Incentives

Lots of sites offer worthwhile rebates and incentives. You can't really go wrong if you're saving money, right? For the most part yes, but be sure you know in advance if the manufacturer gives you money directly (factory-to-consumer cash) or if the manufacturer gives the dealer money (factory-to-dealer cash). The one site I recommend for beginning your savings search is Intellichoice CarCenter (http://www.intellichoice.com). Other good sites are Edmunds (http://www.edmunds.com), AutoSite (http://www.autosite.com) and AutoAdvice (http://www.autoadvice.com).

Venues for Selling Your Car

The best way I know to sell your trade-in through the Internet is to post it on a bulletin board or somebody's used-car cyberlot. The problems of showing the vehicle, getting the price you expect and handling the paperwork still remain (unless you authorize someone else to do it). For fun (and maybe for some money!) you might try auctioning off your vehicle through eBay (http://www.ebay.com) or other electronic auction sites. From what I have seen, however, cars don't do especially well on these sites because they are such high-priced items. A fine car trading site for you to post your vehicle is AutoTrader (http://www.autotrader.com).

Auto Brokers Who Will Help You Buy a Car

A broker could be described as someone who sells something he doesn't have. A real estate broker helps you sell your house; an auto broker helps you find new cars to buy. There are plenty of auto brokers on the Web just itching to do business with you. (I just casually went to one reputable search engine and received 721 hits for the phrase "auto broker.") Most auto broker sites seem to be little more than sophisticated electronic brochures. Know that all brokers want you to know what you want before you go to them. This is how it works: You tell them what you want; they won't tell you what is best.

A few warnings: Most brokers want to handle only new cars (it's a lot easier and cleaner than dealing with used cars) and they won't hold your hand through the entire car-buying process. They will get you price quotes, have a selected dealer call you and then let you handle the rest of the deal alone. Of course, they won't let you off the hook until they collect a fee for their part of the deal (getting prices and having a dealer call you). So if you're buying a new car and considering using the services of a broker, think twice, because a broker can't get you any car or deal you can't find yourself. A broker is just one more person you have to pay, but if you don't have much patience or time for research, the expense could be worth it.

If you want to use a broker, I'd start at Autobytel, http://www.autobyt el.com, which is the most famous online broker. The site will give you quotes and also refers you to a network of dealers. Other Web sites specializing in brokering new cars are AutoSmart (http://www.autosmart.com), Online Auto (http://www.onlineauto.com) and AutoWeb (http://autoweb.com).

Used-Car Cyberlots

A cyberlot is an online place to buy, sell or gather information. It is the equivalent of a newspaper ad listing cars for sale in a dealership.

Not so long ago, there was not even a term for a Web-posted electronic inventory of cars; now cyberlots are all we hear about on the wholesale level. In a cyberlot, the listing party may own some or none of the vehicles and may or may not get a fee for the sale of these vehicles. There are no posting fees because the posting costs are covered by the advertisers. The cyberlot manager may just run the computer and list the vehicles for sale and have the cyberlot connected to search engines. The listing party (the person running the Web site) is probably not responsible for the sale or condition of the vehicle. It is an E-auto mall.

AutoTrader (http://www.autotrader.com), which is fueled by Manheim Auctions (the largest owner of dealers-only auctions in the country), posts on its Web site the vehicles sold weekly at dealers-only auctions. (I post mine there after I buy them at the auctions and so do a lot of other dealers. Don't assume all "for sale by private parties" are not dealers, and don't assume all cars are really available.) AutoConnect has merged with AutoTrader. Dealers who buy at a Manheim dealers-only site get a free cyberlot ad for their car.

Questions to be answered before you buy that cyberlot car:

- Are all the cars on the lot really for sale? Some cyberlots have huge numbers of cars on their site but not all of them can be purchased.
- How dated are the lists?
- Are the cars accessible in your neck of the woods? How far away are they? Will you be able to see and test drive?
- Is the car you want still available? Don't be surprised if the car you find at a cyberlot is already gone.
- Can you view the cars before buying?
- If the vehicles are for retail sale, does the cyberlot also offer retail prices and guarantees?

In some cases cyberlot listings are a bonus offered by dealers-only auctions to the wholesale auction buyers of the cars, regardless of whether the vehicles are for sale or have already been sold. For the wholesale buyer the listing is, at worst, a free ad that might snag a customer looking for a car that's already sold. It is then just a small step for the cyberlot to get the customer another car just like the one he's looking for. Also note that the inventory in cyberlots may not even be real, and if a customer calls up and wants information, he may be told "the car has just been sold but we can get you another one tomorrow."

Cyberlots are challenging to the retail buyer because of the difficulty in calculating what any used car is worth or what shape it is in. Location is another concern. Is the travelling expense of picking up the car worth purchasing it? One benefit of used car cyberlots is that they give you a distance counter so you can set the maximum distance you will go for this car. Cyberlots also can give you a fix on retail pricing.

While cyberlots may not significantly impact people in metropolitan areas, they will open the auto world to people in rural areas. Here's an example of how: Let's say a luxury car buyer living in the middle of sparsely populated Eastern Oregon wants a four- or five-year-old Infiniti. He can't find that car anywhere near him, but he does find it for a great price at a cyberlot. One problem is that the actual car is in Los Angeles. Well, this buyer might be willing to fly down to Southern California to look at a few Q45s. After all, he can get a one-way plane ticket to Los Angeles for about $100 and drive the car back home (gas won't cost that much). In the above scenario, it's definitely a good deal to use a cyberlot. Again, it's up to you, your needs and your geographical location.

Some auctions (like Manheim) put dealers' cars on their cyberlot for free after they are purchased at auction. Such cars can be found on AutoTrader at http://www.autotrader.com, a really fantastic site. Three other good cyberlots to start with are Manheim Online at http://www.manheim.com, AutoSmart at http://www.autosmart .com and AutoMallUSA at http://www.automallusa.com.

What the Internet Can't Do For You

The Internet obviously offers you many benefits, especially access to a wealth of information. But there are some aspects of car buying the Internet cannot help you with. Let's take a look at them.

It Can't Provide a Hands-On Evaluation of the Car

Unless you live close to the seller, you will not be able to check out and test-drive a car you find on the Internet. This is a problem. Sensory perceptions are important to people, and you are likely no exception. How will you know if the color of the actual car matches the color of the car displayed on your computer screen? How will you know if the car drives well? How will you know the car doesn't leak oil? Other points to consider are these: If you are exceptionally tall or short or heavy, you must figure out if you're comfortable in the car. You also have to think about who else will drive the car and whether it's suitable for them. Will your wife have any trouble opening the rear doors of that Suburban? Will she easily be able to take out the removable seats on a minivan?

It Won't Get You a Great Deal on Your Trade-In

The Internet can't help you get the best deal for your trade-in. How can dealers pay a good price for something they haven't seen? If you have bought a new car before getting rid of your trade-in, your allegiance to the trade-in might drop so much that you will be tempted to give it away just to get it over with. For the type of person who hates negotiation, the pressure to just give away that old trade-in you don't want will be very high. The thought of selling it yourself will be repulsive. This doesn't happen if you do the trade-in first, before the new car buy, because then you still know in your heart that your used car is sufficient to carry you for a while. The trade-in section of this book will give you a strategy for handling this part of the car buy.

It Can't Negotiate for You

If you are one of those nice people who get pressured by hard unyielding salespeople, you may go into a dealership to finalize a deal you thought was etched in stone only to find it being renegotiated. Therefore knowing something about the art of and necessity for negotiation, what works and in what circumstances, is still a necessary part of car purchasing and should not be avoided by the savvy consumer interested in getting the best deal. The Internet can help you prepare for buying a car from your local dealer, but it can't do it for you.

It Can't Give You Dealer Costs for Used Cars

As a used-car retail buyer, you can't get into the dealers-only online inventories. Sorry, but you'll need a certified dealer to help you tap into the huge wholesale market. Remember that the difference between new and used cars is there is no wholesale new-car market. Most used cars that hit the wholesale market come from two sources: lease returns and trade-ins. Wouldn't it be great to find out what the price of a Ford Motor Credit Corp. lease return really is? Or how much a trade-in is worth? Or wouldn't you like to buy a used car, before it hits the retail market, at those low dealer prices you have heard about?

Well, you could go into business, advertise to buy cars and then buy your own trade-ins (but then you would be one of those dealers you have always feared). Or you could tap into a dealer who takes people like you to dealers-only auctions and gets cars where the dealers get them. You get the dealers-only price plus you pay a small mark-up for your dealer friend. If the dealer gives you advice, is honorable and doesn't press you too hard, this is a very desirable way to get a quality used car.

✦✦✦

The Internet can give you lots of tools and resources to get the information you need. But the Internet cannot tell you how to best utilize all that information; nor can it make decisions for you. You still have to choose between buying options and make tough, smart decisions to get the most bang for your buck.

Web Sites of Interest

Check out these sites to get started:

http://www.aaa.com. The American Automobile Association (AAA) auto club has a good general site for members (not so good for the general public) that offers financing, insurance and more.

http://www.autoadvice.com/aaguide/negotiate.html. AutoAdvice has sound auto advice about negotiating.

http://www.autobuyingonline.com. Auto Buying Online features some auto negotiating information. Also has a section called "For Sale," by an auto expert who will give you pointers.

http://www.autotrader.com. AutoTrader is the place for car classifieds on the Web. If you want to buy, sell or trade cars, this is where to go.

http://www.carinfo.com. CarInfo features car information provided by consumer advocate and auto expert Mark Eskeldson, author of *What Car Dealers Don't Want You to Know*.

http://www.consumer.checkbook.org/auto/cb-advice.htm. Robert Krughoff's article on the Consumer's Checkbook site has some interesting advice on negotiating.

http://www.edmunds.com. One of the premier sites on the Net, Edmunds is a great place to start looking for just about anything car-related.

http://infoseek.go.com. The Go Network site has some reasonably good access to negotiating and basic car-buying stuff.

http://www.jdpower.com. The J.D. Power and Associates Web site is a great generalized car Web site.

http://www.kbb.com. The Kelley *Blue Book* site is a place where most people go to price their cars for sale or to see what a used car should cost. A good site but these numbers are not what dealers use.

http://www.zbths.k12.il.us/projects/sherwood-wehle/usedcar.html. This site has an interesting Web tutorial that leads you step by step through an evaluation of what a car costs to run, how much it will cost to maintain and other interesting facts.

CHAPTER 3

Who Has the Advantage?

In past editions of the book, I indicated that a well-informed, well-trained consumer could generally do well buying a car even though it initially seemed that all the cards were in the hands of the dealership. My position has moved further in that direction. With the computer revolution making access to information easy, an informed buyer has an even stronger edge. That edge is even more pronounced for new-car buyers than used-car buyers, because a lot more information is available for new-car purchases. But even if you don't have a computer, you can still have the advantage.

The Car Dealer's Advantages

Let's look at the advantages that both sellers and buyers have and then decide how to use the system to give you, the buyer, the edge:

The Salesperson is the Expert in the Field

Traditionally the salesperson is the expert in the field. He does, after all, know the product line, the economy for selling, options, prices and the other numerous relevant details. Times are changing, though, with the salesperson having less of an advantage because a lot of Internet savvy, research-oriented buyers are becoming more knowledgeable before buying a car. This is the age of the informed consumer.

You Are on the Salesperson's Turf

It is common knowledge that dogs are tougher and meaner on their home turf and become more hesitant and passive when on someone else's property. People have similar tendencies. This means that you, the customer, will tend to defer to the salesperson's pushy personality more in his salesroom than you would if you were in your living room. I can't imagine that you would allow yourself to be yelled at and intimidated on your own porch the way you will allow yourself to be in a car showroom.

The Salesperson Sells Every Day

He understands people because he practices on customers every day. He knows what it takes to bring together a reluctant buyer and a dream car. He is well practiced at making a car transaction happen. You, on the other hand, are there on a one-time buy faced with the decision of spending a major part of your disposable income. You probably haven't prepared and may just be starting your car-buying process. The salesperson can spot all these disadvantages and discover what it is that will make you commit to a new car. He is naturally attuned to discovering these things, and his further sales training on how to sell you a car more efficiently will work in his favor.

The Salesperson Has the Personality for High-Pressure Sales

A good salesperson is not a shrinking violet. A car salesperson is a smooth, aggressive person who can force or defuse a confrontation. In many cases, he can impose his will on a customer. He is drawn to sales in part by the strength of his personality. As a rule, he has a much stronger personality than the general population.

You Probably Need a Car Right Now

This means that you have an immediate need that only the car dealer can meet. If you wait until the last minute, when your car is breaking down, to go out and buy a new car, you will lose a lot of your bargaining power. It is tough to fight hard for a good price for your trade-in when it isn't running. It is hard to threaten to walk out of a showroom if your car won't start. In my experience, the average person will buy within two weeks once he starts seriously looking.

The Dealer Is Focused and Decisive

Even if he really needs a car, the average person is torn by a lot of questions: Should I buy a new car? Can I really afford it? Should I fix up my old clunker and make do? The salesperson is single-minded. He wants to sell this person a car today at the maximum profit. He is not wishy-washy. He has his goals laid out for him and knows what he has to do to achieve these goals.

The Salesperson Has Reserve Troops

If he can't sell you a car because of a personality clash or another problem, there are other salespeople who can and will. If he needs other help, he has closers and general managers to convince you, to wear you out or to supply other information. He also has literature, displays, and of course, the car with which you are in love.

Dealers Created the System

The salespeople know the system and how it works. As a consequence of setting up the present car-buying system, the car-selling industry works efficiently to separate you from the maximum amount of your money. This system must be efficient because all the car companies use essentially the same system.

The Salesperson's Authority Is Limited; Yours Is Binding

This is a great tactic used extensively by many great negotiating powers. No matter what you, the customer, say, you are held to your word. Yet, no matter what the salesperson says, he is not held to anything because he has to check with his boss. If you change your mind or back away, you are openly challenged and called a wimp or a dishonest individual. If he backs away from a promise, it is because his big, bad, mean boss won't let him earn an honest living for his wife and seventeen children. (If you want to have fun, ask your salesperson if he has the authority to agree to a price. Don't let up on him until he answers. Most salespeople are trained not to answer that question.)

The Car Buyer's Advantages

I know it sounds as if all the advantages belong to the dealer, but there are some great advantages for you. In fact, the advantages are so strong (as we'll soon see) that car sellers have had to devise a whole system to help them come out ahead. But you can beat the system by making the most of the advantages outlined below.

You Pick the Time and Place

You can pick the time and place to buy a car. While the salesperson is stuck waiting in his showroom, you can go to any dealer you want, anytime you want. This means you can buy a car when it is convenient for you, when you are well rested and when the time is right for buying. These are important factors in an auto negotiation.

Obviously, only you can determine these first two items. But I can tell you definitively the best time for buying a car: one to two hours prior to the dealership's closing time. The best days are those near the end of the month, during bad economic times or during a rainy weekend. If you can combine all of these, your timing is perfect. This is the key time to buy since it gives you a few hours to test-drive the car you want, inspect the car and have your trade-in appraised before you get down to serious negotiations. Salespeople, like other people, like to get home early. In the middle of the day, they will sit and wait and negotiate until you give in. The later you keep the sales staff after hours, the more they want to finish the sale quickly.

Buying a car at the end of the month or the end of the quarter adds even more of an advantage. All dealers are rated by their monthly volumes. At the end of the month, they are more willing to give way on price to get one more sale. Slow economic times, Christmas week and other national holidays are also times when car sellers are more anxious to make a deal and will bend more under pressure. Therefore, your advantage in buying a car is to buy it when the sellers are tired, distracted or in need of a sale. They can't pick a time to sell a car, but you can pick a time to buy a car. This is a big edge—don't underestimate it.

You Can Walk Out

You can walk out at any time; the seller can't. As long as you stay there and argue and negotiate, the salesperson must also stay. He can't walk out and leave you alone in the middle of the showroom, but you can get mad at any point and walk out, and he is powerless to stop you. You can always walk out in the middle of a negotiation and force the salesperson to run out to the parking lot to try to coax you to continue the dialogue. Saying that you will leave if the salesperson doesn't get serious is a threat he can't match. The ultimate test of how far you can go is to see if the sales force actually tries to prevent you from going. You can leave a negotiation and come back the next day and open the dialogue again; they can't. If the salesperson is being confrontational or pushy, your implied threat of leaving is often enough to control his outrageous behavior and to force him to make his best bid quickly, before you disappear. You have the power to initiate selling and to terminate it; the salesperson can't do either. This is another big edge.

It's Your Money

You are the customer. It is your money. The salesperson is trained to respect the customer as king, and is limited to acting in a certain way and to following a "script." You can talk or act pretty well the way you want, and the salesperson has to put up with it. You can make ridiculous statements, change your mind and get away with it because you are the customer and it's your money. You can directly remind the sales staff of this point. Say, "I am the customer, and it is my money." You have a right to spend your money as you wish, when you wish. You are in charge of the money, and they have to defer to you if they have any hope of getting it.

Your Power Grows With Time Spent

As the negotiations progress, the dealer's position gets weaker and your position gets stronger. I know that most people feel that as the negotiations progress and proceed towards completion, their position weakens. This is just not true. In the early stages of a negotiation, if you walk out, the salesperson has not wasted much time on you and won't regret your leaving very much. But as he puts in time and effort and the negotiations progress, he will become more concerned about losing a probable sale. At that point, he may have even told his boss that, "The sale is in the bag." His job or ranking in the company may hinge on just a few more sales, so he doesn't want to fail after investing so much time.

The finance person is in an even more difficult position. After a car has been sold, if the sale falls through in finance, he has to answer not only to the general manager, but to the salesperson, who was already banking on the sale, as well.

Always remember that a car buyer's power increases right up to the point where she puts her signature on the contract, and then it immediately decreases. This means that the longer you keep a salesperson tied up negotiating and dealing with you, the better deal you can drive (since he has invested more time in the selling of this vehicle). So take your time, don't rush, keep him overtime, deal toward the end of the month, pick weak economic times and rainy weekends and believe that as the negotiations progress and he gets more interested your power increases.

Your position is weakest when you first walk in and the salesperson has not yet qualified you as a real honest-to-goodness customer. As you talk and convince him that you are a real prospect, your value to him increases. Therefore, your power to demand and command increases. After all, he doesn't want to lose a potential sale. As you agree on items like trade-in price, new-car price, etc., you become a probable sale and, therefore, even more valuable. By this time, the sales staff will probably be treating you with kid gloves.

Deadlock is an important negotiating situation in which you and the salesperson can't reach an agreement. You can deliberately create a deadlock and resolve it later if you wish. You can give it up for a concession of his later, or you can allow the deadlock not to be broken and just walk out. Don't fear a lack of agreement on all points. It is not a sign of weakness or lack of skill. It is actually the opposite. Deadlocks are especially useful if the salesman has classified you as a real buying prospect. In that case, he will bend over backward to reach an agreement and break the deadlock.

You become the strongest just as you have agreed on everything and are about to sign. But your negotiating position immediately plummets once you sign (it's difficult and awkward to try to demand anything more after you have agreed to a contract and signed on the dotted line).

Never worry about losing control as the negotiation proceeds; you don't get weaker, you get stronger. The benefit of getting stronger is that you do not have to take abuse or give back benefits. Further into the negotiations, you become even stronger and can demand more or can make sure that what was promised to you is delivered. Consider what a salesperson will have to explain to his boss if he is kept two hours overtime to close a sale and the sale falls through at the last minute. Even worse, what will the finance and insurance (F&I) person say to the salesperson and manager if, after everyone has been kept overtime for two hours, the F&I person loses the sale?

You Can Be Armed and Dangerous

An information-collecting car buyer who researches his potential buys, knows what he wants, and has his financing in order has the edge over the auto industry. Such a consumer is "armed and dangerous," and hopefully you are one such person. If not, I'll tell you how you can become one in the next few paragraphs.

Your greatest asset to becoming armed and dangerous is conducting exhaustive research. Thank goodness for the Internet, which offers you the opportunity to acquire superior knowledge and analyze nationwide buying opportunities before you actually step foot in a dealership. You can easily become more knowledgeable than the salesperson.

Think of it from a strategic point of view. If you are armed and dangerous, you will have all you need to make a good choice. So before going to the dealership be sure you do the following:

- Research all the car sites on the Web.
- Become conversant with all the available options.
- Take care of your financing.
- Price your trade-in (know you're getting enough for it).
- Learn the dealership costs.
- Determine whether the car might be "hot."
- Approach a few Internet brokers to see what they can offer you (see chapter two).
- Contact (either over the phone or via E-mail) multiple sellers across the nation and tell each one you are in the market for a new vehicle today. See what prices they give you. (One warning

about contacting a seller over the phone or through E-mail:
You may find some dealerships will not deal with you unless
you visit the dealership in person. The problem is that the sales
force will not believe you're a "real buyer" and will doubt they
can land a sale from a hit-and-run voice over the phone.)

You'll know you've finished your research and have become armed
and dangerous when you can answer this simple question: "What is
a good deal for the car I want to buy?"

Once you know what a good deal is, you need to convince a dealer
that you're a real buyer with resources (which you'll have since you
just did all that research!). Talking with my contacts in the new car
business, I am finding out that if a customer presents a strong
technical knowledge and shows she's armed with loads of research,
the sales force basically just tries to settle. This is good news for you.

Your next step is simply to go to the dealership and take a test-
drive. Since you're already armed and dangerous (and you've kept
the above points in mind), you know the playing field rules and if
you want to play. You even know what to expect for your trade-in
and whether you want an upgrade package (and when to beat off a
push to buy one). The only other thing you must do at this point is
add a little bit of "chutzpah" to your research (not just knowing what
a good deal is but having the courage to get it), and you're on your
way to buying a great car at a great price. If you're convinced you're
getting a good deal after all the test-driving, pricing and negotiating,
feel free to sign the papers and drive your new car into the sunset,
all with the assurance that you got the deal you were looking for.

The armed-and-dangerous approach to car buying is a one-two
punch: You go in with enough knowledge to know what a good deal
is, and you know there are other places to buy your car if this
particular dealer doesn't please you.

Remember, even though the dealership seems to have a huge edge
over the consumer, on closer inspection you see this is not true. If
you're a well-informed, capable car buyer you definitely have the
edge, particularly if you follow the points above.

CHAPTER 4

Doing Your Homework

I'm going to preface this chapter on homework with a true story about rugs, not cars, that shows you what wonderful things can happen to people who diligently do their homework.

The Antique Rug

When we were first married and I was a graduate student at the University of Pittsburgh, my wife, Stephanie, was a teacher. She had to take the trolley to work every day. Pittsburgh weather is not the greatest (which is why we are in California now), and Stephanie used to wait for the trolley in the shelter of the doorway to an Oriental antique shop. Stephanie is an artistic and literary type, and the beautiful rugs in this store were a source of great interest to her.

As her gift for putting me through graduate school, you guessed it, I bought her a beautiful room-size Oriental rug at the same antique shop. It took all of our savings, $800, and meant there was no furniture in the living room, but my wife didn't care.

Fifteen years later when we bought a house in California with wall-to-wall carpeting in the wrong color and no basement, we were forced to store our magnificent rug in the already crammed garage. We decided to sell the rug. Maybe if we could get rid of it and some other things we hadn't used for years, we would have room for our cars. But what was it worth? Was our rug really a beat-up old Ford or a vintage Model T? We decided to try to find out by doing some homework.

The First Bite

To begin with, Stephanie called several Oriental rug stores. One owner came to our house to view the rug. He introduced himself, walked around the rug a few times, lifted a corner, pointed out a few faded areas and worn spots and then asked me what I wanted for the rug. The conversation went as follows:

Rug Merchant: What do you want for the rug? Name a price.

Burke: I don't know. What do you think it is worth?

Rug Merchant: The ends are frayed and it is very old, but name your price.

Burke: What kind of rug is it?

Rug Merchant: It is a Serapi [something else I didn't know], but come now, name your price.

Burke: What is that design in the center?

Rug Merchant: It is a turtle-back center, popular with the peoples of northern Iran. Look, my time is important. Surely you must have some idea of what you want for it.

Burke: I really don't know anything about rugs. I have no idea what it's worth. By the way, what kind of border is that around the outside?

Rug Merchant: It is a serpentine border. Come now, give me your best price, and I will buy the rug today.

This went on for forty-five minutes. I was just trying to find out, from someone who should have known, something about my rug, while he was just interested in buying it for the cheapest price. When I got tired of the stalemate, I put my arm around his neck, walked him out of the house and noted that he drove a new Mercedes. As he was about to drive away, I gave it one last try. "Since I have no idea what this rug is worth, how about you offering me your best price for it right now? It's now or never," I warned. It was only then that he gave up the figure. "The rug is old and so worn it needs expensive repairs. It also needs a good cleaning. All that must be done by specialists and by hand. Maybe then I can resell it. I will give you $500 cash for it today. That's my best price."

Come to think of it, even back then I enjoyed a good negotiation because we went back and forth for a while and he came up with an absolutely "final best" price of $700. Since I had just begun to do my homework, I wasn't prepared to sell it yet, and I let him go.

Two days later, a woman who said she was the merchant's sister stopped by and said she would give me $750 for the rug right then only because it had the exact shade of red as her couch. She admired it for a long time and gradually raised her offer to $1,100. I smelled something fishy. My wife and I had a feeling our rug was worth an awful lot more.

Doing Our Homework

It was then we decided we would take our time and do our homework. We started in earnest. We shopped for Oriental rugs, had other merchants look at ours, went to museums and even read books containing photographs of rugs in museums. It was in one of these books that Stephanie found a picture of a rug with a border that looked like ours. So she and I dragged our rug out of the garage, rolled it out on our back patio, vacuumed it a few times and, with the aid of the bright California sunshine, took about one dozen pictures.

Then we made long-distance phone calls, got the names of museum curators of Oriental art and antiquities and sent letters with the photos enclosed. The response letter was worth waiting for. It was from the curator of Oriental rugs of the San Francisco Museum of Art. He said the words we'd been waiting to hear: "I believe your rug is a significant piece." He said that for a small fee, if we could get it to Butterfield and Butterfield, which we then learned was a famous auction house in Los Angeles, he would appraise it when he was there.

At the auction house, the curator examined the rug, consulted with an associate and then confirmed what he had written in his letters: It was a "major piece" that he estimated would sell in Butterfield's televised closed-circuit auction for at least $10,000. It sold two months later for $14,525.

The next day I wrote a cheerful letter to the first rug merchant thanking him for alerting me to the rug's true value and telling him the price for which I sold it. (I added about $8,000 to the price just for fun.) So the moral of this story is that doing your homework pays off (and revenge is sweet). Read on to see how doing your homework especially pays off for the auto consumer.

+ + +

Let me set the stage for the kind of homework I expect you to do. There is perhaps $2,000 in "profits" that either can be saved by you or can be given to the dealership. The lion's share of this will go to the dealership if you don't do your homework. The lion's share will be saved by you if you do the homework and follow the directions in this book. Doing a buy right will require about twenty hours of pleasurable work. This means you will make about $2,000 in approximately twenty hours of work, or about $100 per hour. This is, of course, after taxes, so to generate this kind of money conventionally, you must make about $150 per hour before taxes. If you were going to pay someone this kind of money to buy a car for you, you would expect a hardworking, dedicated person who did her homework and did the buying well. This is exactly what I expect from you and what you should expect from yourself.

There are two general categories that must be considered: "homework" items and items listed as "at the dealership." The homework items can be done in advance and in any order, but the at-the-dealership items must be done in the order given or you will lose control of the buy. Any time you lose control of the buy, you will lose money. That should be incentive for doing your homework and following the prescribed order once you are at the dealership.

Homework

These homework assignments can be done in any order but must be done before your trip to the dealership to look at cars:

Read About the Cars You Are Considering

Ready, set, go. Start with *Consumer Reports* for information about costs and reliability. Next try *Road & Track* or *Car and Driver* to see how the experts like the vehicle and what specific options and equipment they recommend. Look at other magazines and publications and go from there. Start now.

Suggested Information Sources

• Edmund Publications Corp., 300 N. Sepulveda, Suite 2050, El Segundo, CA 90245. Edmunds publishes a variety of useful guides. These guides cover new-car prices for most classes of cars and trucks, including domestic cars and trucks, foreign cars and trucks and some used-car prices. These guides cost around $7 each and are updated once or twice yearly. Edmund is a great source of information. You might find it useful to buy the guide that deals specifically with the type of car you need. If you are hooked up to the Web, try Edmunds at http://www.edmunds.com.

• *Kelley Blue Book Auto Market Report, Official Guide*, commonly called the *Blue Book*. This great source of used-car price evaluations has page upon page of price information about all sorts of used cars. It makes no recommendations, just acts as a reflection of the current market value. The purpose of the *Blue Book* is to report current market prices for automobiles, not to set them. The NADA *Official Used Car Guide* is similarly used.

When dealers talk among themselves, they refer to the *Blue Book* often. Rather than saying, "I will buy that car for $5,300," a dealer might say, "I will buy that car for $800 back of Book."

Do not take the *Blue Book* prices as gospel. Many factors, including condition, color and local availability, can seriously affect the price. Most dealers in my part of the world evaluate a car by considering the car condition, adjusted *Blue Book* valuations and the local "dealers-only" auto market report, to come out with what is probably the best estimate as to what a car is really worth. To get accurate info fast, go to the *Blue Book* Web site (http://www.kbb.com).

• *Consumer Reports*, especially the annual automobile issue that comes out each April. I look to *Consumer Reports* for good information about reliability and repair records. They also have a whole raft of books on various aspects of car buying.

• Auction sale reports for dealers-only auctions. These sale reports are sent only to authorized dealers who are licensed through the auctions, so while you cannot get them directly, you might be able to work with a dealer who has them. These sale reports give the sale prices at the dealers-only auctions. They let me know very vividly what cars sold for at these auctions on specific dates. These types of reports are what the *Blue Book* is in part based upon.

• Choose which car and options to buy. This part of your homework includes pricing options like stereos and antitheft systems at outside sources. Use the checklists at the end of this chapter to help you think your way through all the available choices. Determine what your needs are versus what your wants are. Prioritize, then get a rough idea of what you can afford and figure out what your payments will be. Some of the Web sites will have a payment calculator which can help you. Start with http://www.autotrader.com.

Some good books I have read on the subject of car buying include:

• *The Car Buyer's Art: How to Beat the Salesman at His Own Game*, by Darrell Parrish (Book Express, 1996)
• *Cheap Wheels: The Complete Guide to Buying, Selling and Enjoying Used Cars*, by Leslie R. Sachs and James S. Bennett (Simon & Schuster, 1989)
• *How to Buy a Car: A Former Car Salesman Tells All*, by James R. Ross (St. Martin's Press, 1993)
• *How to Save Big Money When You Lease a Car*, by Michael Flinn (The Putnam Publishing Group, 1999)

Get Your Financing in Order

Chapters seventeen and eighteen of this book will be useful in helping you sort through the financing maze. Go to a bank, credit union and/or your favorite relative and get your financing in shape before you go into the dealership. Make sure you are approved for enough money at a good interest rate, and make sure it will be available when you want it. It is a horror to lose a car or to pay top financing interest rates because your loan falls through or because you haven't financed enough to cover the car you really want. It is also a horror if your loan falls through because you buy a car through an auction and then discover that your lending institution doesn't loan on auction purchases. (This is rare.) Get all the details of your loan or financing straightened out and completely in order before the buy.

Price Your Trade-In

Chapter four provides you with help in evaluating your vehicle. Chapters nine, eleven, twenty-six and twenty-seven will give you valuable information on what you can get for it in a dealership or by selling it yourself through advertisements. Don't dismiss selling a car yourself without thinking the process through via this book. It may not be right for you to sell it yourself, but then again it might make you some extra money.

Pick the Dealership

I first consider only those dealerships that are close and therefore convenient. It is important that they be large enough to offer discounts easily. In addition, I check for reputation and longevity, and I consider the success of the dealership in fulfilling repair warranties.

Pick the Time and a Buying Companion

As you saw in chapter three and will see elsewhere, your advantages as a buyer are strongly influenced by picking the best time (end of the month, rainy weekend, late in the day, shortly before closing) and having the right people with you. Don't go when it is convenient for the dealership. Go when it makes sense for you to get a great deal.

Practice

If the opportunity presents itself, go with a friend to his car buy and practice. Help him with his buy and use the experience gained for your benefit. Practice makes perfect; if you make mistakes, make them before your purchase. Make them on his dollar.

At the Dealership

Remember, these items must be executed in the order listed for you to maintain control of the sales situation. These things are done at the dealership with the sales staff after all the homework items have been completed. Each of these steps is discussed in detail in later chapters.

- Meet the salesperson and take a test-drive.
- Get a fixed firm price for your trade-in.
- Set a fixed firm price for the new car and options.
- Settle all the financing issues, including payments, leasing, extended warranties, etc.

What Kind of Car Do You Want and Need?

Deciding what kind of car you want and need means searching your soul and your wallet and examining your dreams, reasons and motivations. It is also the most important thing to do before you step into a dealership. The purpose of this section is to help you focus on what you really want or need in a vehicle.

Winging it may be fun, but it is seldom profitable. One of the problems with going to a dealership unprepared is that if you really aren't settled on what type of car you want, the salesperson will certainly help you make up your mind. That usually means switching you to the particular car that is the most profitable for the salesperson to sell. If the dealership is offering incentives to sales staff for selling luxury cars, you will be pressed to buy one of them. You may go out to buy a station wagon and come back with a sports car. The best way to avoid this kind of pressure is to make up your mind logically and carefully in your own home. Filling out this form will help you.

This Car Will Be Used for the Following:

____ driving to work
____ hauling cargo
____ hauling kids and groceries
____ impressing the neighbors
____ improving social life (sports car)
____ long-distance commuting
____ sales calls
____ other _____
____ other _____

I Need a Car With the Following Characteristics:

____ lots of economy

_____ lots of luxury
_____ lots of power
_____ lots of room
_____ holds _____ people easily
_____ 2, 4, 5 doors
_____ other _____
_____ other _____
_____ other _____
_____ other _____

	Want	Need	Comments (Pro/Con)
1. luxury car	_____	_____	_____
2. minivan	_____	_____	_____
3. recreational vehicle	_____	_____	_____
4. sedan four-door	_____	_____	_____
5. sedan two-door	_____	_____	_____
6. sports car	_____	_____	_____
7. station wagon	_____	_____	_____
8. truck	_____	_____	_____
9. other	_____	_____	_____

Conclusions about what kind of car I need:

_____
_____
_____

Here is a sample of the bottom portion of a completed checklist:

	Want	Need	Comments (Pro/Con)
1. luxury car	yes	no	too expensive
2. minivan	no	no	useful, but ...
3. recreational vehicle	yes	no	too expensive
4. sedan four-door	yes	yes	boring, but I need a four-door family car
5. sedan two-door	no	no	need second set of doors
6. sports car	desperately	no	can't afford

7. station wagon	no	no	not useful to me
8. truck	yes	no	fun, but . . .
9. other			

Conclusions about what kind of car I need:
I need a four-door family car. I would love a truck or a luxury car, but the latter is way too expensive and the former would only be used occasionally.

Following is a list of options to consider:

List of Options Wanted

Feature	Selection
air bag	yes/no
air-conditioning	yes/no
antilock brakes	yes/no
antitheft package	yes/no
color:	_____
cruise control	yes/no
door crash protection	yes/no
doors (number):	2/3/4/5
extended warranty	yes/no
exterior protection packages	yes/no
interior package	yes/no
interior protection packages	yes/no
life insurance	yes/no
light package	yes/no
motor size (number of cylinders)	4/6/8/12
power features:	
doors	yes/no
mirrors	yes/no
seats	yes/no
windows	yes/no
roof rack	yes/no
rust protection	yes/no
sound system (buy elsewhere?)	yes/no

special features:

center console	yes/no
other:	yes/no

suspension type: _____

tilt wheel	yes/no

top styles:

convertible	yes/no
hard top	yes/no
moon roof	yes/no
T-top	yes/no

towing package	yes/no
transmission type:	automatic/manual

trim packages:

drink holders	yes/no
exterior trim	yes/no
including special upholstery	yes/no
leather	yes/no
pockets	yes/no
other:	_____
type of seats:	bench/bucket
other specials (CD players, etc.)	yes/no

Some of these options come only in a package that includes a number of items sold together. For instance, you may not be able to get air-conditioning without a package that includes power steering, power door locks, cruise control and a tilt–steering wheel. There is usually no flexibility in these packages.

Now that you have decided what the car will be used for, what type of car you need and what options are essential to you, you can concentrate your homework effort on assessing the performance and availability of your choice and its options. The key element here is to find the areas of the car's performance that are critical to you and to rate the car accordingly. For instance, a person who needs a performance car and who trades in a car every year or two may be less interested in reliability than in acceleration and style. Likewise, someone who buys a family car and holds it for ten years is likely to be more interested in usable back seats and reliability than in styling. Therefore, see how the experts rate your car, and see how their recommendations suit your situation.

Ratings by experts can be obtained from car magazines such as *Road & Track* or *Car and Driver* or other publications such as *Consumer Reports* and specialty books like those mentioned earlier. It also would be useful to talk to friends, relatives, neighbors and others who have purchased cars similar to those you are considering.

On a scale of one (least) to ten (most), rate the following items for your needs. Then see how the vehicle you are considering fits this profile as rated by the experts in the car magazines.

Priority Rating Chart

Characteristic	My Priorities	Rating By Experts
acceleration		
braking		
bumpers		
controls		
cost		
displays		
driving position		
emergency handling		
front seating		
fun to drive		
gas mileage		
heating		
noise		
rear seating		
reliability		
ride		
routine handling		
servicing		
towing capability		
trunk		
value		
ventilation		

Special Items Wanted

Item	Wanted	Rating By Experts
air-conditioning	yes/no	_____
cruise control	yes/no	_____
luxury package	yes/no	_____
moon roof	yes/no	_____
power brakes	yes/no	_____
power steering	yes/no	_____
roof rack	yes/no	_____
special engine	yes/no	_____
special exterior package	yes/no	_____
special interior package	yes/no	_____
special suspension	yes/no	_____
special tires	yes/no	_____
T-top	yes/no	_____
tilt steering	yes/no	_____
towing package	yes/no	_____
other	yes/no	_____

Special Recommendations of Experts

automatic or stick	_____
corporate twin available	yes/no
preferred model	_____
upgrade engine	yes/no
upgrade suspension	yes/no
upgrade transmission	yes/no
other: _____	yes/no
other: _____	yes/no

Additional Considerations

Is the vehicle a first-year design of uncertain reliability?	yes/no
Do the experts say this is important?	yes/no
Do the experts think the styling is dated?	yes/no
Is this the last year the car will be produced?	yes/no
Is the vehicle in great demand?	yes/no

Final List

Now look over all the data you have gathered and list the cars (company and model) that fill the bill.

1. _____
2. _____
3. _____
4. _____

Calculating Affordability

This section is designed to help you calculate how much you can afford to pay for a car.

1. Maximum total price you can afford to pay: $_____
   (You can either put in a number here or you can take the maximum monthly payments you can afford times the number of months you want to pay to get the maximum amount you can afford to pay for the vehicle. For example $300 a month for sixty months is $18,000. Make this a realistic figure, and use it as a guide above which you will not go, even under pressure.)

2. Maximum monthly payment you can afford: $_____
   (Note: Do not tell these numbers to the salesperson because if you say, "I can only afford $325 a month," he will feel you can afford at least $350 a month and probably more.)

3. Realistic price for a suitable type vehicle: $_____
   (You can get this from your literature search.)

4. What is your trade-in worth? $_____
   (Get this from your *Blue Book* wholesale, less $200 to $400.)

5. How much cash can you put down? $_____

6. Taxes, licenses and other fees: $_____

7. Transportation cost: $_____

8. Extended warranty and other extras: $_____

9. Factory rebates: $_____
   (factory-to-consumer or a piece of the factory-to-dealer rebates)

10. Premiums, an AMU or an ADMU: $_____
    (additional dealer markup or extra profit)
11. Options, extras, special tires, etc.: $_____

Total to be Financed

$$3+6+7+8+10+11-4-5-9=$$ $_____

This calculation will give you a good approximation of the car's actual price. Many times, people forget item #6, the costs of the taxes, licenses and fees. In California in 1992, the sales tax ran as high as 8.5 percent. The registration fee of as much as 2.5 percent, plus additional small fees such as a document fee or a luxury tax, could boost the price of item #6 to over 12 percent of the final cost of the vehicle. This is a major item. If you don't know the tax and fee situation in your area, contact your local DMV or any local dealer.

Experiment with your calculation. For instance, substitute various values of your trade-in. Take *Blue Book* wholesale, or auction price, or *Blue Book* wholesale less $800 and see how this affects the total amount to be financed. For item #9, see if the car becomes more affordable if Detroit gives a factory-to-consumer rebate of $1,000 on your vehicle.

Sample Financial Calculation

1. Maximum total price you can afford to pay: $15,600
2. Maximum monthly payment you can afford: $325
3. Realistic price for a suitable type vehicle: $18,000
4. What is your trade-in worth? $7,100
5. How much cash can you put down? $2,736
6. Taxes, licenses and other fees: $1,790
7. Transportation cost: $475
8. Extended warranty and other extras: $1,250
9. Factory rebates: $750
10. Premiums, an AMU or an ADMU: $0

(This should always be $0. This reminds you that you did not pay this extra amount for the vehicle.)

11. Options, extras, special tires, etc.: $500

Total to be Financed:

$18,000 + 1,790 + 475 + 1,250 + 0 + 500 − 7,100 − 2,736 − 750 = $11,429

Amount of Money Available to Spend on a Car

1. Expressed as total dollars: $_____
2. Expressed as monthly payments: $_____

This gives you the dollar amount to be financed. For an accurate monthly payment, go to a book of interest amortization tables and figure out what your monthly payments would be. [Check out *McGraw-Hill's Interest Amortization Tables*, 2nd edition, by Jack C. Estes and Dennis R. Kelley (McGraw-Hill, 1993) or *Monthly Interest Amortization Tables* by Michael Sherman (NTC/Contemporary Publishing, 1994).]

Amount to be financed:	$11,000.00
Interest:	14.5 percent
Term:	48 months
You would expect monthly payments of:	$303.36
Which would be a total payment of:	$14,561.28
Or interest of:	$3,561.28

So it looks like you can stay within your $325 per month limit and afford about $18,000 for a car if your figures are even approximately correct.

Now that you know how much you can afford to pay for your car, find out what cars fall into that price range. (One word of caution: Don't let the salesperson do this type of "What kind of car can I afford?" calculation for you. He may try to confuse you and convince you to get a more expensive car than you really want.)

Now with your decision made, your research done and your financial calculations in front of you, you are ready to make a choice.

You can easily decide if you can afford the new car you want.

One other item of homework to consider is the two types of rebates: factory-to-customer and factory-to-dealer. You will know about factory-to-customer rebates because they are widely advertised and automatically presented by the dealer to the customer. They are paid directly to you, the purchaser of a new car, by the manufacturers. Not so for factory-to-dealer rebates; they are hidden. These rebates come and go. It would be useful to obtain information about what types of cash incentives are given from the factory to the dealers. If you get an unusually low price on your new dream car, this may be a reason for it, but these are not always passed on to the buyer. Nationwide Auto Brokers, at (810) 559-6661, will give you current information on incentives and rebates. You can also look at the IntelliChoice Web site (http://www.intellichoice.com) for current information.

Best Choice
Make it, write it down and never look back.

Now that you know yourself, your needs and what your budget will bear, it's time to strategize on how to get the money you need to purchase your car.

CHAPTER 5

Getting Loans

If you need to get a loan for your car purchase, don't feel bad. Most car buyers don't have the money to make cash auto transactions (in fact, 90 percent of all car buyers must finance their purchases). But a lot of people are embarrassed about their credit histories. They will not risk embarrassment by going to banks, which they regard as so respectable and upscale as to pose a threat of certain rejection. They would rather go to an auto dealership, pay more and avoid the discomfort and anxiety, even though most dealerships ultimately finance through banks. What you don't want to do is worry about your credit to the point that you do not go to a bank, but go to a dealership and throw yourself at its mercy. Let's go over the banking industry's auto loan process.

Banks and Their Function

Bankers in their habitat are a strange breed, and I make no claims to understanding them. Loan officers are usually underpaid; although banks are high on prestige, they are low on salary. However, these same loan officers seem to control our ability to purchase the vehicle we want. We need them in order to get money at lower rates than those available from a dealership, to afford to buy a better car. If you wait until you sell your old car, buy a new car and get all the extras you want before you try to obtain reasonable financing, you may be in for a shock. It is always better to get your money first, then go after the car. This section is going to show you how best to get that loan money.

Let's look at banks and loan officers and see what they are and what they want.

First, the institutions themselves are conscious of security and of making sure that the loans are repaid, that they are repaid profitably and that no one skips out with the bank's vehicle before the loan is paid off. Because of the small margins between depositors' interest rates and loan rates, a bad loan can hurt enough to cover the profit from many good loans. They are therefore very reluctant to loan money if the customer is less than primo. From the customers I have dealt with, credit unions seem to be much easier than banks to get money at good rates. But then, credit union customers own the credit union whereas bank customers don't own the bank.

Second, they want to make loans. Really they do! It's how they make money. If they only took in deposits and did not invest what they received in houses, cars and other things, they would quickly go broke.

The combination of the first and second points is enough to make them schizophrenic. They think, *We will loan you our money because we must in order to survive, but you must treat it right and give it back to us at regular intervals. You must not make us nervous because we want to be safe, and the only way we can feel safe is not to lend to people who make us nervous.*

Third, banks structure their sales staff (loan officers and behind-the-scenes people who spend all day in offices approving loan applications on essentially a salary basis). These people receive no benefits other than pats on the back for making loans. They do not receive monetary incentives. They are not highly commissioned like vinyl siding salespeople and thus tend to judge loans by the consumer loan application. Although bankers get no commissions for making profitable loans, if the loan goes bad, they have explaining to do. If a large number of their loans go bad, they have a lot of explaining to do. They might even lose their jobs. If they make a mistake, it is going to be on the conservative, "I won't loan you that money" side.

Fourth, the people who make the decision about the loan never see the loan consumer. The impression you make with the bank officer is somewhat muted by the fact that this is not the person who approves the loan. However, if you do not make a good impression on the loan officer, you won't ever make it to the approval headquarters.

How Loans Are Processed

The bank loan officer talks to the customer, prequalifies him, helps him fill out the application and then ships it back to headquarters for approval.

The headquarters people approve or deny the loan based on the application and on their own internal factors and ship the results back to the bank loan officer. The application is important because the person who does the loan will not see the customer or know how nice he is and will only go by some hard monetary facts and his credit history.

The branch bank loan officer can, within certain limits, overrule a central bank denial of an application. This override ability seems to fluctuate with the economy and is not a common occurrence. But the fact that it is possible should stress the importance of favorably impressing your banker.

Bankers have assured me that while loans can be processed on an emergency basis in eight hours, routine approvals are done in two to three days. If your bank tells you it will take three to four weeks, ask why and either check another bank or threaten to do so.

For new-car loans, many California banks (as of late 1999) are lending 80 percent of selling price for new vehicles and are lending up to 100 percent of wholesale *Blue Book* for used vehicles. Obviously, this is subject to change depending on economic conditions. The right bank may even loan for tax and license for used vehicles. This goes to show you how much better a bank feels a used-car purchase is than a new-car purchase.

You may be an inventive and imaginative person. I may be a person who evaluates people and things uniquely. Bankers are not like that. They are paid to evaluate things only on a conservative, conventional and financial basis. How do they evaluate a vehicle conventionally and financially? They base the loan on the price of the new or used vehicle as defined by the manufacturer (list price), the selling agency (dealership) or a recognized used-car expert (*Blue Book*).

This can create problems. For example, for a used car, *Blue Book* is only an estimate. The *Blue Book* and others like it cannot hope to show all the factors that can influence a car's price. These factors include regional preferences, seasonal differences, the effect of paint color, interior condition, etc.

In its introduction, the *Blue Book* says, "Wholesale values are based on clean vehicles fully reconditioned and ready for resale with acceptable mileage as indicated by zeros on the mileage chart." It defines suggested retail values "as an estimated dealer asking price. The actual selling price may vary substantially." It also indicates that, "Condition is of prime importance. Appropriate amounts should be added for exceptionally clean vehicles and vehicles which are under warranty by the factory or the dealer. Appropriate amounts should be deducted for needed reconditioning."

How do banks do this? Do the bankers come out of their air-conditioned offices and go over the vehicles they are going to loan on? Do they check the oil and listen to the engine run? The answer is obviously no.

I have taken purchase orders (the documents dealers give to banks to inform them what is on a car), a VIN (Vehicle Identification Number) and other useful data and gone to a bank. On a hot day, the loan officer didn't want to go out to see the vehicle and wouldn't even bother to take a look out the window to see if it was a ¾-ton truck or a Volkswagen bus.

Some other bank officers with whom I have worked are so inexperienced that when I took one to see the car in question, she didn't know where the VIN was located, what items on the car to compare to the purchase order or anything else. If she was protecting the bank's investment, that bank was in trouble.

The bank officers compare *Blue Book* values to what is reported on the purchase order. They seem not to care about the condition of the vehicle or any of the really practical stuff. Yet we all know that color, condition, options, smell, rips in the upholstery or cigarette burns in the carpeting can drastically affect the desirability of the vehicle and, therefore, its price.

How can a set of values for a car that does not cover all the really important items affect the loan value, which is a measure of the worth of the car? There is no other way to evaluate what a car is worth, or really what the car will be worth if you don't make payments, and the bank has to repossess the vehicle and sell it to get the money back. You then come back to the major value that determines a loan: how the bank can get its money back if it must.

If your ability to pay back were so solid as to be absolute, banks would lend you whatever you wanted on your vehicle, even if you grossly overpaid the dealership.

Therefore, as a borrower, your job is to make yourself appear so solid on a loan application that you can get the best terms possible, both in rate and in percentage of the value of the car. How do you do this?

• Look like a good loan candidate. It always helps to dress up, look solid and financially conservative. My banker says the way you look doesn't matter because the loan approval officers are in the central headquarters of the bank and they never see you. Yet, he also indicates that he has the power to overrule a negative loan recommendation if he feels strongly that the loan is viable. What does he base his opinion on? I will bet it is partially on his personal evaluation based on your meeting with him. A large part of this evaluation will be based on your behavior and dress.

• Never mention troubles such as divorce or layoffs. The loan officer will wonder if you will still be able to pay off the car loan with the other demand on your money. Make it look like as much of your income as possible will be available to go toward the loan.

• Make it look as though there are fewer people enjoying a piece of your income. If you have kids and an ex who get a piece of your pie, your significant other has kids and an ex who get a piece of that pie and the two of you have kids together, the bank is going to be aware of the constraints on your salary. Of course, the bankers will consider your income with deductions, but they will also consider you, your whole tribe and all your financial obligations and then look at whatever remains as available for repayment of a loan. You get no points for being a good parent.

• It is best not to even try to receive an out-of-state loan. It has to be a nightmare to repossess an out-of-state car, so the loan process is nearly impossible. One exception to this is for those who are members of an out-of-state federal credit union.

• Do your best to show long, steady work history based on salary and not commissions. Banks object to commissions as a basis for a loan because they fluctuate with the economy.

• Show long-term stability in your residence. Banks like to know where to go if it is ever necessary to repossess their vehicles.

• If you feel your loan history may be marginal, and most of us know our credit history will have some flaws, it may be good to get a copy of your credit history from Experian Credit Reports and look at it before the loan interview. You can get your Experian credit report by calling (800) 392-1122. This will prepare you to answer questions about any questionable items such as any late payments or disputes.

• A lot of people are embarrassed about their credit histories. They will not risk embarrassment by going to banks, which these people feel are so respectable and upscale. They would rather go to an auto dealership, pay more and avoid the discomfort and anxiety, even though most dealerships ultimately finance through banks. What you don't want to do is worry about your credit to the point that you do not go to a bank, but go to a dealership and throw yourself at its mercy.

• Make sure you ask for enough money to be able to get what you need and want. Don't starve yourself; make sure you borrow enough money for the vehicle you want.

• Just for fun, ask for 1 percent less on your interest rate because of some made-up reason. You could say that times are good and you *know* that a lending institution on the Net loans 120 percent at 1 percent less than the bank does. See if it works. It can't hurt.

How the Internet Is Affecting Banking

Thanks to the Internet, you can now get the best financing available. Banks and financial institutions no longer have the power to get you by default only because you live locally, you bank there or you have a personal relationship with the loan officer. Without telling you where to finance, let me tell you to look around, get your best rate or get a bank that will loan as much as you need. People who go on the Net for car information are also going on the Net for insurance and financing. And almost all of the big auto Web sites have information about getting a loan. So point, click and investigate, and see how Web rates compare to your local banking sources. Some useful Web sites to check out are:

Edmunds, (http://www.edmunds.com)
Autobytel, (http://www.autobytel.com)
CarPoint, (http://www.carpoint.com)

Wrap Up

Be sure you go to a bank or credit union armed with a preview of your own credit report. Argue for the best rates available, and come out of the bank with a loan in advance of your trip to a dealership. This will enable you to go through with an automobile transaction without worrying about how you will pay for the car.

It is important when going for a loan on a new or used car that you make sure the bank knows from whom you are buying a car. Banks have a right to know if you are buying from a dealer, from a private party or at auction. Providing the bank with this information upfront will prevent the bank from canceling the loan based on a misunderstanding. For example, some banks won't finance a buy of a vehicle that's older than five years, some won't finance salvage titles, etc. Once you know how to secure an auto loan from a bank, you are ready for the next part of your homework: finding out what your used car is really worth.

Web Sites of Interest

These Web sites will help you with a loan:

http://www.banx.com. The BanxQuote site provides comparisons of different bank lending rates. There is a fee.

http://www.carloan.com. Car-Loan will help you get a loan even if you are not the most loan-worthy person because of bad credit history. This is also a good place to begin to look for the best interest rate. Essentially, though, sites like this one (and there are thousands on the Web) are just brochures that send your personal information to an online loan company. There is a fee.

http://www.equifax.com. If you want a second opinion about your credit, check out Equifax. There is a fee.

http://www.experian.com. Experian will provide you with a credit report. There is a fee.

CHAPTER 6

Determining the Value of Your Trade-In

The first step when negotiating with a salesperson is determining your trade-in price. This initial step may be the most difficult one because your car is a part of you and selling it is an emotional issue. To get the best price for your trade-in, you have to know what it is really worth to the dealer. He won't give you more for it than it is worth, but he will certainly try to give you a lot less.

Everybody knows you really love your used car, and everybody knows it got you through the snowstorm of 1992, and through the flood of 1988 and was the best of the litter in 1985. But you must evaluate your car realistically, as a potential buyer would. Someone who just needs transportation, nothing more, and does not regard rusted-through holes as increased ventilation.

Here's how to see what your vehicle is really worth so that when you try to get maximum dollar for it, you are trying for a realistic figure.

Check the *Blue Book* or the NADA *Official Used Car Guide* (use a local bank or library), and evaluate the worth of the car. Try to get hold of the dealers' edition of the *Blue Book*, not the consumers' edition. The consumers' issue says "Consumers' Issue" on the cover. Find a copy machine and copy both the base page and the mileage page for your records and calculations. Banks will be glad to give you this information and to show you how to read the figures. Tell them you want to buy a car and are considering using them for the financing. Make sure you receive a current reference book, not one that is months or even years old.

Blue Book base wholesale value:	$_____
estimated value of options:	$_____
estimated value of mileage:	$_____
total wholesale value of car (base + options + mileage):	$_____
Blue Book base retail value:	$_____
estimated value of options:	$_____
estimated value of mileage:	$_____
total retail value of car (base + options + mileage):	$_____

You may find that different evaluations do not come out the same. That is to be expected, as these evaluations are approximate. The evaluations do not take into account a variety of factors, including condition, color and whether the car is currently "hot." Also, the *Blue Book* does not always reflect market changes in the value of a vehicle. For instance, Audi was a highly regarded upscale automobile. Then an exposé on unintended acceleration was aired on a television news program. This destroyed Audi's reputation in the United States. The actual street value of an Audi deviated wildly from the previously published wholesale values. Audi has staged a well-deserved comeback and the valuation is now closer to *Blue Book* values.

Remember, the *Blue Book* and others try to follow and report the market, not predict it. Naturally, they will deviate strongly from it in some circumstances. Use the *Blue Book* as a first look at a vehicle's worth. It is great for that.

The next step in evaluating your trade-in is to see what a dealer thinks it is worth. If you have a friend who is a dealer, ask him to check recent dealers-only auction prices for your vehicle. The figures the dealer gives you, if accurate, are good indicators of what another dealership is going to use as the maximum to pay for your trade-in. This data is very important because it tells you the dealers alternative acquisition costs. (The auction valuation is how dealers look at your trade-in, and what they must expect to get from a quick sale at the auctions.)

Read the newspapers and see what price people are asking for vehicles of this type. Usually the asking price will fall somewhere between (dealer's edition) low *Blue Book* (wholesale) and high *Blue Book* (retail).

first newspaper price: $_____

second newspaper price: $_____

third newspaper price: $_____

How the Internet Influences the Price for Your Trade-In

The Internet can help you handle your trade-in. If you have Internet capability, you first want to go to the *Blue Book* site (http://www.kbb .com) and evaluate your vehicle. Remember that this site uses consumer figures.

The Net provides you with a lot of easy alternatives besides the conventional ones to sell your own car. You can place your car on a cyberlot, thereby listing it for sale on the Net (for more on cyberlots, see chapter two). You also can post your car for sale on a bulletin board, even if it doesn't pertain to cars. People do this all the time. I do (it's free advertising for my car business). For fun you could try to auction it off at some Web auction site, like eBay (http:// www.ebay.com), but car sales rarely go to completion on eBay. Trader Online is on the Web (http://www.traderonline.com/auto), as well as most newspaper classifieds. The more places you can advertise your car the better you can sell it. This is especially important for people who live in more rural areas where the options are limited.

Here are some good Web sites that can help you price and sell your car:

AutoWeb.com at http://www.autoweb.com
Carlist.com at http://www.car-list.com
CarPrices.com at http://www.carprices.com
Excite Classifieds at http://www.classifieds2000.com
Edmunds at http://www.edmunds.com
Kelley *Blue Book* at http://www.kbb.com

Trader Online at http://www.traderonline.com/auto

Here are some typical bulletin boards that contain discussions about particular types of cars. Type the following into your search engine to get started.

alt.autos.bmw
alt.autos.ford
alt.autos.mercedes
alt.autos.volvo
alt.autos.toyota

By checking out the above bulletin boards and looking at what other people want for their cars (private parties and dealers alike), you get a good idea what your vehicle is worth. Also, in your travels over the Web, you may come across other people looking for a car. Try to sell them yours, all from the anonymity of your own home.

Traditional (NonInternet) Ways to Help You Price and Sell Your Car

Don't be shy. Respond to some ads for vehicles similar to yours and see what kind of action the sellers are getting. Also, get any facts they are willing to share. Most people are so anxious to sell their cars they share information easily. If a vehicle does not have an automatic transmission, ask if this has been a barrier to the sale. If the car is fully loaded, ask if that has helped the sale even though it raised the price. If the vehicle has sold, get the figure and see how it relates to your vehicle. The prices sellers quote will be useful in determining how high a price you can expect to get from a dealership. If people are selling vehicles on the street that are similar to your trade-in and they are getting good prices, perhaps you should try selling your car yourself. Street prices do reflect the retail market; you may be surprised at the low price the dealerships will first offer for your trade-in. Remember, they are selling to the same retail market and should be able to pay more for the car since they can sell it for a profit, even though they have to fix it up and guarantee it. (When you respond to ads, make sure the seller is truly a private party and not a dealer masquerading as a private party. In California, as many as 60 percent of the ads are placed by dealers in sheep's clothing. There is nothing wrong with buying from a dealer at the same price, though. See chapter twenty-six for more on this.)

Check with some used-car dealers and see what they want for a car of this type. What would they buy or sell it for? Check the market. Is your car hot or cold, a seller or a sitter? If it is a hot seller, be firm on the price you want from a dealership. If it is not moving, you may have to drop considerably below *Blue Book* wholesale to sell it.

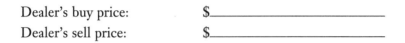

Dealer's buy price: $_____

Dealer's sell price: $_____

If you have the contacts, see what your car would sell for at a dealers-only auction. See if someone will sell it there for you for a small commission. You may come out ahead if you do it that way. We do this for people all the time.

The auction price of a vehicle at a dealers-only auction is interesting. If a dealership takes in a car as a trade-in, it may decide it doesn't want to retail this particular car itself. The reasons for this vary but may have nothing to do with the car's condition. Dealers-only auctions provide a marketplace where vehicles can be bought and sold quickly. Auction advantages are the possibility of a quick sale at a reasonable price. Therefore, if a dealership "steals" a car from a customer at $2,200, it may sell it at auction for, say, $2,950 and pocket the $750 (minus expenses). If a dealership can't get a car below auction prices, it may not buy the trade-in but may buy a similar car at auction and save money.

New-car dealerships also "wholesale" their trade-ins to wholesalers who eventually sell them to retailers. So new-car dealerships must buy trade-ins low to be able to resell them. If they pay too much, they must cover this by charging too much for the new cars to make their money. A later section in this book details how certain buyers are labeled as trade-in sensitive, so new-car dealerships pay them more for trade-ins but also charge them more for their new-car purchases.

Dealer Quotes

Auto dealers will try to lowball you and tell you they can't even give you *Blue Book* wholesale for your vehicle. They will say that now everybody gives only auction prices for a used car. They will then quote you a much lower price than auction prices. For instance, if *Blue Book* retail is $5,900 and *Blue Book* wholesale is $4,500 and a typical auction price is $4,100, they will offer you $2,900 for your car and may go as high as $3,200 if pressed.

Dealerships believe they can get away with this and often they do. This is true for a number of reasons:

- Most people don't know what their cars are worth. The initial reaction is that their car is worth a lot. When pressed, however, car owners just give the vehicles away with a whine and a whimper because they don't really know how high a price is realistic.

- Most people are either embarrassed by negotiating or don't know how to fight for a better price. This discomfort is exacerbated if the other party is strong willed, seems knowledgeable and is intentionally intimidating. Consumers feel they have only two choices when presented with a deal: take it or leave it. They rarely negotiate for price or conditions. They are basically ignorant of the value of a vehicle even though they are sure the dealers are giving them a low price for their trade-in. People generally give in if anything resembling a reasonable explanation for the low offer is presented to them.

- Salespeople are experienced negotiators and leave themselves some maneuvering room so they can later raise the price if they must. Who knows, the customer may just take the lowball offer or the dealership may not have to raise the offer much. When a customer hears a salesperson say, "I will give you $1,850 for your Buick," what the salesperson is really saying is, "My initial offer for your vehicle is at least $1,850 and is probably more." What the customer thinks is, *I either have to accept his $1,850 or walk out and not get a new car here.* Since the customer really wants a new car, she is not likely to refuse the $1,850. In reality, this is only the opening gambit in a negotiating scene. The salesperson is just fishing to see what will be accepted.

He is hoping this first price is taken. But remember, it is just his first move in a bidding cycle. It is certainly not a take-it-or-leave-it situation. As soon as you begin to understand his offer as just that, an offer, it will be easier for you to counter rather than feel pressured to take it or leave it.

• Who knows, maybe the customer won't argue at all. She might not care and more than likely just wants to get this unpleasant task over with. It is worth a try just to see. If the customer accepts a lowball for $1,000 less than her vehicle is worth because she really doesn't want to argue, the dealership can make $1,000 in just a few seconds.

• Dealerships don't have problems financing customers if they make their profit with a low price for the trade-in. Banks have rules about financing. The main concern of a bank is not financing a customer as a public service, but insuring that if the customer defaults on the loan, the bank can retrieve its investment. How does the bank do this? By loaning less than 100 percent of the car's value. If the dealership makes its money by selling a car at list or—heaven forbid—above list, the bank may be reluctant to lend all that extra profit. If the car has to be repossessed and sold, it will not return enough money to satisfy the bank's investment. So what better way to make your profit than to get it on the nonfinanced portion of the car deal—the trade-in?

• People usually buy their new cars first and then determine what their used cars can bring. By that time, they are so emotionally committed to their new cars they don't even care about getting the best prices for their trade-ins. They have devalued their old cars in their own minds and won't fight hard for better prices for them. This is why it is better to get your price for your trade-in first, before you psychologically feel that the beautiful new car is yours and switch allegiance from the old vehicle to the new one.

• Many people are unable to sell their cars themselves, so they have no choice but to accept the dealers' prices. This is a tough situation to be in. The customer needs a new car and wants to get rid of his trade-in. He is not comfortable selling it himself, and for the same reasons, he is not comfortable negotiating with a dealership for a better trade-in price. What does he usually do? He just gives in and gets the trade-in negotiation over with.

Remember to try for *Blue Book* wholesale for your trade-in, but be prepared to settle for something less. If you can get wholesale, congratulations. Never settle for less than auction price; you can always get that. A good price through a dealership would be wholesale minus $300. If you are unable to get that and feel comfortable doing so, try to sell the car yourself. One interesting item to note here is that dealerships never give *Blue Book* price credit for low miles but always deduct for high miles. Always fight for every dollar for low miles. Dealers prize low-mileage, clean older cars and will eventually pay for them. Also, it is generally known among used-car dealers that for cars older than six years, the mileage in the *Blue Book* is not realistic. The figures for average miles driven are so low the deductions don't make sense. One final point: Some used vehicles command over *Blue Book* wholesale prices. How do you find this out? Get your "friend" to give you some recent auction prices.

Negotiating Trade-In Prices

Remember, always negotiate trade-in price before you negotiate new-car price.

dealer's first offer on your used car:	$_____
dealer's next offer on your used car:	$_____
dealer's best offer on your used car:	$_____
How does it compare to wholesale?	$_____
auction?	$_____
retail?	$_____

It is important you get the maximum price for your trade-in. One of the best ways to do this is to repeat the following points.

First, tell the dealer it is very important that you get the very best price for your trade-in and that after you get your price for the trade-in, the rest of the sale will go easily. Sales staff look at each customer to see what is important to her. If the trade-in price is important, the dealership will give it if the salesperson feels the rest of the deal will go down easily. The salesperson needs to feel sure the necessary profit can be picked up in other areas of the transaction, such as on the new-car price.

Second, tell the salesperson you need a good trade-in price for your car in order to afford a down payment. This is a great reason. Even if it is not relevant in your case, it is a great reason. Many people have good jobs but live right to the limit of their incomes. They can make payments of $200, $300 or more but find it tough to come up with $3,600 in cash. The best way to raise cash for a down payment is to get a good price for the trade-in to apply to the down payment, thereby keeping the cash portion of the down payment low. Lead the salesperson to believe that this is your situation.

After you have been promised an acceptable price for your trade-in, you can stress the importance of other elements of the transaction. Initially, the only important thing is getting a good price for your trade-in. Later, when the salesperson tries to get a higher price for the new car, take the position that the only thing important to you is a good price on the new car. The salesperson is trapped at that point, having already agreed to a good price on the trade-in. He has already invested a considerable amount of time on you and does not want to risk losing the sale at this point.

When you've settled the trade-in issue and have a firm commitment from the dealer on a price, your mind is free to decide on a realistic price for the new car. How well you can do this determines how well you and your pocketbook will fare in the important second phase of the car buy, getting that new car.

CHAPTER 7

Knowing and Calculating Dealer's Costs

The best way I can relate the importance of knowing dealer cost is to tell a story about my poker-playing days.

During my transition from scientist to used-car guru, I entered a seven-card stud tournament. The format for a tournament like this is to take three hundred players and distribute them seven to a table. Then, as people lose their money and get eliminated, the stakes rise, the number of tables gets smaller (from fifty to twenty to five to eventually one table). Finally, by night's end only two happy people are left, surrounded by big piles of chips. On this particular occasion, another woman and I were those two happy people. There were still about one hundred unhappy people standing around waiting for one of us to "off" the other. From what I had seen earlier, the woman had a great streak of luck, and a lot of those unhappy onlookers were casualties of her pulling a miraculous "river card." Anyway, during that final round she was smiling, laughing and luxuriating in her lucky run—and she was showing off her cards to the crowd behind her. I was squeezing my cards and keeping to myself.

At one point I looked up at the crowd behind her, and a man in a cowboy hat was trying to get my attention, making hand signals at me. I realized he was telling me her cards. He held up two fingers and mouthed the words "kings," and I had nothing so I dropped. The lady showed the two kings, smiled and laughed. The next hand the cowboy gave me a "thumbs down." The lady bet her share, and then I bet the farm. She dropped because she had nothing. The rest of the evening went like that and eventually I won the tournament.

The point of this is that I won with only a mediocre run of cards but full knowledge of her hand. Because I knew what she had, I could bet big. The same can happen for you when buying a car: Knowing what the dealer paid for his cars and what he will sell them for is like having your own cowboy. Giddy-up!

Calculating Dealer Costs

This next important operation, calculating dealer costs, can be done after a preliminary walk-through. It should be done before your serious visit when you come armed with all your research data, before you take your test-drive and before serious negotiations begin.

Wouldn't it be nice if you could know beforehand the dealer's cost for the new vehicle you just fell in love with? Wouldn't it be even nicer if you knew how much to offer him over his costs, a price he would just barely be able to accept?

Well, you are in luck. You can find out exactly what the car cost the dealership. This chapter provides guidelines to show what dealerships will reluctantly accept as a profit margin for their vehicles. Later chapters will tell you how to factor in such things as factory-to-customer rebates or hidden factory-to-dealer cash backs, commonly called holdbacks. With this information, you will know exactly how hard you can push the salesperson to accept the price you offer.

First, let's work on a formula that will allow you to calculate what a vehicle cost the dealership. There are three ways to get this new-car cost figure:

1. For a nominal fee, you can contact a service that will quote you the dealer's cost for a vehicle with the options you request. Consumer Reports Online (http://www.consumerreports.com) does this for about $12 and gives you a lot of information, more than just the manufacturer's suggested retail price (MSRP) and list prices. It seems like a good deal if you like lots of data. Ditto for Edmunds Online (http://www.edmunds.com), but that site doesn't provide as much information. The only problem with obtaining information this way is that if you are pricing three or four different cars, with different engines or options, you could spend a lot of money to be spoon-fed the figures you want. It would be much

cheaper to get the information yourself.

2. You can look up the information yourself in appropriate publications, such as the annual April auto issue of *Consumer Reports* or Edmunds "specialty" auto books. Remember that you are paying yourself $150 per hour to do a good job buying a car. That good job requires spending as little money as possible to get all the information you need to make a good buy. This means doing your homework, but do it well and you'll have peace of mind knowing you're working with accurate facts because you obtained them yourself.

This research will give you both the dealer's cost and MSRP for the base car and the various options. All you have to do is add the desired options to the dealer's cost for the base car. If this number differs from the sticker price on the vehicle, it may be that there has been a recent price increase by the manufacturer for the car. The MSRP is also called the sticker or list price. It is the undiscounted advertised price for the vehicle as recommended by the manufacturer.

3. Take the factor for the car and the factor for the options and use them in conjunction with the figures on the sticker. The factor is the percentage of the price the car cost the dealer, and it's typically between .80 and .90. For example, the factor for a Chevrolet Lumina is .86 for the car and .85 for the options. A factor of .85 means that the car cost the dealer 85 percent of the sticker price on the car. In other words, a factor of .85 means a 15 percent profit on the car because the dealer paid 85 percent of the sticker price for the car. If you want to get 25 percent off the sticker price, you will find that the dealer will not treat you seriously because that is 10 percent below his cost. Knowing the factor helps you calculate dealer's cost from the sticker price on the window of the new car, and thus lets you know if you're getting a fair deal.

If in your research you can't find the factor but you can find the dealer's cost, you can calculate the factor yourself by dividing the dealer's cost by the published MSRP. For example, let's say the sticker price for the car is $12,000 and the dealer's cost is $10,000. The factor is .83 ($10,000/$12,000). Also note that even though car prices change, the factor usually stays the same for a given vehicle from year to year. Again, knowing the factor of the car you want to buy is helpful because it allows you to evaluate a salesperson's price. If he says he can't give you your proposed offer because it is below his costs and you know it's not . . . well, you know you're dealing with a liar.

Understanding Sticker Price

Here's how to interpret and utilize the information on the car's main sticker, which is usually placed on the side of every new car up for sale. In many cases, there is more than one sticker, a main one and one or more smaller stickers. These smaller stickers deal with extras, such as a wax job, special wire wheels or pinstripes.

Since you have come to the showroom with your homework done and you know the factors for your car and its options, you can calculate dealer's cost from the sticker as follows:

1. Locate the main price sticker on the car.
2. Disregard the other small stickers charging for special services.
3. Locate the base price for the car (without any extras), and enter the figure in (A) below. This number is usually located on the top of the sticker.
4. Total up all the extras you know you want, and enter this figure in (B) below.
5. Write down the factor for your base car in (C) below.
6. Write down the factor for your extras in (D) below.
7. Completely disregard any charge for AMU or ADMU, which are simple additional dealer markups (extra profit).
8. Disregard all charges for things you don't want, such as a wax job, undercoating, etc.
    - (A) $
    - (B) $
    - (C) $
    - (D) $

The dealer's cost for this car with its extras but without the special services like wax and pinstripes is $(A \times C) + (B \times D) +$ transportation (from the sticker).

Here is an example. You want to buy a Mitsubishi Eclipse GS. The published factor for the car is .90, and the published factor for the extras package (air-conditioning, etc.) is .94.

List price for the base car $17,910

Air-conditioning, etc. package list price $1,869

You would calculate the dealer's cost for the car with air-conditioning, power windows, etc., as

(car factor × MSRP for car) + (options factor × MSRP options) =

(.90 × $17,910) + (.94 × $1,869) =

$16,119 + $1,757 =

$17,873

Also add destination charges (transportation) to the final calculation.

These figures are on the main sticker on the car. On this car they are $343.

$17,873 + $343 = $18,216

Be sure you always add destination charges at the end of your calculation. The factor is not used on the transportation cost.

Compare this to the total sticker price for the car plus the options plus the transportation:

$17,910 + $1,869 + $343 = $20,122

If a dealership sold this car at list price, its gross profit on this segment of the transaction would be list price less his cost.

$20,122 − $17,873 = $2,249

Granted the dealership has other costs, but do you really want so much to come out of your pocket?

Researching Dealer Costs on the Internet

Surfing the Net makes it easy to get information that can help you calculate dealer costs and thereby help you construct your negotiating strategy. Here are three ways you can get dealer prices on the Net.

First, you can obtain dealer costs from a number of Internet sites. I would start at the Edmunds site (http://www.edmunds.com). Play around on the Edmunds site for a while and then focus on the new-car prices section. You can effectively design your own car and accessories and even come up with dealer costs. You can also simply search the Web by typing in "car prices," and hundreds of possibilities pop up. This is easy and fun to do. The only hard part is staying on target, because all the good sites have lots of great information.

Second, you can find places that will allow you to buy cars directly over the Net. These sites will either refer you to dealers or will have you fill out a form and have the dealers call you. What also is happening now is that these sites (AutoBytel at http://www.autobytel.com and AutoWeb at http://www.autoweb.com) will sell you a car directly. Use the information about dealer costs obtained above to see if you can get a good deal; then act accordingly. If you have no trade-in and are self-financing, the process is easy.

Finally, if you are the kind of person who likes to find scraps of information that may prove useful, browse around the Web and see what you find—you'll probably find a lot of helpful stuff. For instance, I recently found on the Edmunds site the best write-up of "dealer holdback" I have seen. You can check it out at http://www.edmunds .com/edweb/advice/Car.Buying.research.htm

Constructing a Bid

Let's say you need to negotiate for the Mitsubishi Eclipse GS mentioned earlier in this chapter. The price to aim for would be the dealer's cost plus $300 profit for the dealership, which for that car would be $18,216 plus $300, or $18,516. To end up here, initially bid $18,100 (about $100 less than dealer's invoice). Now, if the Eclipse is a hot car or if it is a seller's market, you may well have to pay more than this bare-bones price. But at least you know where to start. Offering within a few hundred dollars over a dealer's base costs puts the salesperson in a terrible fix. Your opening price is not so ridiculous that he can just ignore it. It is just low enough to lower his expectations and still keep him interested.

Some dealerships will try to itemize out their costs for such things as advertising and charge you for them separately on top of the agreed-upon price. These costs are certainly a part of the dealership's operating expenses, but whether you should pay part or all of them as a separate item on the car is another matter. In addition, the dealerships have other costs that are to come out of that $300 in profit you are trying to leave them, like the commissions and the floor plan (financing) that they pay on the cars. But that's not your problem; it's theirs.

◆ ◆ ◆

See how easy it is to find out exactly what cars cost the dealerships? You can do this either by conventional methods or by using the Internet. You can also determine the factors that will allow you to calculate their exact car and accessory costs using the stickers on the cars. This is useful in case there has been a price increase since the list you read was published. Knowing such information is like playing poker and being able to see some of your opponent's cards; it gives you a great advantage.

Your Visit to the Dealership

CHAPTER 8

Going to the Showroom

You are now ready for the big dance with the dealer. This chapter will cover what to take to the lot, how to dress like a real customer and what attitude you must have to convince the sales force you are a person to be reckoned with. Remember, by this point you have done all your homework and have that information at your fingertips. You are ready to visit the showroom.

What and Whom to Bring

A Distractor

If you are inexperienced and/or have a gentle personality, take someone else with you who will pull you out of the fire if necessary. Here's why it is desirable to take along a distractor, or a "third baseman," as this person is often called. From your normal, everyday life experiences, you probably think it's best to have all the power in your hands so you can do whatever is necessary to ensure closing the deal. Sorry, but my experience has shown me that it is actually better not to have the power to make the final decision when you enter into a car negotiation. It is still better to have someone with you whose only job is to make sure things don't happen according to the plan of the sales staff.

Car salespeople, as we shall see in a later chapter, work on the theory of limited authority. From his position of limited authority, the salesperson verbally agrees to any kind of deal you want. He does this in order to find out what you can really afford. Later, he claims not to have the authority to finalize the deal. Then his manager reworks the arrangement and demands more money from you.

Each time you have to negotiate with a manager or a new salesperson, you start from a more vulnerable position and in the process give up more. It works to your advantage if the salesperson feels you can't make the final decision. It is also helpful to have someone with you to distract the salesperson and relieve the pressure when "teams" of experienced sales staff start pushing you to make decisions.

The following exchange is a good illustration:

Salesperson (closing in for the "kill"): Now that we have answered all your objections, what will it take to get you to buy this car today, right now? (This is known as the "California approach.")

You (feeling a lot of pressure): Well, the car is nice and I really can't think of a reason not to buy it now, but. . . . (You are now getting ready to give away the store.)

Third Baseman (giving you time to think): Excuse me, but does this car come in yellow? I really like yellow.

Salesperson (really irritated that his "close" has been inter-rupted and the mood broken, but unwilling to attack the idiot who is with the buyer because he looks like the buyer's best friend): No, it doesn't. Now, as I was asking, what do you want to pay for this great car that we have spent the last three hours looking at?

Third Baseman (still giving you time to think): Why not? It would look great in yellow.

Salesperson (ignoring the third baseman): Why don't you just give me a bid to take to my manager and then we can see if he accepts it?

You: Why doesn't it come in yellow?

Salesperson (frustrated but unwilling to offend a "real" buyer): The manufacturer makes that car in only four colors with four matching upholsteries.

You (having had time to think and to resist the pressures of the salesperson): Let's talk a little bit more about getting a better price for my trade-in. As you know, the trade-in price is very important to me in terms of my ability to make a good down payment.

In this example, the pressure position has passed and you can go on with your bid to buy a car. Often, the sales staff are very practiced in their presentation. Interruptions of this sort take them off guard, and it is not easy for them to find their way back to the practiced flow of their high-pressure pitch.

A Yellow Pad and Two Types of Pens

These are necessary so you can write notes with a fine-tip pen and write big agreement items (like trade-in price) with a big colored marker so the salesperson will see them. Anything written down has more significance than the spoken word. Verbal "agreements" can later be misinterpreted or forgotten. An agreed-upon price or figure carries a lot more weight if it is put into print. If the salesperson has a casual attitude toward his claims and prices and a talent for making figures appear and disappear at will, writing down the figures makes his utterance more permanent. If he then gives you a variety of prices for your trade-in, you can quote—and point to—the highest when it is suitable. If you feel comfortable, show the numbers to him as you go along, ask for a verbal confirmation and ask him to initial the figures. His initialing of the figures does not bind him to them, as he is operating from his position of limited authority, but it does force him to stick with that figure in your discussions. This prevents him from confusing you by throwing around numbers at will.

The Results of Your Homework

Keep your homework results out of sight until needed. I went on a car buy with a young woman (maybe twenty-two or twenty-three). Prior to going to the dealership, we had worked out the prices we would accept for her trade-in and for her new car. We wrote down the figures so we could remember them and refer to them during the appropriate time in the negotiations. She put those figures on the bottom of her notebook. After the test-drive, she held her books and papers to her chest—facing out—as we were talking to the sales staff outside the negotiating room. The figures were exposed, giving the salesperson a pretty good idea of where we were going to end up.

We were still able to get close to our prices for the deal because they made sense. The economics of the situation still determined what could happen. We had allowed for the dealership to make some money—although less than they would have preferred.

Remember, do the preliminary library work and the figuring and keep the figures handy but out of sight.

Reference Books and Papers

Treat reference books and papers just as you do your homework: Keep the books handy but out of sight.

Calculator

Use your calculator whenever the salesperson is working with figures. Don't blindly accept what is told to you. Do the figuring for the salesperson if you can. It makes you more active and the salesperson more passive. It also takes away his ability to confuse you with inaccurate figures. He may still try to finagle the whole system of numbers, but it is more difficult if you are doing the math. Be careful not to let the busywork of doing the calculations pull your attention away from your main job—getting the best deal. It is a common tactic for salespeople to give interested buyers something to do so they are not thinking about whether the deal is a good one.

Interest and Payment Tables

At the end of the buy, after the trade-in has been worked out, the new-car price agreed upon and the financing arrangements determined, pull out your interest and payment tables and double-check the figures presented to you. It gives one a great feeling of confidence to be able to check the dealer's calculations of monthly payments. It increases your level of confidence in the negotiations. You are assured that the figures given you for the payments are accurate. The finance person knows that if he tries to change the numbers at the end, you will catch the changes. Also inform the finance person that you will check the payment figures later on the Web. A lot of Web sites have payment calculators (AutoSite at http://www.autosite.com is a good one). If you get an approximate figure for monthly payments before you go to the dealership (and you do end up buying a car), be sure that after you arrive home in your new car you use an Internet calculator to double-check your contract.

Payment or Financing Verification From Your Lender

As we discussed earlier in the homework section, it is to your advantage to provide your own financing. If you have obtained your own financing, have all the paperwork handy and ready to show at the appropriate time. You lose a lot of negotiating power if you have to promise to return the next day with loan confirmation. Have all of this completed before you visit the salesroom. If you come into the dealership with an approved low-interest loan, you can probably get the dealer to reduce his rate.

Proof of Insurance

In many places you must have insurance to drive. Make sure you have the details of your auto insurance handy. An insurance card will do nicely.

If you have a trade-in, here are a number of other details you should have in order:

A Clean Car

I am always amazed that people who take good care of their homes or clean up articles for a garage sale do not take the same care in presenting their cars to dealerships as potential trade-ins. A potential trade-in should be as well detailed as possible, be immaculately clean and have all personal papers removed. Repair records and items pertinent to the sale of the trade-in vehicle should be left in the glove compartment. Nothing else should be in the car.

When dealerships put cars out for sale in their lots, they detail the inside and outside of the vehicles and in many cases steam clean the engines to make them show better to customers. If the dealership is your customer for the trade-in, should you do any less to secure a good price? Your intention should be to leave your old car at the dealership and to drive away in a new car. It is important that it be ready for them to put on the lot as it is (without further cleaning). This will increase your bargaining power on a price for the trade-in.

Documentation of Debt

If you owe money on your vehicle, get documentation showing the exact amount of money left to be paid off. If you have your vehicle paid off, bring verification of this. This can be found on the title; the lienholder had to sign off once the debt was fulfilled.

All of the Keys to Your Car

Give one set of keys to the dealership's used-car evaluator, but keep the rest with you until the transaction is complete. This way if the deal goes sour, you can still drive off in your trade-in and not be held hostage by the dealership's staff. Yes, they do it if they can.

The Title for Your Trade-In

Bring the title for at least two reasons: first, to show that your car is paid off and second, to show that the title is a normal title and not some "limited" title like a salvage title. The value of a vehicle can drop dramatically if the car has a salvage title. In states that have salvage titles, they indicate that the car has been "scrapped" (for reasons such as a bad accident) and then rebuilt and the title reactivated. A vehicle with a salvage title may run well, but its perceived value, and therefore its resale value, is substantially lower.

Service Records

Nothing sells a car like a verifiable history of good service. This is especially important for the more expensive, luxury cars, but it is also useful for the less expensive models.

How to Dress

Wear comfortable, presentable clothes. You are going to be at the dealership for several hours, and you need to give the impression of being a real buyer. Tight clothing will make you uncomfortable; ripped or torn clothing will not get you a better price on your car, nor any sympathy—but it may get you a higher interest rate on your financing. Make sure you can stand, sit, yell and negotiate in your clothes without being embarrassed or uncomfortable.

Dressing well (but not outlandishly) will help you look prosperous.

You want to look as though you can afford to buy a car. People usually get better car buys and better financing if they look as if they are well educated and can afford the vehicle. Interestingly enough, the time in negotiations will decrease if you look prosperous and competent and do not allow yourself to be tricked.

Stay away from low necklines or distracting clothing. You can't be tough if you don't look tough. Keep the issues on the car, not on any other topic. The typical car salesperson may be influenced by style, fashion or skin exposure, but in most cases, it will be business before pleasure.

The Best Car-Buying Attitude

It is important to enter the showroom with certain attitudes firmly entrenched. Your body language should match your clothing and the thoroughness of your homework. You must be clear in your mind that you will buy a car today if the price is right and if you are treated well both personally and financially.

Remember that you are the customer. They have the car and they must sell it. You can live without it for a while longer. Do not allow yourself to feel pressured. Remind yourself that the salesperson is the one who is desperate. Go with the attitude, "Treat me right or I am out of here; I will not be messed with." Let them see that you have changeable moods and cannot be trifled with. If this is not your basic nature, bring a third baseman who can act this way. Try acting this way for a short period of time yourself, and see if you can pull it off.

Here is how to get that winning attitude:

• Clear your mind of extraneous details. Don't go to a buy with a head full of troubles. Once you enter that showroom, the car buy should be your first and only priority. Get the other items out of the way before you buy. If other items are pressing you and crowding your mind, put them off. If you have no car and need one, rent a car for a few days.

• Know that your financing homework is done and that for all intents and purposes, you have the cash in hand. This will give you confidence and will prevent you from being held up by later financing problems. I cannot emphasize enough how important it is that you have your financing lined up before you physically start shopping. That way, you will never have to worry if you can get your dream car financing from the dealership. You will never have to take a bad deal in order to get dealer financing; you will have your own.

• Limit the negotiations to one car, two at the most. The sales staff will look at you as a browser if you negotiate in general rather than on one specific car. Negotiating for a particular blue Taurus on the lot right now is very different than negotiating for a family car. In addition, it is hard to do "general" homework of the depth described earlier.

• Know what your trade-in is worth, what you can get the new car for and what options you will want. Be prepared. You can wing it, of course, but it will cost you in your wallet.

• Remember, it's your money. You are the customer. If the dealer presents it well, treats you well and gives you a great deal, you may buy his car. Your money can be spent at another dealership, or it can be spent on things unrelated to automobiles. If the dealerships want your money for their cars, let them court you and treat you well.

• Demand good treatment. A lack of warmth and some reserve will keep a distance between them and you, which is what you want. Most salespeople believe that if you like them, they will have more success making the sale. They will go out of their way to make you like them in order to facilitate closing a deal. Don't give them that edge. Keep them at enough of a distance so that friendship (which really doesn't exist here) does not become a factor.

How to Act

Don't be emotional—be neutral. Remember not to gush about the car. If you do, you will pay more for it. But don't be too negative either. This only makes the sales staff defensive. If you are constantly negative, they assume it means a sale is not in the near future. It will not buy you respect or a cheaper car. It will not make you look like a real buyer. Be a little unpredictable and cool. If you feel you are being treated badly or not taken seriously, be firm and let them know about it.

Don't be afraid to speak up. You must ask for a good deal to get one. Be ready to deal if the price and everything else are right.

Salespeople are trained to determine in the first several minutes exactly what kind of customer you are. Once this is settled in their minds, they choose a game plan to follow in order to "handle" you to their best advantage. It is definitely to your advantage—and very disconcerting for them—for you suddenly to show them that their whole strategy for selling you a car is not working. They have to rethink their strategy at the last minute, and it is difficult to change pace and negate all the things they have said previously to make you buy a car.

Tell the salesperson only what he needs to know. He will probe you for information about your job, why you want to buy a car and your financial situation. He will also want to know if you want to buy or lease. Tell him only what you want him to know when you want him to know it. Everything he learns will be used against you. Consider having a friend give you the following "Miranda warning" before you go onto a car lot:

Do you understand that you are going to spend a lot of money?

Do you understand that a lot of pressure will be put on you?

Do you realize that every scrap of information you give a salesperson will be used against you?

Remember, the salesperson doesn't care if you love Buffalo or the Forty-Niners, but if you indicate that you have season tickets to the Raiders, he will become an instant Raiders fan. He may also assume that if you can afford season tickets, you may be interested in a sportier and more expensive car. Striking up a football friendship may make it easier for him to sell you the fancier car.

Even your most casual comments are important to a good salesperson. A simple question like, "Does this dealership finance at competitive rates?" tells the salesperson you are a real buyer because you have already come to the point in your reasoning process to be concerned with interest rates. If you talk about leasing, the salesperson knows that people who lease usually pay a higher price for the car. He will then try to focus on lease terms rather than car price. If you give the impression of being financially strapped, needing a car, and you act interested in leasing, you will get a very high-interest-rate lease, a low price for your trade-in and a lot of talk about your bad credit report and how lucky you are to have financing at all. The salesperson probably will not deal with car price at all, and you may not even know what the vehicle cost you.

So reveal only what you want the dealer to know—no more, no less. When in doubt, say nothing.

Play dumb if it helps you. Saying, "Huh?" or "I'm sorry, I just don't understand," will put them off guard. You don't have to know everything to do well in a negotiation. During the meeting of the salesperson and the test-drive, when the salesperson is still trying to classify you, you can appear to be a little confused, uncertain and weak. Later, when it is too late for him to change his tactics and attitude, let him realize you are in control. When hit with technical or sales mumbo jumbo you don't understand, repeatedly saying, "I don't understand," may put him off guard.

Say, "This deal is just not good enough," but don't tell the salesperson why. Let him offer concessions. Force him to guess if it is the price, the trade-in, the type of car or the competition. If he is scrambling to make a deal, he may throw in things you never considered to make the deal go down. If pressed to explain why the deal isn't good enough, just say, "I don't know, it just doesn't seem good enough." Later, ask for a better price or something more specific.

When you are near an agreement, say no just one more time and see what happens. You never know—something else might fall from the tree, especially if it is late at night.

When trying to sell your trade-in, tell the salesperson that the only thing standing in the way of a sale is getting a good price for your used car and after that, everything should be downhill. Then when buying the new car, tell him that the most important thing is getting the best price for your new car.

What and Whom Not to Bring or Do

Now that we have discussed what to bring, how to act and what to do, let's look at the process from the other side: Let's see what not to do.

- Do not bring anyone who won't be able to help you. If you need someone just to help choose the color or style, send him away to a movie or anywhere before the negotiations begin. I have seen people in dealerships negotiating for a car with their young children spread out playing on blankets in the doorway of the negotiating room. How can the parents leave, walk out of the room or get upset with those kids blocking the door? To save a few dollars on child care, the parents gave up their mobility and locked themselves in a room with a salesperson (something I would hate to do). This probably resulted in their loss of several hundred dollars.

- If the person who is supplying the money is not going to be helpful in the buy, have him do something else during the negotiations. This may be difficult, but if the person is coming along just to see how you are spending the money and will get in your way (not the salesperson's), it is in your best interest not to have that person there.

- Don't put a time limit on yourself: You need the freedom to wait them out or to walk out without encumbrances. If you have to buy a car in order to get to work before 4:00 P.M., you will give away the store to get out of there by 3:30. The salesperson will feel your deadline and will stall until you panic and close the deal in his favor. The best strategy—more on this later—is to put the dealership under the time limit. Do your buying late in the evening, when the sales force wants to go home.

- Don't bring any sort of fear or apprehension. If you have done your homework, you have no reason to be anxious. You will feel more than ready for whatever happens.

Total Image

Since you want to be treated as a person who will buy a car today if treated well, tell them so. Then act and look like it. You want to be perceived as a real buyer. This gives you a lot of latitude in the way you operate and in how much the dealership will tolerate. Come prepared, looking and acting like a real buyer. Show that you are the kind of person who will buy a car today if everything is right. This is the kind of person for whom car dealers make allowances and with whom they will willingly spend a lot of their time.

Web Sites of Interest

Check out these two Web sites to get a different perspective on the whole negotiating process. Their negotiating tips may prove useful.

http://www.autoadvice.com. AutoAdvice has good information.

http://www.fightingchance.com. James Bragg's site *Fighting Chance* is great; it reflects his combative personality.

CHAPTER 9

Order of Operations

A major goal of this book is to help you develop a winning system for getting a great deal on a quality car. I believe I'm achieving my goal by providing you with lots of solid tips and information. That's my part of the bargain. Your part is to move beyond what you read and translate it into buying success. After all, it is one thing to read a book on how to buy a car; it is another thing to be able to utilize what you've read. That's why you need a well thought-out plan to guide you through the car-buying process.

Remember that as a buyer you have many strengths and you should not hesitate to take advantage of them all. Don't feel sorry for the dealerships or the salespeople, and don't feel that you have to play by the dealerships' rules or follow their agendas. Do what you have to do to control all parts of the car purchase. Most important, you must execute the various car-buying operations in the right order. If you do the "first thing first," you will not be confused or influenced by the tactics a sales force uses to control the buying situation. As a result, you will save more money and they will make less profit.

The only way to know if you are really in control is to make sure every step gets done correctly, gets done in order and leads you closer to your new car. You should know exactly how much you got paid for you trade-in and how close this price is to *Blue Book* wholesale. You should know what your new car cost the dealership and exactly how much profit they are making. You should know exactly what factory-to-consumer cash is available to you and what factory-to-dealer incentives are available to the dealer. If you know these figures, you will know if you are getting a good deal at every step of the transaction.

How do you know what a good deal is? By studying costs and

knowing what profit amounts to allow the dealership. The alternative is to keep grinding away on price, not knowing if what you are asking for is realistic or not. The key to being able to negotiate is to watch ALL the costs, not just the price of the new car. A dealer can practically give away the new car and still make plenty of money by "handling you well" on other issues like trade-ins, interest rates, extended warranties and other options.

The driving force for the dealerships is profits. That means making money on the total of the various parts of the negotiation. If they only break even or even lose money on one part, they will make it up on others. Let's look at the parts of a car purchase and examine the order and logic of each.

The Four Basic Parts of an Auto Buy

There are four basics parts of a car buy in which money can change hands, and all of them must be controlled by you. These parts, in order, are (1) the used-car trade-in; (2) the new-car price; (3) buying special packages/options/extras; and (4) financing.

Most car buyers focus only on one aspect of buying a car, the new-car price. You don't want to be such a buyer, because it's unwise to neglect the other three points. If you are to get a great deal, you really must consider all four aspects of car buying. Now let's look at them in their preferred order.

The best way to control the negotiations is to operate in the following order. Do not deviate from this order. Don't go on to point two before settling on the first point. Don't settle for allowances, and always know the dollar value of each point. Allowances lose you money.

The Used Car Trade-In

The dealerships want to make a profit on the used-car portion of the transaction even if they don't plan to sell the cars from their lots. A dealer might plan to sell your car to another dealer or to a wholesaler to auction. Auction prices are considerably lower than the retail price the dealership might get for selling your trade-in off the lot. The dealer will offer you a still lower price in order to make a profit selling your trade-in at auction.

Fight hard for a good realistic price. Indicate that it is the most important thing in the world to you, that you demand a good price for your used car. Do not begin to discuss the new-car price until you have received a good price for your trade-in. Be prepared to walk away in order to emphasize the importance of this issue. You must make the salesperson believe that you are a real buyer and that once the trade-in price is settled to your satisfaction, the rest of the transaction will go more smoothly. If the dealership agrees to a good price and then tries to take it back later, get mad and be prepared to walk out. If you get a firm fixed price for your used car, the dealer should stick with it. Dramatize the importance and the permanence of the price offered for your trade-in by writing it down with your colored marker. Have the salesperson initial that price or at least acknowledge it. Do not accept an allowance toward the purchase of a more expensive car. Get a hard price.

It would be ideal if you could easily get *Blue Book* wholesale for your used-car trade-in. At best you won't get more than wholesale for your car from a dealership unless it is an unusual circumstance. Realistically, you may not get wholesale for your car. A good price would be *Blue Book* wholesale minus $300. Even more realistically, you may be forced to settle for less than that. Again, remember that some cars are in demand and will bring more than wholesale. Others are not well regarded and will get considerably less.

The best price for your used car might be obtained by selling it yourself. Usually, cars sold through the paper or auto trader magazines advertise between *Blue Book* wholesale and *Blue Book* retail. A hot car in cherry shape may sell for more, while a car of average shape and popularity may sell for closer to wholesale or even below.

Remember, car sales staff immediately categorize buyers. They recognize people who fight hard for a good trade-in price, people who must have a good new car price, impulse buyers, etc. Your first job is to convince them that you are a person who needs a good price on the trade-in. They will assume that the remainder of the sale will be easy.

The New-Car Price

You have done your homework and you know what your new car cost the dealer. A great price to aim for would be $300 above dealer's cost as calculated in chapter seven. Remember, do not begin talking about new-car price until you have a firm price for your trade-in— not an allowance, a firm price.

If the dealership demands that you discuss new cars first or wants to run a credit report, play at it for a while and then steer the discussion back to used-car price. To emphasize this, toss the salesperson the keys to your trade-in, and ask him repeatedly if he has looked at it and what the word is on the value of the car. Act as though you can't concentrate on anything else but the trade-in. Eventually he will give in just to keep the negotiating going and not let it bog down. Dealers rarely consider the used-car price as a set price. They count on being able to go back to this price later or to confuse you so it will be forgotten.

Negotiate now for the best car price, using all the techniques you will soon read about. Fight here for your best price. Do not allow the dealer to cut the price given for your trade-in as you strive for a good price on the new car. Stop negotiating immediately, point to the figure on your pad (which the salesperson has already acknowledged) and insist that that number does not change. Once he acknowledges the figure again, resume the new-car price negotiation. If you are forced to do this more than once, he will soon get the point and will no longer try to change the price given for your used car. Do not discuss financing or terms of payment or buy versus lease here; go strictly after car price. There are two things you should say over and over again: "I really want to buy a car today" and "It is most important that I get a good price for this new car; if we do that, everything else will happen more easily."

At the end of the negotiations, you should have a fixed firm price written down for the new car—not a monthly payment, not an allowance deal with a used car, not a difference, but a dollar value for the new car including all the accessories you want. As with the trade-in, write the agreed-upon price in your notebook with a colored marker, and get the salesperson to initial it if you can.

Remember, you may be forced to take some things you don't want to get items you do want. Many items come only in packages. For instance, you may have to take tilt steering and cruise control when you buy the air-conditioning you want.

If you can couple a wholesale trade-in minus $300 with a wholesale plus $300 buy, you are an incredible car buyer and my hero.

Buying Special Packages/Options/Extras

This occurs in the office of the finance person. Remember, take only those extra items that you decided beforehand you needed. Think carefully about getting insurance, special exterior packages, rust prevention packages, etc. The best advice I can offer is to steer clear of the items offered in financing. These items are usually high priced with large markups. In the event you want something like an extended warranty, negotiate strongly for it. Try to knock down the price by as much as half; this is not an unreasonable expectation given the markup. Threaten to terminate the whole deal unless you get it.

Financing

As we discussed earlier, it is important to feel confident about your financing. Get your financing through outside sources before you come into the showroom. This may be the financing you eventually choose. Alternatively, you may decide for one reason or another to take the dealer's financing. Show the lowest outside financing to the dealer and see if he can do better for you. Get him to quote his interest as an APR (annual percentage rate), and try not to get a "Rule of 78" interest payment (this will be explained in detail in the chapter on financing). This may be impossible, but if you keep the car until the end of the financing, it won't make a difference. However, there is an advantage to getting straight declining balance interest. If you do take a dealer's financing, make sure you get a reasonable drop in interest to compensate for the disadvantages of Rule of 78.

Remember, for best results, things should be done in a certain order. If you negotiate for your new-car price before you have settled on your trade-in price, you face the probability of giving away your trade-in because you have fixed your allegiance on your new car.

It is critical to do these four operations in the correct order. Do not mix them up or go from new car to financing to trade-in price to get a better car price if you take an extended warranty. After you have finished the test-drive, have picked out a car you want and are ready to go into the negotiating room and buy that vehicle, do it in the following order:

1. Negotiate and settle the trade-in price. Don't do anything else.
2. After the trade-in price is settled, determine the new-car equipment and purchase price.
3. In the finance room, figure out what extras you want.
4. Determine how you are going to pay for the vehicle with the finance person.
5. Set payments, if any, and financing terms before you leave.

Finally, summarize the whole deal in your mind and look at all the costs. You should know exactly what factory-to-consumer cash is available to you and what factory-to-dealer incentives are available to the dealer. You also should know what your new car cost the dealership and exactly how much profit the dealer is making. If you know these figures, you will know if you are getting a good deal at every step of the transaction.

Web Sites of Interest

You'll find good helpful buying information at these sites:

http://www.autobytel.com. Autobytel is as good a place as any to get initial Internet quotes to use in bargaining for a new-car price.

http://www.carloanhelp.com. Carloanhelp.com might be of use for financing if your credit is not so good.

http://www.warrantygold.com. Warranty Gold is a great source for extended warranties.

CHAPTER 10

Test-Drive and Inspection

Congratulations—you're ready to take a test-drive! I know this is really exciting (most buyers simply can't wait), but try to put your excitement at bay for a bit because there's something you need to do before you go to the dealer and step foot in that car.

I'm talking about reading professional test-drive evaluations of your car. The single benefit to doing this is that after you read what the pros think of your potential car, that information will stick in your mind and you can then determine if the vehicle's alleged weak spots are a problem for you—they may not be.

You can go about reading up on your car in two ways: You can either purchase some of the more notable car review magazines, or you can get on the Web. I'd recommend doing the latter first. Many good Web sites evaluate all parts of the test drive, from how the car steers and drives to how it feels being inside the car's interior. With Web sites, you get current information, and often researching on the Web first can point you, if necessary, to the right publications to find reviews of your car.

Three notable and helpful sites I recommend are *Consumer Reports* at http://www.consumerreports.com, *Road & Track* at http://www.roadandtrack.com and *Car and Driver* at http://www.caranddriver.com. (The first is good for solid professional evaluations; the last two allow you to see what car nuts think of your potential car.)

Again, your test drive will be much more productive with an expert's comments about the car's strengths and weaknesses tucked into the back of your mind. Now let's get on to what happens once you decide to head to the dealer and take that test-drive.

Taking the Test-Drive

Nothing is more pleasant for a prospective car buyer than the test-drive. It is usually a time of minimum pressure and maximum enjoyment, but for you, the serious buyer, the test-drive should also be the beginning of an extensive evaluation that will show you if the car you have chosen is one you will be happy with.

People who are unhappy with the car they have so carefully chosen can often trace their problems right back to something they didn't notice or failed to seriously consider during the test-drive. As with anything having to do with cars, the stories abound: One friend never uses his BMW's fifth gear because he can't reliably shift into it from fourth. An acquaintance is afraid to drive on freeways because her new car won't accelerate fast enough; another has a terrible time getting out of her car's seats because the lateral side supports on the driver's side impede her graceful exit. And the list goes on.

Take the test-drive seriously. Enjoy it, but don't get so caught up in the excitement of buying a new car that you are careless. Allow yourself plenty of time, perhaps an hour for a complete inspection, preferably of the exact car, with all the options, that you want to take home. Of course a salesperson will be there with his own agenda and goals, but don't let this deter you from your appointed task. When he sees your detailed checklist, he will know you are a buyer to be reckoned with.

The test-drive usually occurs soon after you arrive at the dealership. Most buyers can't wait. Before you get behind the wheel of a car that looks just like the one you want, make sure it is exactly the one you want, complete, if possible, with every option you want. Also, before the test-drive, you should ask the salesperson to have your trade-in evaluated while you're gone. It is best not to be present when the used-car evaluator finds all the items with which they will devalue your old car and justify a low offer. If you are not there, you are in a psychologically stronger position later to negotiate for a better price.

The salesperson who invariably accompanies you during your test-drive may now seem more like a guide, more chatty and relaxed. But, for strategic reasons, consider the test-drive as another part of your negotiations. Tell him only what he needs to know. Don't be too negative about the car unless you have already decided that you absolutely don't want it. Also, avoid giving buying signals. It is best to remain coolly analytical and to appear neutral at this time. There is nothing wrong, however, with showing him that you are knowledgeable and have done your homework.

Don't forget that your evaluation of the car really began with your own research so that now you are competent to say something more than, "It's really a beauty." You are in a position to assess, firsthand, the validity and relevance of the professional ratings. For instance: Does its reported lack of power at high speeds pose a problem for you? Perhaps not if you are a slow city driver. It will take time to think, consider and evaluate your priorities. Above all, be willing and determined to take your time. With these factors in mind, you are ready to start your test-drive.

The Predrive Inspection

- Do you love the exterior? If not, you should look at another vehicle.
- Do you love its interior ambiance, or is it just adequate?
- Are the doors so heavy or the door handles so awkward it is a strain to use them?
- Do the doorstops keep the door open easily? (This is of special concern on larger cars.)
- Can you lock and unlock the doors easily from the inside?
- Are you comfortable in the car? Do your feet fit the pedals?
- Test the seats in all positions. Can you get in and out of them easily? Are they adequately adjustable?
- Do the seats have good back support?
- Is the headrest adequately adjustable?
- Does your head hit the roof? (This may prevent you from buying a car with a sunroof. Sunroofs are little lower than normal roofs.)
- Are the lights, wiper switches, cruise control, radio, etc., easy to find and use?
- Is the horn easily found and easy to use?

- Is the interior lighting adequate?
- Are there map lights? Do they work well?
- Will the lights automatically turn off when the engine shuts down? (This prevents the battery from draining if the lights are left on.)
- Can you easily read the gauges, radio and computer readouts, both day and night?
- Are the controls usable, or are they too complicated?
- Are both mirrors adjustable from the driver's side?
- Are there adequate pockets? For instance, where would you put a map, a book of maps, a pocketbook, your garage door opener, extra keys, cigarettes and other small items?
- Are there vanity mirrors on both visors of the car? Are they lit?
- Are there coin slots and cup holders?
- Is there a front seat console for tapes, CDs, etc.?
- Can you easily attach and adjust the seat belts?
- Can you easily see over the hood?
- Can you see over the back and front of the car?
- Can you easily see into the backseat to talk to others or watch your kids?
- Are there air bags on both sides?

The Moving Inspection

- Did the car start easily? Turn the car on and off several times.
- Is the steering column easy to lock and unlock?
- Does the radio work well? Is the sound adequate for you?
- Does the car maneuver easily at low speeds getting out of the parking lot?
- How is the turning radius? Can you make a U-turn in the road?
- Can you parallel park easily?
- How is the acceleration? Can you zip around in comfort and in control of the situation?
- Is there enough acceleration to easily fit into traffic—even freeway traffic? How about going up a hill?
- Is the car powerful enough? Does it pass easily? Does it have enough power to get up hills when loaded?

- Is there power at both low speeds and high speeds? Many cars have drive trains that are fine at lower speeds and die at higher speeds.
- Is the car so big it feels like a boat or so small it feels vulnerable?
- If the transmission is manual, is it smooth? How does it feel while shifting? Is it too easy to mix up the gears?
- If the transmission is automatic, does it shift smoothly and at the right times?
- Is the steering responsive at higher speeds? Does it understeer or oversteer around corners?
- Do the brakes work smoothly without needing a lot of pressure? Would you feel comfortable in a panic stop?
- Is the car quiet when stopped, moving and accelerating? Turn off the radio to really hear it.
- How is the wind noise at higher speeds?
- Is the car stable at cruising speeds?
- Is the ride too hard or too soft? Do you need a different suspension?
- Does it "porpoise" when hitting bumps?
- How is the vibration at high speeds and on rougher roads?
- Does the engine idle smoothly at stops?
- Can it tow anything you have to tow?
- Is this the exact car you are buying or a similar one with significant differences (like a different engine, etc.)?
- Is visibility good in all directions? Do you notice any major blind spots?
- Are the instruments visible? Can you easily reach all the features, including the radio, windshield wipers, lights, temperature controls, dash, etc.?

The Postdrive Inspection

After you have driven the car and are back at the dealership, look at the following:

- Will the vehicle fit in your garage?
- Is the trunk adequate?
- Try the backseat. Is it comfortable for both sitting and reclining?

- Do both front seats recline?
- Can you open the hood easily?
- Is the motor easily set up for servicing? (This is of particular interest to those of us who change oil, etc.)
- Are the oil, water, power steering fluid, etc., marked and easily accessible?

At the end of the test-drive, you should know if you must have this car at any price, if you want it only at the right price or if you still want it at all. If your answer was you only want it at the right price, which is the only satisfying and "no regrets" way to buy a car, you are now ready to have some fun negotiating for it.

CHAPTER 11

Getting the Best Price for Your Trade-In

OK, this is it. It's time to buy the car. You have done your homework, seen the dealerships' products, read all the literature available, seen what you can afford and what the experts say about your choice of vehicles and finally taken a test-drive. Now is the time to decide: Are you going to buy this car or not?

If the answer is, "No" or "I don't know yet," don't feel pressured by the dealership or the salesperson. Get your keys back and walk off the lot as quickly as possible, and go somewhere either to see other vehicles or to decide what to do. But whatever you do, don't do your thinking in the dealership's negotiating offices.

Negotiations

If the answer is, "Yes," now is the time to remember to stick to your order of operations and concentrate on getting the best price for your trade-in. Why? Because most car buyers use their trade-in money as the down payments for their new cars. Getting the best trade-in price for your vehicle is critical to making a good car buy. The standard tactic of most dealerships is to give you reasonable prices on their new cars and to absolutely destroy and lowball you on trade-ins. Don't be misled by low new-car prices alone. Your first order of business is to get the very best price for your used car. You know what it is worth because you did all the homework. Now let's go after getting that price from some pretty hard characters.

Here is the way to achieve this goal. First, examine and change your attitude. You must appear colder, more detached and more irritable than you did during the test-drive. Allow yourself to be lured into the salesperson's office to discuss a possible car purchase. Be a little reluctant, and go at his insistence. I usually stay outside the dealership leaning on a test model for as long as possible because I know where I want to end up price wise and because I know my hanging around outside the "safe" office makes salespeople and sales managers uneasy. During the test-drive, you should have been a little more mild-mannered and a lot less knowledgeable than you will appear now. It is always best to appear naive at first to throw off the sales staff who make fast judgments about people and to gradually appear to be tougher and more knowledgeable as the negotiations progress.

Remember, the dealership's salespeople are trained to classify car buyers in various ways. One classification is the "trade-in buyer." This type of person is concerned primarily with getting a good price for his trade-in. Once this is taken care of, he is less concerned about car payments, new-car price or any other issue. Thus the dealership gives him a good price for his trade-in and makes money by dealing hard on the other parts of the auto transaction. Your goal at this point in the transaction is to convince your salesperson that you are a trade-in buyer. Later you will convince him that you are a "new-car price buyer." A new-car price buyer is one who is interested primarily in the price of the new car and will not concentrate on trade-in price or any other issue. Your goal is to be a trade-in buyer when it suits you, then to switch and become a new-car price buyer later in the transaction. This way you can garner the advantages of high trade-in price and low new-car purchase price.

Once you have begun to change your attitude and are in the office, reiterate that you would like to buy a car today but that you want the best price for your trade-in before you discuss the new car. Tell your salesperson that if this point is handled to your satisfaction, everything else will go smoothly. You want him to mark you as a trade-in buyer and treat you as one. Remember, a trade-in buyer is given a great price on her trade-in in the hopes that she will be locked into buying a new car and will provide the profit the dealership needs in the other areas of the transaction. The salesperson hopes to make his profit on the new-car purchase, the financing and the financing extras. Let him think this will happen for now.

I can't stress this enough: Get the dealer's price on your trade-in first. Don't give a definite figure of what you want. It is a general principle of negotiation that whoever mentions price first loses. Indicate how important it is for you to get a great price. If you can, send the salesperson back to his boss many times by indicating that their price for your trade-in is unacceptable. If necessary, get huffy and upset and appear to have your feelings hurt. Keep saying the trade-in price is critical to buying a new car. Don't give your bottom-line figure early. Reiterate that you really want to get a car today, and ask them why they won't let you do so. Remember, you want to be classified as a trade-in buyer.

If anyone came with you to approve the car choice and pick the color of the upholstery, ask that person to leave. (Obviously, you want to work this out in advance of your arrival at the showroom.) This is the time to ask the person (mild-mannered spouse, etc.) who is approving the choice but would not be good in a negotiation to go away and come back later after the car has been bought. This may be tough to do because you surely don't want to hurt this person's feelings. Is it worthwhile paying hundreds of dollars to avoid some hurt feelings? This is your call, but you can buy your helper something nice with the savings.

Make sure you have all the details of your trade-in handy to support your claim that the car is a cream puff. You should have brought details on extra features, recent repair records, etc. Show these details even if the car is not a cream puff, but later settle for a lower price. Remember your strongest negotiating posture at this point is one of a trade-in buyer who loves the old car and is a little irrational about it.

If used-car prices are high, remind the salesperson that you are aware of that fact. State that you know your car is a cream puff and you know used-car prices are high, so the dealer will be able to sell it immediately. Tell the salesperson you want the dealership's best figure now.

After you are given the dealer's first price (which will most certainly be low and unsatisfactory), try a new technique. Simply say, "You have to do better than that if this conversation is to continue." Send the salesperson back for a better figure. Send him back frequently for a better price. Think of it as exercise; it's good for him and good for you. My rule of thumb is that a salesperson should make a total of five to ten trips back and forth between you and the boss for a standard car transaction. Emphasize that this trade-in price is critical and is the only thing standing between you and a new-car purchase.

If the price comes back low, ask to see his boss or the person who evaluated the vehicle. Tell your salesperson that if you are treated right, you may come back for future vehicles as well. Stick to the topic of used-car price; don't meaningfully discuss new-car price at this time.

Hold fast to the price you want for your trade-in. Don't accept his low "auction" price. (Your research will tell you what the auction price really is, or at least what the wholesale price is based on car condition, mileage, etc.)

Remember, you came in late—one to two hours before closing. You will be there for several hours after closing. They are tired—you are not. Let the negotiations go slowly. You want them to be the ones to try to speed things up by giving concessions. The longer this deal takes and the later it goes, the better it is for you. Fatigue on their part will make for better prices for you. Tire them out; make them want to get the transaction over with. Make absolutely sure that they consider you a real buyer; keep saying, "I really want to buy a car today."

Chapter fifteen (Your Best Tactics) lists a series of techniques or tactics designed to help you get your best deal. For this part of your car-buying process, go to that chapter and read "Broken Record" and "You Have to Do Better Than That." These techniques will be of great use to you here.

In a perverse way, salespeople expect you to be unreasonable when defending your trade-in. Don't disappoint them. Hold fast initially. Don't give your expected price first; try for *Blue Book* wholesale for your car, and then let your price slip below wholesale. If your car is a wreck, you will get a much lower price. If it is cherry with low mileage, you can get closer to wholesale. Remember, a great price is about $300 less than *Blue Book* wholesale. If your car is a hot vehicle, you may get that price, but be prepared to accept less.

Firm Price vs. Allowances

Get a firm fixed price for your trade-in; don't settle for an allowance. An allowance is where the dealer says, "I will give you $2,000 for your car if you buy this particular upscale model at full price." You eventually don't know what you got for your car or what you paid for the new car. It all becomes very confusing. Compartmentalize each individual transaction; a trade-in negotiation is a trade-in negotiation and should not be tied in with any other part of the transaction. If you are offered an allowance, get a little huffy and get back to price. Make it clear that you will not accept an allowance but will proceed with the transaction only after a firm price for your trade-in has been agreed on.

This is a final reminder: Be persistent; be firm; threaten to walk out. Don't just melt away at the first touch of dealer resistance. If the dealer won't give in at all, walk out and try your tactics at a different dealership. But always indicate that you are a real buyer and that you "want to buy a car today."

Remember, you have the edge: You are the customer, and it is your money.

CHAPTER 12

Examples of Bad Negotiating

Most people don't remember the details of their last car buys. All they know is they ended up with higher payments than they expected. Some people don't even know what their cars really cost them. All they know is that the cars weren't paid off when they were ready to sell them. I've heard so many car war stories and been to so many dealerships that I've decided to show you how these undesirable situations occur.

As you drive your mud-spattered old car into the lot of a local new-car dealership, it backfires, thus alerting the sales staff that you have arrived. You, your spouse and three kids get out. You are tired after a twelve-hour shift and are still wearing your work clothes. As you enter the showroom, a salesperson comes forward to greet you.

You: Can you show me some cars?

PROBLEM. Your body language tells the salesperson you are really tired and are doing this after work. Your clothing indicates that in spite of your immediate need for a car, you may not be able to afford one. Your car looks as though it may not make it out of the lot, and your frazzled-looking spouse and kids indicate that you want to get this over with as quickly as possible.

The salesperson is thinking, *These people may be a credit risk. I bet their credit report is really marginal. At least they could have spiffed up the trade-in. With the whole family here, they will probably agree to almost anything. If they give me a hard time, I will blow them off. But if they do buy, they will definitely pay full price.*

Friendly Salesperson (FSP): Hi, I'm Joe Carshark. How do you like these cars? They are the best to come out of Detroit in years. I am really glad you came today because this is our once-a-year founder's sale, and we have been doing so well that we only have a few models left in stock. We are going to put you in the seat of the car of your dreams right now. Are you ready to buy a car today?

You: Slow down, slow down. I haven't even decided what model I want yet. I like to take my time and not be pressured. I've had a long day. I just came in for a test-drive and to ask a few questions.

PROBLEM. All you have done here is indicate to your FSP that you are irritable, can't stand pressure and may not be a serious buyer. These kinds of statements at the beginning don't buy you credibility or a better deal. There is plenty of time to show him who is boss later on. If anything, it's smart strategy to be easy and enthusiastic initially and hard later on.

FSP: I understand how you feel about pressure. A lot of people feel the same way you do about buying a car. But people who come to this dealership have complimented us on our friendly, civilized approach. We realize that buying a car is stressful, and we plan to make the whole experience as easy for you as possible. We even have some toys for the kids. By the way, I also hate salespeople, especially insurance salespeople. You don't sell insurance, do you? Ha ha. (The salesperson is using the feel/felt/found technique to defuse your resentment. He is also trying to qualify you as a real buyer by probing your financial situation.)

You: No, actually I work at Consolidated Aircraft. I'm a junior engineer and have been working part-time for a few months now, but I hope to be called back to full-time work soon. Probably in two to three weeks at the most.

PROBLEM. Bad, bad, bad. The FSP now knows you are practically unemployed and may not be able to afford a new car. This means higher interest rates, a higher down payment and more pressure on you to prove you qualify for credit. In addition, now he'll have less patience with you if you prove to be a difficult buyer. In general, do not divulge any personal information. Remember the Miranda warning from earlier in the book: Everything your FSP finds out now "can and will be used against you."

FSP: Yes, I've heard that times are tough, but with our special incentives and rebates we're seeing a lot of action. Speaking of action, did you see the Cowboys last weekend? (The FSP is now trying to become your friend because people buy more easily from people they like and trust. He has pegged you as an amiable person who needs to establish a personal relationship with someone before he buys.)

You: Well, I'm actually not a Cowboys fan. I like the Giants.

FSP: Yes, me too. They are having a great year. (You can bet he will like whatever you like whether it be football, politics, polo or collecting bottle openers. At this point, your FSP is concentrating on defusing your earlier perceptions about salespeople and trying to find out what emotional buttons to push.)

FSP: What kind of car were you considering?

You: I need a station wagon, and I don't want to pay more than $17,000. I can afford monthly payments of $400 or so a month.

PROBLEM. As soon as you mention price and payments, the FSP thinks you will be willing to pay at least $17,000 and at least $400 a month, probably more. Since you weren't shy about mentioning money—a delicate subject for most customers—the FSP feels he can get as much information out of you as he needs. He is encouraged and immediately launches into his pitch.

FSP: Before we go on, tell me, did you see our ad or hear about us from a friend?

You: Well, my dad always had good luck with your cars, my old car is about dead and the whole family hates it. (Spouse nods obviously and emphatically.) We want a new car now.

PROBLEM. Bad, bad. You've just told your FSP where all your hot buttons are. You need, not want, a car now, and you know your trade-in isn't worth much. So the FSP will feel free to give you a low price for your trade-in. You also told him that pleasing your family is a factor in this buy. They are pushing for a new car. He will load you with lots of options—that means extra profit for the dealership. Now that he has this valuable information, he will hold out the carrot of the test-drive while he probes for more information.

FSP: Well, now that I know where you stand, let's go for a test-drive. What sort of equipment do you want on your new car?

You: I really don't want much more than a bare-bones car, but my spouse wants power everything.

FSP: I can understand that. Some people like every comfort in a car. By the way, before we take the test-drive, do you plan to buy the car for cash, or are you going to finance through us? Also, what about the down payment?

You: We have enough cash for a good down payment, but the monthly payments will be a problem.

PROBLEM. You have just qualified yourself as a payment buyer, so later complaints that the car costs too much will be ignored and countered with talk of better payments or a larger down payment. Also, since payments are your big issue, he will not worry about giving you much for your trade-in.

FSP: Trust me. If you can come up with a good down payment, we can get you really good monthly payments.

PROBLEM. He has already decided that you sure aren't going to get that down payment from your trade-in. Also, those "really good monthly payments" will be spread out for seventy-two months—six years

You: Boy, that's a relief. I was really afraid of high payments. Let's take that test-drive.

FSP: Fine, but just to save time later, fill out this credit application before we go for a test-drive. That way we can do a credit check on you and have all the information by the time we get back.

You: No problem. (But you are wondering what your credit report really says; you haven't checked it recently. This is the beginning of a panic attack.)

Finally, your FSP takes you all out for a drive in an upscale model with all the extras including a bigger motor so you will be safer getting onto the expressways. When you question the costs of all these extras, he assures you they are easily within your price range.

During the test-drive, the FSP continually probes and endeavors to discover (and answer) any objections you might have. He makes comments like, "Do you like this type of upholstery?" or "We have an upgrade sound system available" or "By the way, did you notice the pinstriping as you got in? We have a special deal on it this month."

After the test-drive, you and your FSP take a look at your old car. As he walks around it, he doesn't say anything, but he taps on parts of the car that are dented, stained or imperfect. He fingers rips in the upholstery and makes sure you know he hears noises in the engine. Each time he discovers a "defect" that you knew was there but had sort of grown used to, your heart stops and your hope of getting a good trade-in price further decreases. He won't directly say the car is bad, but the FSP lets you infer it from his actions.

FSP: Let's go inside now. I'll have our used-car manager really go over your car. It's really not my department, so I can't quote you a price. I just hope he feels it is worth more than I do. Hopefully, he will let us use it as a trade-in. But I have to warn you, he is a really difficult person. He may not want this vehicle at all (at this point he notes the panicked look in your eye), but I can handle him. By the way, have you ever considered selling this car yourself?

You: No, I haven't. I hate writing ads and staying home all weekend. Besides, I'm a terrible salesperson; I just can't stand haggling with people.

The FSP now knows what you will do if you are offered a low price on your trade-in. You have left yourself no options. You will not sell the car yourself, and you have admitted you do not like to argue or haggle. At this point, the FSP is setting the stage for hooking you into the new car first, then confirming what you already know—that your used car isn't worth much.

> **FSP:** Now let's really talk turkey. It's obvious you like the car with all the extras, the bigger engine, the sunroof, the upgraded upholstery. Don't you? (This is a technique: He is making a statement and getting you to agree to it by asking you a question that has only one answer—yes.)
>
> **You:** Sure, I mean, what's not to like? But I'm not sure if we can afford it. I already told you how much I can afford to pay monthly. Is it within that range?
>
> **FSP:** You quoted me a figure of $400 a month, but that was for a bare-bones car. If you can go just a little higher, to $450, and put down about $3,000, we can put you in the driver's seat right now. What do you say? (A big silence here. Soon both you and your spouse nod; this is called a silent close and is very powerful. Notice that he has gotten you to forget about the price of the car. All he will talk about from this point on are payments.)
>
> **FSP:** Think of it this way. It isn't what you pay for the car; it's your monthly payments that are important. Don't you agree? (Another big silence here, and you both nod in agreement.)
>
> **FSP:** Since you both like the car and can afford the payments, let's do the paperwork right now. OK?
>
> **You:** I guess so.
>
> **PROBLEM.** At this point, you have essentially agreed to buy a car today, and if there is a later problem, the FSP will remind you of this. Remember, he negotiates from limited authority; he can say, "My boss won't let me do that." But if you agree to something and then back away, he will accuse you of being dishonest or not playing fair.
>
> **Spouse:** I agree that the payments are important. We really do love the car, but I think we should backtrack a little. What about our trade-in? It really is a nice car.
>
> **You:** (You vividly remember the friendly salesperson noticing

all the defects in the car.) Well, honey, let's not go overboard. You know it has dents, and it doesn't start real well. (To FSP) Has your manager decided what he'll give us for the car?

At this point, your salesperson excuses himself to find out, leaving you alone to worry for what seems like an hour. Finally, he returns.

FSP: I have bad news. Our used-car manager feels it is only worth about $500 to $600 at best. It's not really the kind of vehicle we usually even keep on our lot. Look, let's sit down and talk about the new car first and then handle the trade. It might take me some time to convince him, but as soon as we're done here, I'll try again. Maybe I can get you a better allowance.

You: Please tell him that it's in good shape for a six-year-old car. It starts a little hard in cold weather, but otherwise it's a great little car.

PROBLEM. The FSP thinks his position is solid because you have accepted him as your advocate. He takes strong control now.

FSP: If we do take your trade-in for $600 with your $3,500 cash down—it was $3,500 you were going to put down in cash, wasn't it? (You nod yes even though you really don't remember.) If you can give me, say, $475 a month, we can work out a deal.

The conversation will go on and on like this with you giving in a little and him waffling until a final monthly payment (not a car price) is agreed upon.

Several times during the negotiation, another person will wander into the room and speak to you and your FSP. This person will say things like, "Let's finish things up here as soon as possible if you can. It's already an hour after closing time, and we've been keeping the financing staff waiting" or "I just want to let you know that I just got a chance to speak with the manager about your trade-in, and we're giving you top dollar. He says we'll probably have to junk it, so I just want to let you know that we're doing all we can."

In most dealerships, the closer is the real salesperson. He is the person the dealership depends on not to let the customer get away. Your FSP assures you that he has everything under control and tells you not to worry about the closer.

Sometime later, after giving up and agreeing to whatever it is you have agreed to, you will go for a chat with the finance person, who will dismiss your FSP and usher you into his office. Even though you are thinking that you really need a break here (by this time you're really tired and a bit confused), you are also anxious to finish the deal and get home, so you don't protest.

Finance Person: You people really look beat, but don't worry. It's almost over. I'm as anxious as you are to get this over with so I can hand you the keys to your new car. It is a beauty, isn't it? (He then stops and waits for an answer.)

You: Yes, we just love the car, but can we afford it?

Spouse: We really do want this car. We haven't spent all this time here for nothing. It's getting late, and the children have to get to bed.

You: What do we have to do to get it now?

Finance Person: Well, we do have a little problem with your credit report. You do know that, don't you?

You: Well, I did have some problems three years ago, but I am in pretty good shape now. That old problem wasn't supposed to be on my record. That was some time ago, and I am making regular payments now. Does this mean you can't get me financed?

Finance Person: Don't worry; we will figure it out somehow. I know we are going to have trouble getting you the low interest rate we promised. That is only for people with good credit. Lucky for you, we are a large dealership and have been in business for years. We have special credit sources available to help you. You may have to pay an extra point or two, but I can't see any other way of obtaining the financing. You do understand, don't you? (Nice guilt attack and a little bit of "I am the good guy" routine. You now feel so unsure of yourself that you probably will not even contest the higher interest rate that will be artfully buried in the finance charges.)

You: Well, we certainly appreciate your help. (Like most people who have had credit problems, you feel guilty and fully expect that most institutions will not lend you money. So the friendly person helping you now seems like your only hope.)

Finance Person: Come to think of it, I do have another suggestion that might help you. Do you have any other sources of money? Instead of $3,500 down, if you can come up with about $1,000 more, we can probably keep the interest rate lower, say, only two or three points higher than conventional. I would like to be able to do that for you.

You: I guess I can come up with some more down money as long as the payments are still within the $450 a month we agreed on.

Finance Person: Also, I would like you to consider getting our extended seven-year guarantee on the engine and drive train. It only costs $995, and it's a guarantee you really can't afford to be without. The engine and drive train are the most expensive parts of the car, and our guarantee protects you.

You: I really can't afford it.

Finance Person: We can finance the cost and just add it in your monthly payments; you'll never even notice it.

You: Well, yes. But it seems like a lot of money.

Finance Person: If we can finance it for $20 a payment, can we just add it in? You do want it, don't you?

You: Well, yes. If we can finance it. . .

Finance Person (interrupting): What about an antitheft protection system? (Here he goes onto a new topic and thus assumes an agreement in the absence of an objection.) And what about a protective coating for the outside of the car as well?

You: How much more is that?

Finance Person: Oh, about $18 a month.

You: I don't want it.

Spouse: I think we should definitely get the antitheft system. After all, I work at night and some of those neighborhoods are pretty bad.

You: OK, OK. But I really don't want anything else.

From the tone of your voice, a good finance person knows that it is time to stop. He has pushed you to the limit. To push you further might endanger the sale. So he ushers you to a waiting room and offers you some drinks and donuts. He says he needs a few minutes to prepare the paperwork and make some phone calls. The mention of phone calls worries you, and as you wait, your anxiety level rises as you anticipate additional complications.

Fifty long minutes later he comes back in saying he has finally put together something that may work, but you will have to pay three points over conventional loan rates. Your credit was worse than you thought, and the bank has to be protected. You give in with a sense of relief. He pushes the stack of contracts over for you to sign. You do, glad that your ordeal is finally over.

As you drive out in your new car, your family regards you as a hero. But all their excitement and happiness can't keep you from feeling bad. You chalk it up to tiredness, but the real truth is

- You put down more money than you had intended (a lot more money).
- You paid a higher interest rate than you had intended.
- You got practically nothing for your trade-in.
- You paid top dollar for your new car.
- You didn't get the bare-bones model you wanted.
- You really don't know the exact cost of the car.

Don't let this happen to you—ever again.

CHAPTER 13

Negotiating Basics

Well-brought-up, professional, white-collar, middle-class, intelligent, educated people have a hard job preparing themselves for a down-and-out, face-to-face "commando raid" type negotiation because they usually never have to do it. Culturally, they are conditioned to avoid conflict, and they fear the worst. These talented professionals would rather deal indirectly with difficult situations. They temporize by writing letters. They handle things indirectly by utilizing E-mail, and they deal with difficult personal interaction through a computer. This is not good. Gentle, nonconfrontational, empathetic women seem to fear confrontations the most. Their stomachs turn when they realize they must fight for what they want, which in the case of buying a car is usually a good price. They dread the tension of a direct negotiation without the guidelines of take it or leave it. Even veteran negotiators are not immune to tension, but they feel it to a much lesser degree. They may experience some discomfort sometimes but not in their areas of expertise.

The Bullfighter Concept

To overcome our cultural bias against negotiating, I have found something that works for me and I am sure will work for you in your quest to buy a car as cheaply, as quickly and as painlessly as possible. I call it the "bullfighter concept." I think I stole this from someone else, but I can't remember who, and since I personally use it myself all the time, I will teach it to you. Here is how it goes.

Envision yourself as a bullfighter facing a large, mean and ugly bull (the sales manager, your boss, etc.). If you panic and bolt, you will get gored with the bull's horns. If you panic and freeze, the bull will sense it and hurt you. The bull is unpredictable, and neither of you knows what the bull will do. If left alone, the bull might leave you alone for a while. However, you are both locked into a face-off by chance or circumstance, and this truce won't last long.

To survive this bullfight or any negotiation, you must be cool, detached, calm and confident that you can handle this negotiating opponent, whether it's a salesperson, sales manager, girlfriend or irate husband. I have found that if you let your opponent get close to you, let him talk his talk first, make him make his move first, you will know what kind of opponent he is and what he wants. As does a bullfighter, you have to let the bull get close before you can be effective. When your opponent has given you what you need in terms of information and when he is close to you, then you will do what you have to do. You will also do it with ease and professionalism. A proximity to the bull will make you unafraid and comfortable with him. It will not do the same for him.

Therefore, whenever I have to deal with a car negotiation, handle an unhappy customer who had his car repossessed or deal with a major problem, I let the other guy get in close and lay out his problem, request or sales pitch. All I do at first is concentrate on getting him to talk. Be cool, be cordial, offer him a cup of tea, inquire about his situation, get him talking.

How to Withstand the First Rush

As you listen, lo and behold, you become less anxious because listening allows you to think, plan and gather courage. Talking does not allow you to think or plan. As your adversary talks, all those horrible things you thought were going to happen, don't. He is nervous, he gives way, he explodes, then weakens. He compromises his position, and still you have done nothing but listen and perhaps nod. In 60 percent of the cases, the other party is troubled and wants to make peace and settle (not yell and scream) or is just looking for an easy way out; he will tell you what he needs to surrender. In another 35 percent of the cases, the person exhausts himself after a few minutes, while you remain calm. Like a bull after his first rush at the toreador, your opponent, his anger spent, usually rolls over and agrees as soon as you offer a conciliatory suggestion.

Even in the other 5 percent of negotiations, the outcome is not nearly as bad as you might have thought once you understand the situation.

Wait out the other side, gather intelligence, wait for him to give it up, and then do your thing. Have the courage to allow this closeness of the other party, and have the courage to allow him to do his thing first. It will work; it is a great negotiation attitude.

Look at Las Vegas blackjack: The house must play according to a fixed set of rules. The house must stand on seventeen and hit on sixteen. If the house goes over twenty-one, it loses. The house can't draw again if you have a higher number. The player can do all sorts of things but invariably (before the advent of card counting) loses. Why? Because the player moves first and frequently busts before the house has a chance to do anything. That's the house's only edge. Do the same thing in your negotiations: Give the other person the chance to bust before you do anything substantive.

The laid-back-bullfighter strategy works particularly well during auto transactions. When you deal with irate and pushy people in those transactions, use these principles. Remember: Wait for the opponent to make his pitch as loud, vocal and vituperative as it may be. Remain calm and detached. Don't fear close contact; welcome it. Believe you have the superior position. To be able to use the bullfighter strategy, you must have the respect of the other side, so suffer no personal attacks, and consider anything less than respect from the other side as unacceptable. Do this and you can handle any negotiating situation. This I guarantee or, at least, warrant.

CHAPTER 14

Dealer Tactics and How to Counter Them

How did he do it? How did that last salesperson twist your mind into a pretzel and convince you to buy that car, which wasn't the one you came in for? That car you bought only five years ago, that car you didn't need, that car you are trading in right now to avoid further hassles. He did it so skillfully, you weren't even aware of what was happening. Well, it is no great mystery. As I said before, professional salespeople have the edge on their own turf with an uninformed consumer. They learn tricks and techniques from the masters, spend years trying to apply them, and spend even longer discovering the type of person who is most susceptible to each technique.

Knowledge is power. If you know when a "technique" is being used on you, it becomes easier to ignore it and single-mindedly get on with your business, that is, buying the car of your choice at the lowest possible price. You cannot be confused or bamboozled if you can dismiss anything that even remotely resembles a manipulative technique. Once you recognize the techniques, you might even want to learn to use them yourself. Some might come in handy if you try to sell your own car.

Techniques

The following is a list of some of the most common and most successful techniques used by professional salespeople.

Take It or Leave It

Take it or leave it is the standard marketing policy all Americans have grown up with. You go to a restaurant or a furniture or clothing store and you take it or leave it at the price marked on the item. However, in the auto business, you don't have to take it or leave it. You can negotiate for it. You can, of course, leave it and later come back and take it. It is a good negotiating practice always to leave it before you take it. The tactic is usually a ploy to force you into an early decision, but eventually it may really be the way it is. You'll never know unless you test it.

Making You Feel Guilty

"I really need the sales" or "You're just wasting my time" or "Are you serious about buying this car?" or "I may lose my job if I don't make this sale" or "I consider you a friend" or "One more sale this week will win me a trip to Hawaii," pleads the salesperson, trying to make you feel guilty.

If any one of these attempts at playing on your emotions succeeds, you will be had. Remember, the problems of the dealership staff are dealership problems, not yours. Remember why you are there; you want to buy a car, and that's all. You are not there to make a friend or solve the world's social problems. Showing empathy will merely encourage further appeals. Hard as it may be, try to keep a businesslike distance between you and the salesperson.

Write Makes Right

Somehow or other if things are written down, we are not as apt to question them. The written word has a certain power of legitimacy. Car dealers are armed with an array of written facts, figures, forms and rules that they say are etched in stone. You should always assume that anything written is negotiable, that prices are meant to be tested and that any item can be adjusted. If you do your homework, you will know what all items cost, which costs are fixed and which are not. The fact that a dealer has something written down doesn't mean it is true. Question everything.

The California Approach

"What do I have to do to get you to buy a car today?" the salesperson queries, over and over again, each time more forcefully, until the buyer's objections are understood and countered one by one. Hopefully, the buyer will peacefully sign on the dotted line just to end the pressure.

Many times the sales force will accept what you say you need and pretend to reach an agreement with you about the car (in the process they find out that you are a real buyer). What happens, however, is you are then taken in to see the boss who says, "The sales guy is wrong. We can't do this. And we can't give you that price, etc." The counter to this is to know what a good deal is, ask for it and demand that the salesperson stop pressuring you. The broken record technique (explained later) works well as a deterrent to the California approach.

Good Guy/Bad Guy

In this scenario, the salesperson becomes your friend and helps escort you through a maze of roadblocks. His sales manager keeps bringing up problems, and your friendly salesperson helps you solve them— usually by having you give way on point after point. Your best tactic is to keep a formal distance between you and the salesperson and to verbally and overtly indicate that good guy/bad guy is such an old tactic you are surprised anybody is still using it.

Control Through Questioning

Since the person who asks the questions and demands answers is in control of the situation, it might as well be you. The salesperson does have a need to ask some qualifying questions to find out what it is you need, want and can afford, but he has no right to demand answers or to answer each of your questions with a closing question. For instance:

> **You:** Can you get me that car in red?
> **Salesperson:** If I do, will you buy the car today?

His response shows that he is asking you to make a decision about buying prematurely. Your reply should be:

> **You:** I would like an answer to my question please. Can you get

me that car in red? When I get my answer, I will be better able to determine if I am going to buy or not.

The Team Approach

In some dealerships, there are layers of salespeople. Each layer has a different responsibility. One greets you, another takes you for the test-drive, another starts the sale and yet another closes it. Sometimes several salespeople will gang up on you in sequence and work on you until you wear out. The best way to handle this is not to allow more than one salesperson at a time to work with you and to arrive so late that there are few salespeople around. Don't allow them to double-team you. Leave if you can't control this situation.

Delay

Sales staff can extend negotiations in several ways: by running in lots of other salespeople, losing your keys or having you wait around so long that you get anxious or tired and just want to consummate the deal as quickly as possible. However, they will only do this if you have signaled that you are susceptible to this type of treatment. So when you are sitting and waiting for the salesperson to come back with a counteroffer, make him uneasy. Get up, walk around, go outside. The customer who can successfully control the pace of negotiations is more likely to have them go his way. A typical delaying scenario can go something like this:

> **Salesperson:** Your credit report seems to be presenting some problems. It will take about sixty minutes for us to check with our bank. Why don't you have a cup of coffee in the reception area and we'll get back to you soon.
>
> **You:** My credit is fine, and I'm late for dinner. Why don't I just go home and have you call me tomorrow when you finish your investigation?
>
> **Salesperson** (panicking—he is afraid you will walk off): Wait just a minute. Let's see if I can speed this up.

Going, Going, Gone

Saying that the dealership only has one car left like the one you want is a great way to force you to make an immediate, perhaps premature, decision. By making you feel that your choice is the dealer's hottest car and that the supply is limited, a salesperson thinks he can force you into a commitment. If this tactic is tried, you should be willing to let your dream car go if everything else isn't exactly right.

Another version of going, going, gone is the line, "This deal is good for one day only—today." The only response to this variation is to say, "Well, then, I may miss it." A deal is good for as long as anybody wants it to be good. There is usually no reason for a time limit on any offer. Call his bluff by adhering to your own agenda. If you lose it, you lose it.

"Only the Payments are Important ... Right?"

Wrong. Sometimes, the real cost of a car can be obscured when the salesperson says, "We both know that the only important thing is to get your monthly payments down as low as possible." Beware of this ploy. Before you know it, you will have a lower payment, a much longer payment time and a higher down payment. If you are not careful, you won't even know the price you actually paid for the new car. This tactic is usually used when the buyer stalls on a high price because of sticker shock. Never worry about payments until you talk to the finance person. Always know what you actually paid for the car, and always fight hard for the lowest car price.

"Only the Difference in Price is Important ... Right?"

Wrong again. Often the salesperson will try to convince you that all that really matters is the difference between the new-car price and the trade-in price. Your salesperson is deliberately trying to confuse you. In actuality, the difference between the new-car and trade-in prices is important. But it is even more important to know the exact price of each to avoid being confused. If you are not careful, every time you get the new-car price to drop, somehow the agreed-upon price for the used car will suddenly drop also. Determine the price of each separately, and keep track of each separately. This will prevent you from becoming confused as the buying progresses. It will also prevent you from losing money on your trade-in. It is also easy to be confused by allowances: "I will allow you $XX toward the purchase of your new car at $XX." Get fixed, firm prices for each item in the negotiation. The price of your new car should not be dependent on the allowance for your trade-in. Allowances never work for you.

Lowballing

To enhance their profits, car dealers usually strongly lowball trade-ins. This is because their profits on the new cars are sometimes limited by the amount of money banks will lend toward new-car transactions. Remember, there are several parts to a transaction, and even though you get a low price for the new car, you still must get a reasonable price for your used car. Lowballing is used when the salesperson determines that you are very concerned about new-car price but are relatively unconcerned about what you get for your trade-in. He will try to focus your attention on a reasonable price for the new car and yet lowball you on the price of your trade-in. While your attention is focused on saving hundreds of dollars on the new car, you may forget to watch the trade-in sale and can easily lose thousands.

The reverse could also be true. If the salesperson feels you are adamant about getting a good price for your trade-in (for the down payment on a new car), he will give you an unbelievable price for your trade-in, charge you above list for the new car and tie both prices together as a package deal. To counter this, first make the salesperson believe the only thing of importance is a good price for your trade-in. After you get it, make him realize that the only important thing is a low new-car price—but don't give back the great trade-in price. Having previously written down the agreed-upon trade-in price will be helpful, especially if you have had the salesperson acknowledge it at some point in the transaction.

Bait and Switch

If you are not careful, you can walk into a dealership to buy the car you have thoroughly researched, the one that suits your needs and price structure, and come out instead with one you just fell in love with. When you find yourself switched, for any reason (perhaps away from a low-priced sale car), leave until you can think your way through the new situation and do the necessary homework.

Verbal Promises

During your buy, a lot of things will be promised to you verbally. Every time something is offered, write it down and keep a list. Even better, have the salesperson or his boss initial the items agreed upon. Save this list for the closing when they will probably try to take back some of the items they have given you.

Limited Authority

Having a lack of authority would seem to make a person's negotiating position weaker, but, in actuality, the best negotiating position is to have no authority at all. Then you can back off any agreement you have made by merely indicating that you aren't authorized to make it. Automobile salespeople operate effectively by relying on this lack of authority. This allows the salesperson to make an agreement with you and also say, "My boss may not go for this." You, however, are expected to be able to make and stick to all your agreements. Ask the salesperson at the onset of negotiations if he has the authority to make a deal. His usual response will be not to answer, to answer or ask a different question or to be evasive. At this point, indicate that if he has no authority, you want to deal with someone who has. Do not let his lack of authority control you.

Getting You to Say "Yes, Yes, Yes"

The theory is that if you say yes to a long line of questions, it will then become easier for you to say yes to accepting a less than adequate deal. When this happens, get obstinate and say no or "Maybe, if . . ." a few times. Other options are to change the subject or to get the salesperson to say yes to one of your demands.

Nibbles

Car dealers are good at asking for small concession after small concession. Before you know it, you have given away the store. If this is happening, counternibble. Don't give away anything without asking for something back. For instance, if the salesperson wants you to agree to a higher price before he presents the offer to his boss, use it as an opportunity to ask for free air-conditioning and an upholstery upgrade. Who knows, he may just say yes. Never let a nibble go unanswered. Ask, ask, ask. No one will give you anything unless you ask for it.

Temporary Concessions

Many times things that have been granted to you at earlier stages of negotiations disappear in financing—usually at about the time you start to feel good because you have almost bought a car. All those things you have fought so hard for sometimes get forgotten when you can smell the leather seats. To keep this from happening, write down all the agreed-upon items, and don't sign until you have everything you were promised. Get really upset if promises don't materialize. Concessions tend to disappear when the salesperson has promised you the moon and the person in financing knows nothing about it. Your best tactic here is to walk away quickly if one doesn't honor the other's commitments.

Refusing to Negotiate

Some car companies, like Saturn or other companies that feature car types that are in high demand, claim they don't negotiate. While they may not be flexible on new-car price, they may give you a much higher trade-in price, throw in extra accessories or allow you a lower financing rate. Claiming not to negotiate is a great negotiating tactic or, at the very least, an interesting initial negotiating posture. Don't take them at their word. Even Saturn dealerships do sometimes negotiate on car price. In reality, a small percentage are sold below sticker price. My advice: Keep probing for other concessions that effectively lower the price of the car, or shop elsewhere for a better deal.

Quoting Averages and Statistics

Do long lists of facts, figures and averages confuse you? If so, then block them out. Another way of dealing with your confusion is to profess complete ignorance, then move the conversation to a more comfortable topic. Here's an example:

> **Sales Manager** (for the third time): And as you can see, you don't have to worry about price when you lease a car because the average cost of a Rule of 78 lease is much lower than even a conventional declining loan balance.
>
> **You:** I still don't understand. What about color of upholstery? What choices do I have?

Appealing to Your Sense of Fairness

Sellers are the only people who ever demand that you recognize their need to make money and get what they consider their due. It is Detroit's responsibility to price its cars correctly and to make profit for the dealerships and sales staff, not yours. Don't get sucked into this kind of debate. This is just a variation on the guilt tactic.

The Silent Treatment

When you notice that the salesperson has stopped talking and you begin to feel awkward, you are experiencing the silent treatment. This is your signal to start talking politics, baseball or cooking. If that doesn't work, it is time to see how quiet he becomes when you walk out of the negotiating room into the parking lot toward your car. If silence makes you feel uneasy, don't stand for it.

"I'm New Here"

Any good salesperson will attempt to make you his friend and to elicit your sympathy. If he is really new, and naive, you can be sure he has an experienced, strong and competent sales manager backing him up. But who is going to intercede for you if you make a costly mistake based on his false information? Now is the time to take him at his word and to ask for someone more experienced. It's as simple as that.

The Good Faith Deposit

Giving a deposit is perhaps one of the strongest signs of commitment. Don't do it unless you are prepared to really go through with the deal. If the salesperson will not take an offer to his boss without a check or deposit, demand that he do. Let him know that until a firm price is agreed on, you will not commit to the sale. If he refuses, threaten to walk. I guarantee he will chase you into the parking lot.

Taking Your Keys and Registration

It is everybody's nightmare to have the dealer "lose" the keys to the customer's car so he must stay and negotiate. Always bring an extra set of keys, and don't negotiate until you get your keys and registration back.

"If I Can, Will You?"

This is a great technique and is used all the time to get a buying commitment from the customer. This technique is designed to see if you are a real buyer, and perhaps to probe your limits. A typical example follows:

Salesperson: If I can get the car in blue at your price, will you buy it right now?

or

Salesperson: If I can get my manager to buy your trade-in at your price, will you accept our price for the new car?

The best way to handle this tactic is to become a broken record. Keep restating your terms. If he gives you what you want, of course you will buy right then and there, if you want to. Later on, you can change your position if it suits you. After all, you can negotiate from limited authority as well as he can.

Intimidation

At some point in the negotiations, usually an impasse, your salesperson will try to intimidate you by cheerfully inviting you to meet his manager. This is not like meeting the queen of England. This is the real strong arm and he looks like he probably eats pit bulls for lunch. He also is pretty busy, so the best way to handle him is to delay, waffle and then stick to your demands without being intimidated.

The manager's job is to spend as much time as it takes to close the sale, so be prepared with some killer tactics.

Stonewalling

Stonewalling, a classic negotiating position, is the granting of concessions slowly and grudgingly. The average person quickly becomes impatient and discouraged and compromises just to get the negotiations going. To beat this technique, you must be willing to outwait the salesperson or to come in at a time that is so inconvenient that all he wants to do is get the transaction over with. This is why starting the buy one to two hours before closing will work well for you.

Upcoming Price Increase

This is a scare tactic designed to get you to move really quickly. Typically, the salesperson tries to speed you toward making a decision by indicating that there is going to be a large price increase soon. Therefore you must buy this car now because the price will be 6.8 percent or 10.2 percent or $500 more by the weekend.

The way to handle this is to ask the salesperson to document, through a bulletin or some other printed document, that there is going to be a price hike soon. Note the amount and the date it becomes effective, and see if the price rise applies to your chosen car. Make sure it does apply because some price increases are not on all models.

If the salesperson can't produce documents, consider the statement as hot air, disregard it and go on negotiating at your own speed. If it does apply, note it and go on negotiating at your own speed.

CHAPTER 15

Your Best Tactics

The *Los Angeles Times* recently ran a story about a garage sale bargain buyer, and the man made a really good point that I think can help you. His technique was to ask for an item he didn't want, and then when a price was quoted he would wince and quickly put down the item. The message he gave was clear: "Your price is way too high." The bargain buyer would then touch another item he didn't particularly want, but one that he knew was inexpensive. He would ask a price, and always this second price was much lower than the first price. Then our bargain buyer would say, "OK, I will take this item at that price if you will throw in this old lamp and this small table." Usually the seller would toss in all three. The trick to this story is that the lamp was what he wanted all along. He never made that clear, however, and he got it at the price of the cheaper item. Essentially, the bargain buyer acquired what he desired, plus he came away with a couple other things—all for less than he was willing to pay for the desired lamp. This chapter is devoted to equipping you with similar tactics that'll help you work similar magic when purchasing a car.

First Things First: Forget About the Win-Win Philosophy

An acquaintance of mine who has taken a number of courses in negotiation wonders why I don't subscribe to the current win-win negotiation philosophy, which is so popular with professional negotiation aficionados. Let me first state that I really do believe in a win-win scenario when feasible, because a massive win-lose scenario usually does not make for any sort of a lasting agreement. All deals, by the way, are usually win-win: If a dealer really thinks he's losing, he won't sell you the car at the price you're willing to pay for it.

The primary reason why I don't like the concept of going into a negotiation with a win-win mindset is because it encourages you to leave too much on the table. This is a common problem with those who don't negotiate often, which is probably you if you're reading this section of the book. To me the ideal solution is a win-win with you getting the big win. (And as I said before, the salesperson will win, too—he'll still make a sale—but you'll be a bigger winner.) Unfortunately, there's usually not a cute, delicate, politically correct solution where everybody wins big. Sometimes you just have to slug it out to get the best deal, and all the techniques in this chapter are designed to help you achieve that end. So forget about win-win negotiating, and utilize the following strategies.

Broken Record

Of all the techniques in a car buyer's arsenal, the broken record tactic has got to be the best. It is used successfully by kids to grind down parents, by people with energy to wear down tired people and by buyers with plenty of time to spend on car salespeople anxious to go home. Badly done, it is a transparent and annoying strategy. Combined with other techniques and done well, it can be subtle and powerful.

Did you ever deal with a person who wouldn't budge from his point of view? Someone who just keeps repeating himself endlessly, waiting for you to give in? If you are under time pressures, you usually give in just to get it over with. If you don't have to deal with broken record people, give them a wide berth. You see this technique used ad nauseam by groups like the National Rifle Association and the antigun groups when they confront each other. Each group just states and repeats its position. There is no real discussion—or progress.

In its simplest form, the broken record tactic is a constant restatement of your point of view. In its more refined form, it is a restatement of your position with a reasonable explanation added. Here is an example of the skillful use of the broken record tactic:

> **You:** Yes, I know that you want to sell your car for $18,500, but I can only afford $16,500.
> **Salesperson:** I would love to make a sale, but my boss just won't

let me make a deal with almost no profit. You have to come up with more money, and maybe we can help you in terms of payments.

You: Yes, I know the deal is not great, but at $16,500 you will be making a good profit.

Salesperson: We are losing money at that price.

You: But you will make a decent profit, and if you look at my figures, you will see that $16,500 is fair. Other dealers are offering the same car at $16,000.

This cycle is repeated continually until a deal is reached or you (not they) leave. There is really no counter to this technique as long as it is done well. The technique is exceptionally powerful because there is no real way a salesperson can shut off or throw out a stubborn customer who may be a buyer and just keeps plugging away.

Yes, But

The buyer's main use of the "yes, but . . ." mechanism is to counter the salesperson's arguments without being obnoxious. Let's see how it is used in the following situation:

Salesperson: The list price for the car is $17,750, and at that price, these cars are almost flying off the lot.

You: *Yes*, I understand how you might want to get full price for your car, *but* I won't pay that much money.

This method of fighting for a price is much less confrontational than other methods.

Feel/Felt/Found

Another version of the "yes, but . . ." tactic that is often used on you to diffuse a confrontation is the feel/felt/found technique. In the hands of an experienced salesperson, it operates as follows:

You: I have heard from my friends that diesel engines are terrible.

Salesperson: I know how you feel. (Sales staff never disagree with you initially.) I felt the same way when I first got into this business, but I found after I researched the subject that diesel engines make a lot of sense in circumstances like these.

Now that you see how this works, you will be able to use this technique on the salesperson:

Salesperson: Your offer is just too low; I can't take it to my boss.

You: I know that you feel my offer is low. My friends felt the same way when I discussed the car buy with them, but I found there was a lot of justification for my bid considering your cost structure and today's market.

You Have to Do Better Than That

Just saying, "You have to do better than that," is a great technique because it forces the salesperson to do something to rescue the sale. Sometimes the salesperson will make a concession without even knowing what it will take to save the situation. This technique works well when neither you nor the salesperson will budge.

Here is an example of how to use this technique in combination with the broken record tactic.

You: You have to do better than that.

Salesperson: If I can get my boss to accept $300 less, will you buy a car right now, today?

You: I didn't make myself clear. You have to do considerably better than that, and, yes, I really do want to buy a car today.

If the technique is used on you, the way to beat this technique is to ask exactly what is it you have to do better and get him to explain how much better and in what ways. Insist that he be specific. For example:

You: I want to pay $15,500 for the car.

Salesperson: You have to do better than that.

You: Tell me exactly what it is you need to make this deal go through.

Salesperson: I need more money.

You: Tell me exactly how far apart we are.

Salesperson: I know he won't let the car go for less than $17,200.
You: You will have to accept considerably less than that.

This combination of techniques is doubly powerful when used correctly.

Why Won't You Let Me Buy a Car Today?

Asking, "Why won't you let me buy a car today?" is a technique designed to shock the salesperson. Usually, the salespeople spend their time trying to get you, the customer, to make up your mind to buy a car. They think the customer is the only one standing in the way of the sale. When you place the blame squarely on their shoulders, they are understandably confused. It is tremendously frustrating for them to try to explain why they won't let you get a car. When you use this technique, they will flounder around for a while before working their way out. Don't use it more than once. Its value is its initial impact as a shocker.

Delay

Delay—especially if you arrived late in the day, it is the end of the month and you are a real buyer. Usually customers get nervous because salespeople use delay as a tactic. However, at the end of the day, the salespeople want to go home and no matter how cool they look, the longer you keep them late, the more they resent it and the more they speed up the whole negotiating process. Keeping them two hours over the end of their normal twelve-hour shift really tries their patience, especially if you are fresh and don't seem to be in a rush (and worse yet are a real customer). They can't kick you out. They don't want to kick you out. They just want to get the deal over with, even if they don't make as much as they would in another situation.

Change the Pace

In the usual car sale, the salesperson first closes on you for a commitment to buy a car and then he closes on you for a price. In the ideal sale, you should make up your mind to buy a car and then close on him for a better price. Change the pace.

This is a role reversal with the salesperson defending his position and you trying to find out what it will take for him to make a deal (the California technique reversed). Salespeople don't handle this well because they are put in a passive defensive position with a tough buyer who knows what is possible. My feeling is that you can get very close to the final figure if you have done your homework, know your prices, have made yourself a real buyer, go in late and are set to buy.

Play the Dumb and Injured "I Accept Your Apology Game"

The basis of this strategy is to entice the salesperson to treat and retreat you badly. It's really a three-part play, in which you play dumb, allow him to walk all over you like you're dumb, and then fire back on him all his mistakes when it comes time to close the deal. Before you know it, he will give in because he's been confronted with evidence of his errors. If you think this creates a lot of tension, you're right. And we'll get into the value of creating tension in a few minutes.

First, let's go over how you need to act and what you need to do:

- Initially seem incompetent, naive and weak. Let the salesperson take limited advantage of you, but keep mental notes. Don't forget that last part: Keep mental notes.
- Next politely pose a few possible errors but not all of them: miscalculations, reneging on the price they promised on your trade-in, switching you from total price to monthly payments to masking the true cost of the vehicle, etc.
- Once the salesperson agrees he made a mistake, ask for your deal again. Each time he tries to dig in his heels on price, you list another misdeed. Remember, you can't expect him to lose money on the deal, but you can expect him to give way on several points to make up for his misdeeds (to sweeten the deal for you). He may not mend his ways permanently, but he will give in more easily because of the guilt after the incident. Also, he will accept a marginal deal, just to dig himself out of that awkward hole.

Here are examples of how not to play and how to successfully play the "I accept your apology" game:

Salesperson: And these are the figures as to what the car will cost you.

You (mad and showing it): This is the second time you have added extra costs into the price you quoted me and the second time I caught you. I can't believe you did this.

At this point the salesperson may get angry and harden his position. You don't want that. An alternative way to handle this scenario might be like this:

You: May I ask a delicate question here?

Salesperson: Go ahead. (effectively giving you permission to act anyway you want)

You: Is there something going on here I don't understand? According to my notes, these items were included in the original price quote. I may be wrong, but I think you added them on again.

Salesperson: Shoot. (To himself: *I just got busted trying to squeeze all that cash out of that buyer!*)

The salesperson at this point is essentially stuck. If you really caught him adding in extra costs, he can't easily defend himself. You now have the advantage.

Create Tension

Most people will do anything to reduce the tension in their lives. They are basically nice folks who get through life compromising and pleasing others. These are great people to marry or to have in a family, but they are not the right people to negotiate with a strong personality type. Car dealers handle these people by continually pushing them to the maximum. The salespeople constantly create stress and force the customer to find solutions to the problems they fabricate.

When you sense you are being put under created tension, raise the tension level yourself. This is hard for most people to do, but the only other alternative is to give in. Here is a typical response to created tension:

> **Salesperson:** I am sorry to say this, but your car is not worth $2,250. My figure was only an estimate, and my manger just told me this. I was pretty surprised that my used-car manager will only give you $1,200 for it. Can you come up with another $1,000 so we can wrap up the new car?
>
> **You:** I am really upset about this. You gave your word that the car was worth $2,250. This is ridiculous, and I am going to terminate this discussion right now. Get me the sales manager, I want to complain.
>
> **Salesperson** (Suddenly scared because he has obviously misjudged your reaction. He was hoping you would easily accept the lower price.): Wait a minute, wait a minute. Let me talk to him again. Maybe I can get you a better price.
>
> **You:** I will give you exactly five minutes to get this straightened out. Then I am leaving.
>
> **Salesperson:** Let me take care of this right away. I assure you it won't happen again. (He knows he will have to treat you with kid gloves from now on.)

When someone has to reduce the tension level, let it be the dealership, not you.

Laugh It Up

I can't always read body language, but I know when negotiations are about to end because someone thinks he's made a decision. Reading body language is not a perfect science, but it is the best indicator I have found. Once I pick up that someone's made a decision, I use my self-deprecating sense of humor as a probe.

Here is how it works. (You don't have to have a great sense of humor to do this.) People can usually laugh only when the tension is off. So you joke to test their tension level. If the situation is delicate, if serious points have yet to be settled, a funny joke or a stupid remark will not elicit a laugh. Usually all you'll get is just silence or a stern look. However, if all issues are settled and if the other party has made up his mind, a person will usually allow himself to laugh at a silly surprise one-liner. Look at this:

Salesperson: I might be able to talk my boss into paying $3,100 for your trade-in.

Burke: I've done my research. I know that's way below *Blue Book*. Even my mother-in-law would give me a better price on that car.

If the salesperson looks at me like I am out of touch, I know he won't give in on price. The issues are not settled yet. But if he laughs at my dumb remark, I know I have a chance. So use humor to gauge the progress of negotiations. The interesting thing about this technique is that no matter how many times you use it, it still works. It even works if the person is cognizant of the technique. The use of laughter as a sign that tension is down (and therefore a deal is at hand) is signaled by a reaction to a bad joke. Try it.

Just Ask—American Style

As I said before, because in the United States most things have a fixed price, we are not accustomed to negotiating. Our only decision is usually whether to buy something or not. Now, you can just settle for paying somebody else's price, or you can wave your magic wand (just ask) and do something that will give you more options. So many savvy consumers are asking for more and getting what they ask for that I think I can safely say that we have developed our own unique negotiating style—the "just ask" style.

The importance of just asking for something you want, even something small, will give you the confidence to challenge our fixed-price economy. Amazingly, you will discover that the mere act of asking guarantees your getting as much as anything in the world. I don't know what is wrong with the rest of the world, but if you just ask for something, you will probably get at least some piece of it. I don't know why, but it happens. Below is a "just ask" scenario by an American-style buyer. The negotiation might proceed as follows:

American Style Buyer (ASB): So you really do need at least $3,500 for your used car?

Seller: Yes.

ASB: If I gave you $3,100 cash right now, could we settle on the vehicle?

Seller: I might do it for $3,250—cash—today.

ASB: Could you throw in the extra set of four tires you have in the garage at that price?

Seller: I don't know. I guess so.

ASB: And you will give me that thirty-day warranty on the engine and drive train we talked about, won't you?

Seller: That was at the higher price, but I guess so if we can settle right now.

ASB: Also, isn't it a law that the horn has to work? I presume that you'll fix it.

Seller (getting more impatient): Yes.

ASB: I'm afraid to get the car smogged. What if it doesn't pass? If you can get that done for me and include it in the deal, we can settle right now.

This goes on forever until the seller puts a stop to it as follows:

Seller: I will do all of that for $3,500, or you can take the car as is right now for $3,250. Your choice.

Another approach is to handle asking by counterasking.

Buyer: Can you give me a better price on my vehicle?

Seller: I sure could if you would buy both of these cars I have for sale.

Buyer: Oh. Well, never mind.

This style of asking for more and more, usually politely, pays off. Some of us do it very well, but many of us back off at the first sign of resistance. The secret of the "just ask" American style is to keep on asking until you get what you want. Do it until you get serious resistance, not just a whine ("I don't know").

You: I think $4,500 is too much for your used car. I would pay $3,750 right now, and I think that is fair.

Seller: Awe, man, I can't believe it. Everybody comes down here and whines about the price. This is a prime condition

Chevy Blazer, and it behaves like new. Get real.

You (usually nervous): Well, it is a nice car, so OK.

What should have happened:

You: I have to agree with you. It is a nice car, and I really want to buy it today. See I have cash on me, but I need a better price. What can you do for me?

Seller (under pressure to name a price): I would never let this beauty go for anything less than $4,200.

What you should have said: I have $3,750 here in this envelope (spread it out on the table), and I really want to wrap this up in the next few minutes.

Seller (his eyes on all those hundreds all over his kitchen table): I want to wrap this up soon also, but I won't settle now for anything less than $4,000.

And so it goes. So just keep on asking until you meet enough resistance to sense that the end is near and pushing on might erode your gains.

Say "No" One More Time

When you get to a point where you are almost in agreement and the sales manager (you are long past the salesperson) offers to split the difference, don't do anything right away. Don't look happy; don't look anxious. Just say no one more time and see what happens. No matter how pleased you are with the agreement, make yourself say no one more time just to see what else falls in your plate (even if doing so makes you uncomfortable).

Finally, do not forget these two important points:

1. He who mentions money first usually loses. A premature mention of money marks you as the person who is more anxious, the one who is feeling the strain. Also, when you mention a price, either as a buyer or a seller, it is tough to retract it.

2. Don't discuss money until you know what you are buying. Money belongs at the end of a negotiation, after you have determined

exactly what it is you're getting and what a good price is. The person who mentions money prematurely will probably amend his amount (probably several times) before the other party even begins to negotiate. If you make a mistake and the quality turns out not to be so good, you'll have a hard time taking back the price you mentioned.

CHAPTER 16

Examples of Effective Negotiating

In chapter twelve, you saw how negotiating should not go. Perhaps you even saw what happened to you on your last car-buying excursion. Now, let's see how it should go if you do it correctly. I hope the following scenario will give you a good idea of how to apply everything you have read so far in this book. Make this buyer your model, and you will fare well in your next car buy.

You arrive at the lot, your four-year-old car fairly gleaming with the polish job you have given it. The blackwall tires are really black. There is no dust or dirt on the car, and it looks far better than the used cars already on the lot. (During the negotiations, you see used-car customers looking at your car.) You get out. If you feel you are a competent buyer, you may have come alone; more than likely you have some support with you, but you surely don't have crying children or anyone else who won't help you.

You are well dressed, well rested, lightly fed and have all night to buy a car. You have done your homework and have the results with you and committed to memory. You also have priced your trade-in and know its approximate worth. You have obtained outside financing that you are prepared to use if you have to. At this point, you are ready to deal and are not afraid of any salesperson who has ever lived. You would like to buy a car today but can wait until next week or even next month if necessary.

The date is within the last three days of the month; the time is one to two hours before the dealership's closing time. (If everything is perfect, it is Christmas Eve, there is a snowstorm and the salespeople all have the flu. But, what the heck, you can't have everything.)

You: If I can find the kind of car I want, I would like to buy a car today. Do you understand? I really want to buy a car today.

Friendly Salesperson (FSP): Hi, I am your friendly salesperson, and I would love to sell you a car today. And let me tell you, we have some great cars, and we are willing to deal. What type of car are you interested in? (He thinks your body language, your clothes and the condition of your trade-in all indicate you are capable of affording a new car and are probably a good prospect to buy one today. As today hasn't been a really good day for anyone in the dealership, he is already anxious to make this sale work.)

You: Can you show me your full-size sedan? Oh, I would also like to look at your full-size station wagon. By the way, I know it is late. Will the dealership stay open long enough for us to talk and make a deal today, or should I come back next week?

FSP: We will absolutely stay open until we conclude our business. No question about that. By the way, good choice; these are some of the best-selling models in the good old U.S.A.

Note: He has just committed himself to staying as late as you want. This makes it tough for him to complain about how long it is taking to make a deal, how late it is or how badly he wants to go home. Also, don't think that this person doesn't notice everything about you or your trade-in as he tries to figure out what is going on in your life and mind and how best to control you.

FSP: I see from your parking sticker that you work for Consolidated Aircraft.

You: Yes, great company. Been there seven years. We are really going to beat this recession with the new products that will be coming out soon.

Note: No need to tell the FSP you haven't worked full-time for several months; just act upbeat. The fact that you are buying a car while practically out of work is none of his business, so don't tell him. This is not an endorsement to buy a car while on layoff, but an indication of how to handle a difficult situation.

The FSP will now show you things about the car and will take you on a test-drive. Meanwhile, he will be asking you questions about how you like the car and if you can afford it. He is prequalifying you.

Before you go on the test-drive, toss the salesperson the keys to your trade-in and say, "I am serious about buying one of these cars, but to save time, have your used-car manager look at my trade-in so he can give me a price when we come back from the test-drive."

> **FSP:** The used-car manager usually likes to have the seller of the car with him when he goes over the car. We also need to have a credit check done. Can you fill out a credit application so we can qualify you?
>
> **You:** It's late now, and I don't care to go over my car with him. I know its condition, and if he is a professional, he will know it also. Let me give you my social security number and date of birth so you can check my credit, and I will gladly fill out an application now or can do so when we get back. Is that satisfactory?

Note: Do not be around when the used-car manager evaluates your car. He will spend most of his time trying to devalue it in your eyes. He will also fish around for you to commit to the lowest price you will accept for it. Let him guess without you. There is no advantage for you in being with him. The credit qualification is legitimate. Make it easy for the dealer to get the information; it makes you more of a real buyer.

The FSP then takes you for a test-drive.

> **FSP:** Isn't the ride great on this car?
> **You:** It's nice.
> **FSP:** Isn't the engine quiet?
> **You:** It's fine.
> **FSP:** Isn't the interior roomy (etc.)?
> **You:** Sure is.

Note: The trick here is to indicate to the salesperson that the car is adequate and that if the price is right, you may buy it. Don't gush all over about how great the car is. Don't be too critical unless you plan not to buy the car. The neutral attitude will leave you with the most negotiating latitude. Be pleasant, noncritical and unemotional. Give few buying signals.

> **FSP:** I hope you like the car as much as I do and that you will buy one because there are only a few of this type left, and you don't want to miss out on a great car. (The going, going, gone tactic. In my way of thinking, when a salesperson starts the battle and uses one recognizable technique, it is morally OK for us buyers to do what we must to counter the offensive.)
>
> **You:** I understand that I may not get the car, but I can live with that. I am certain that you have others I may be interested in.

Note: This is the counter to going, going, gone. The FSP may also try variations on this theme, such as:

> **FSP:** That lady over there is interested in this car, and if you don't hurry up and buy it, she may get it first.
>
> **You:** If it happens, it happens. But you do understand that I really want to buy a car today, don't you?

Note: It is in the salesperson's job description to find out how you feel about the car and to determine how best to hook you. He will try to create a need for immediate action in you. You can neutralize him by continually indicating that you want to buy a car today if everything goes right.

This is the time for you to ask him about details of the car that bother you. If the suspension is too soft, ask if you can get an upgrade in suspension. Some of these people know the cars they are selling and can handle questions you may have from your readings.

> **FSP:** Shall we go into the showroom and put some numbers down on paper and see if you can afford this beauty? (This is where he sees if you are really serious.)
>
> **You:** Absolutely, but first I want to see the price you are going

to give me for my used car. I feel I should tell you that this price is very important to me. If I can get a good price on my trade-in, the rest of this transaction should proceed quickly. If I cannot get what I consider is an adequate price, I will walk immediately. I do not expect to have my intelligence insulted. You do understand that, don't you?

FSP: I will get the sales manager's figure as soon as we go inside. But let me warn you, he is a tough person to get a high price out of.

You: Yes, I understand that you have to make a profit, but I must get my price for the car, or I can't go any further with this transaction, and I really want to buy a car today. Do you understand that? (Notice the "yes, but. . . ." tactic.)

FSP: I will do my best for you. What sort of price did you want for your trade-in?

You: Let's go inside, get the figure from your used-car manager and see if it meets what I need.

FSP: Yes, but what kind of figure do you need?

You (playing broken record): Let's get the figure from the used-car manager and see what it is first. Do you understand that if the figure is too far off we may have trouble making a deal?

Note: This speech is designed to prevent him from lowballing you on your trade-in price. Do not name a figure. Wait and see what is offered first.

Go into the negotiating room, but don't do anything substantial until the price of the trade-in comes back. Many dealerships prefer to sell you a new car first and then to give you a price on your trade-in after you are committed to the nice new car.

FSP: My manager is looking at the car and will have a bid for you in a few minutes. In the meantime, why don't you tell me if you like the car? We can discuss the price, options and other details while we wait.

You (Now is the time to show him who is boss.): I would love to discuss these items, but I feel that I can't do much else until my mind is clear about how much I am going to get for my trade-in. Then I can plan the amount I will pay for the new car and other such things.

FSP: Why don't we start now and let the trade-in price catch up with us? I'm sure it will be here soon. By the way, if the real problem is payments, I am sure we can get you very low payments. Let's look at leasing; we can get you super low payments by leasing. Incidentally, have you paid off your car? If not, we can tie the payoff into your new lease payments. Would you like to lease?

Note: He is now trying to close the sale on a minor point, which then assumes that you have closed on the major points of the sale itself and the car's price—the sticker price at this point.

You: Yes, I have paid off my car. Payments are not the problem, and I prefer not to discuss them now. I hope that the trade-in price comes soon and is reasonable; otherwise, I am just wasting my time and may not be able to conclude this negotiation tonight.

FSP: Well, we definitely want to put you in the seat of the car you want, and we want to do it tonight. Let me go see our used-car manager and push him along. Oh, one more point. If I get you a good allowance on your trade-in toward an upgrade model of the sedan with all the bells and whistles you wanted, would you consider buying it tonight, right away?

You: I am not interested in talking about allowances or payments. Let's just find out what price you are going to give me on my trade-in, and then we can see what kind of price you can give me on the sedan. It is too early to talk financing or those sorts of issues.

FSP: OK, I'll be back in a minute with the trade-in price. (Under his breath, "This is one tough customer; it is going to be hard to switch and confuse this one.")

Note: He tried to confuse you with payments, then he tried to confuse the issue with allowances, and he tried to get a new car decided on before giving a price on the trade-in. He wants you to commit to the new car, and this in itself will devalue your trade-in. He tried and failed to get a commitment to buy this car tonight under any circumstances.

The FSP returns with a number that is below the auction price for the car. You know this because you have done all your homework and know what your car would go for at auction.

> **You:** I indicated that the trade-in price for this car was important to me, and yet you come back with a figure that is not only below retail and wholesale, but below auction value as well. I am very disappointed. Let me say this one more time: The trade-in price for the car is of paramount importance to me. I need a price near *Blue Book* wholesale for the car in order to continue this sale. If we can work this out, I'm sure the rest of the transaction will go smoothly. I really do want to buy a car today. Do you understand?
>
> **FSP:** This is the price he gave me, but let me go back and talk to him in a little while and see what I can do. In the meantime, let's talk about the price of the new car.
>
> **You:** Let's settle the trade-in first. I have made myself clear as I possibly can. I need about *Blue Book* wholesale in order to go on with this negotiation. If you can't get near it, tell me now, and you can save us both a lot of time and energy by cutting this discussion short. I won't discuss a new car until this issue is settled.

Note: For the FSP, this is a worst-case scenario. He knows now that he must eventually come within $200 of your asking price and hope to make his money elsewhere in the transaction.

After the trade-in price is finally settled, the FSP tries to move the negotiation along.

> **FSP:** Now that we have the trade-in price settled, and you know that I got you the best price I could for your car, let's deal on this beautiful new car you picked out. You do love it, don't you?

You: The car is great, but first let's talk about what equipment is on the car, what the guarantees are and what upgrades make sense to give me the performance I want. Then we can talk new-car price. By the way, I have written down the figure you gave me for the trade-in. This is correct, isn't it?

FSP: Yes, that is correct, and you must admit it is a good price.

You: Yes, it allows us to go on with our discussion.

Note: Some time later, the technical details have been established, and you have either decided on a car with all the features you want, ordered a car from the factory or settled for what is on the lot at this time.

FSP: Now that we have decided on all the details, how much do you want to buy the car for? I can get you really great payments.

You: I know you aren't going to like the price I am going to mention, but if we can agree on it, I will buy this car today. This new-car price is the most important item left to discuss. By the way, it is important to me that we settle on a price and discuss payments later.

Note: You tied down the trade-in price by having him acknowledge it. Now you are going to shock him with a figure for his new car that is just barely within the acceptable range. You will not talk allowances or financing, just new-car price in dollars.

The FSP comes back about five minutes later.

FSP: I got the price down to $23,900 and that is the best I can do. These vehicles are hot and they are flying off the lot.

You: I know you have to make a profit, but it is going to be a small one. I checked the Internet last night and I know you are into the vehicle $18,700. This will include all the present equipment on the car and transportation. I will pay you $200 over this to end up at $18,900. I am not going to pay for ADMU, or the cost for the rust proofing that you haven't put on yet or the stain protection on the upholstery.

Note: The FSP winces as you mention the price. (Any good salesperson will wince or jump or make some involuntary gesture when you mention a price. It gives the impression that the price is ridiculous.)

> **FSP:** That's too low. Our sticker for this car is $22,436 even dropping the ADMU, which is put on all hot cars—and this car is hot. I might manage to give you a $500 discount and even drop the ADMU for a serious customer. This would get the price down to $21,500—if I can get it by our sales manager. By the way, you probably know that the manufacturer is giving rebates of $750, so this price would be really close to what you want.
>
> **You:** Yes, I understand that you might want more for your vehicle, but times are tough, and all I want to spend is $18,900 for the car, as it is. Of course, the tax and licensing are separate issues, as are the rebates. I expect to get them regardless.

Note: Keep the discussion focused on your price. Play "yes, but...." and sound like a broken record with him. Occasionally, give a few dollars away and try to settle for $400 to $500 (if the car is really in demand) or less over his cost. With a hot car, you will pay more; with a slow seller, less. Walk out if you must, but if it is late in the evening and after closing time, he will eventually settle for what he can. Be patient, wait him out, be insistent. You should realize, of course, that a superhot car (like the Mazda Miata in 1995 or the new models of Dodge trucks now) may go for list or even above.

> **FSP:** I can't give you your price without giving you a smaller allowance on your trade-in.
>
> **You:** Excuse me; I thought we had that settled. You have already acknowledged that the trade-in price is a fixed firm price. It is definitely not an allowance. If this causes a problem with you, let's stop where we are and renegotiate the trade-in price. By the way, it looks like we aren't going to finish by closing time. Is that a problem? I really want to buy a car today.

Note: Don't let him change the trade-in price. Don't let him call it an allowance. Stick to the new-car price, and tell him repeatedly that you want to buy a car today. He will try lots of these tricks. Keep this line of discussion going. Be sure not to give much away. Never discuss the list price for the car; keep the discussion on your offered price. The list price is irrelevant, and you should not hesitate to tell him that you know that. Don't let him switch you to another car or work in an allowance. Stick to price only. Threaten to walk out. Ask to see his boss. Waste his time, and make it clear you are in no hurry to leave. Remind him that you are a real buyer. Close in on him for a price. Some time later, you will have finally settled on a fixed firm price for the new car.

> **FSP:** You got a really good price, but I guess you knew that. Let's put you in with our finance person and see what we can do to help you afford the car. By the way, we are having a special on alarm systems, and the outside protection package we put on the car is the best available.
>
> **You:** Thanks for the help. You were a very helpful and professional salesperson, and I will pass on your competence to your boss when I meet him. I do appreciate your efforts. I will take up the optional items with your finance person. By the way, I need to take a break for a few minutes. Is it possible for me to have a cup of coffee alone to think about the sale?

Note: The FSP will show you the waiting area and will nervously leave you alone. After you have taken a fifteen-minute break and gotten some coffee under your belt, you feel ready for dealing with the finance person. The time now is at least an hour after closing, and everybody wants to go home but you. The salesperson, sales manager, finance person and all the other people who are waiting around for you to finish up all want to go home. You may be anxious, but so are they, and they are tired after a twelve- to fourteen-hour day. If they press you, turn the pressure back on them by becoming somewhat unpredictable. Don't be rude or abrasive; it doesn't pay. But remember that your power is almost at its greatest now, and you do not have to take any garbage from anyone.

Finance person: I know you are worried about not being able to afford this new car, but I am sure we can get you really great financing so your monthly payments are low. But first, have you considered getting our outside care package? Normally it costs $600, but it is on special this week for only $375.

You (interrupting): I don't want any of those items you mentioned at any price, including the insurance. But if you can get the price of the extended warranty down from $995 to something reasonable, I might consider it. Give me your best figure on it, or else drop the subject. I did a little checking on the Web and I know what a good figure is for these extended warranties. Also, I am not worried about the loan. I already have one at an amount large enough to cover the new car at 9 percent from my credit union. Can you beat it?

Finance person: I can get you down to $895 on the extended warranty, but we have so little profit on this deal that you have to let us make a profit on some of these other items. I mean it's only fair that we make some money, right?

You: I hope you make enough money on the next deal to live long and prosper, but if that is the best you can do on the extended warranty, let's pass for now. What is the best you can do on the interest rate? Let's discuss monthly payments later. Can you beat 9 percent?

Finance person: We have a special with our bank, and I know we can get you lower rates and a lower payment. Tell you what, if you pick up the exterior care package for $350, I will get you an interest rate of 8.5, which will pay for the car care package over the lifetime of the car. So, not only will I get you a cheaper interest rate, but you will have the car care package for free. Doesn't that sound great?

You: Your loan is Rule of 78 isn't it? (See chapter eighteen for more about the Rule of 78.)

Finance person (amazed that you have even heard of Rule of 78): Of course, every loan in the business is.

You: Well, my loan from my credit union is simple interest on the declining balance. If yours is Rule of 78, I will need more than a half point off the interest rate. If you can get me 8 percent, I would consider it. Oh, if you can get me the extended warranty for $500, I might consider it also.

Negotiations will now go back and forth, and the finance person and you will eventually reach an agreement that you both can live with. But you will not give back anything on the trade-in or the new-car price, and you will not be scared of losing the new car because of financing problems: You have a loan already, so what can he threaten you with? All you will do is buy the best items at the best price and nothing else. After you agree on interest rate, you specify the number of months and check his figure against the figure you got from the bank or looked up yourself (maybe from sites on the Net).

At this stage, two or three hours after closing, everyone wants to go home, so there is less pressure on you but more on the finance person. If he drops the ball, everybody has stayed overtime for nothing. You are essentially home free, and he is under the gun. You have a good buy almost under your belt, but don't drop the ball just yet, because you still need to explore your leasing and financing options, which we'll cover next.

CHAPTER 17

Leasing

Congratulations! You're a long way into buying a new car at this point in the game. The trade-in price has been settled, the decision to buy made, the price on the extras determined. Now comes the job of deciding how to pay for that new car. To buy or to lease? That is the question you must answer. In many cases, it is unclear which is better. The rule is that leasing makes sense if you are short on your down payment and/or need low monthly payments. Let's explore the options.

Pros and Cons of Leasing

Leasing is great because your down payments are usually lower and your monthly payments are considerably lower. However, leasing also has its drawbacks. Let's look at them:

- At the end of the contract, you don't own the car.
- There are usually a lot of turn-in fees at the end of the lease.
- You may also not know what you paid for the new vehicle, the used vehicle or anything else—just the payment amount per month and the number of months you are to make the payments.
- Manufacturers and dealers love leasing because more people can afford the monthly payments and at the lease end, they are back in the market for another car. If manufacturers and dealers love something, you should immediately be wary of it.
- Leases customarily run for three years. At the end of that time, you will be looking for a new car (or lease).
- The idea of leasing is so good, people may not even fight for a good buy; they just roll over.
- Leasing is so complex that more profit can be hidden in the leasing structure.

If you decide to lease, be aware of your motivation. Don't use leasing just to get low payments after you have failed to get a good enough price on the vehicle. Fight hard for a good trade-in, a great price on the new car and everything else outlined above, and then negotiate hard for the best leasing terms.

Leasing Considerations

Following is a list of items to discuss before getting into the complicated topic of leases.

Initial Considerations

• Do you want a closed or an open lease? The car will have a fixed or a nonfixed value at completion of the lease. In a closed lease, the leased car has a fixed price at the completion of the lease. This is called a residual value. Most leases now are closed-end. The advantage of a closed-end lease is that there are no surprises at the end of the lease period.

• Do you want to keep the car after the end of the lease? For a lot of people, getting rid of an older car is a problem. Leases make sense here. However, if you may want to give a good, conditioned off-lease car to your kid, you ought to prepare to keep the car if you like. At the very least, negotiate a good interest rate so your kid can take over payments at the best rate possible.

• How much security deposit does the dealer want? Try to keep it to a minimum. A security deposit, usually refundable, protects the bank or leasing company from excessive wear and tear. A security deposit is typically one month's payment. Try not to let it exceed that amount. The best argument to give is that you don't want to pay this fee at all because you are a neat, careful and conscientious individual who will take great care of the car.

Price Determining Items

• Price for the car. Did you negotiate the best price for the car? This is usually called the capitalization cost. How close was it to the dealer's cost? (Remember, you do not want to pay over $300 to $400 above dealer's cost.)

• Price for your trade-in. This may be referred to as a capital cost reduction. How close was it to *Blue Book* wholesale? (Remember, your goal is to get within $300 of *Blue Book* wholesale for your trade-in.)

- Did you pay for an ADMU, AMU, dealer advertising or dealer prep (cleaning up and maintaining the vehicle)? I hope not.

- Is there a factory cash back to be used toward the car? How much? While factory-to-consumer rebates are usually advertised, factory-to-dealer incentives are not. Ask the dealer directly if he is getting any factory-to-dealer rebates. Demand an answer. Don't let him put you off by telling you it is none of your business. If he won't give you a figure, estimate it at a level that is to his disadvantage.

This works even better if you have checked the Web. I recommend IntelliChoice at http://www.intellichoice.com or Edmunds at http://www.edmunds.com. If you find the right site, you will know exactly what the cash-back situation is. If you catch the salesperson in a small fib here, never let him forget it, because that will eventually translate into money during other parts of the transaction.

If, for instance, he refuses to tell you anything, say, "Well, then, I will assume that you are being given $1,000 from the factory for each of these you sell. Therefore, I will expect the price to be considerably lower." This will usually force an answer. Insist that it is critical to the sale that you know the answer to this question.

- What kind of options did you pay for? Did you take any options you did not want?

- How much do you have to finance? (This is called your acquisition price. You figure it by subtracting your trade-in price, rebates and discounts on equipment packages from the best car price. Make sure you write down that acquisition price as a number).

Interest
- What is the dealership's interest rate for leasing?
- How does it compare to a bank's interest rate?
- How long do you want to lease?

Points to Argue
- What residual value is the dealership going to give you? (The residual value is the car's value after the lease is over.) Try negotiating

it upward. If it isn't reasonable, have the dealer look at another leasing institution to get a higher value. One way to see if the residual value is reasonable is to compare the depreciation percentages of previous years. Use the *Blue Book* for this. For instance, for a three-year lease, see how much a similar car sold for in 1992 compared to its worth in 1995. See how much a similar car sold for in 1993 compared to its 1996 worth, etc.

• If buying a performance model of a car, are you being hit with a lower residual value? Argue that performance cars usually sell for more than their usual value.

Things to Negotiate

• Negotiate the lease-end purchase option (the price you would pay to buy the leased vehicle at the end of the lease). Try to get the same interest rate as the initial lease. Make the purchase optional. A side note: You can usually buy your own car back for a cheaper price at a dealer-only auction than what the lease company will sell it to you for.

• Negotiate any premature buyout option. Try to make it inexpensive to get out of the lease. Whatever they offer, try to cut it down—flinching should work well here. The biggest complaint I see from people is having to live out a long-term lease.

• Negotiate any involuntary buyout option.

• What happens if the car is totaled?

• Discuss prepayment options.

• How much is gap insurance? If a car is stolen or destroyed, the insurance payment is usually less than the amount of money still owed on the vehicle. Gap insurance covers this gap.

• What about repairs and guarantees? Who does the repairs? Are they covered in the warranty from the factory? Who handles damage due to accidents or acts of nature?

• What sort of insurance requirements are demanded?

Things to Clarify

• Discuss the condition of the car at lease end. Make sure you are not stuck buying new tires. Ask about any small dings, fabric rips and equipment that doesn't work (e.g., power options). Get a firm written description of what is allowable and what is not.

• How many miles are allowed yearly? What sort of penalties are assessed for overages on miles? Are there credits for mileage under the allowance? If you drive a lot, see if you can get a higher allowable mileage before penalties kick in. The penalties for mileage overage are not trivial. It has been my experience that for newish cars (two years old), mileage costs as per the *Blue Book* are about ten cents a mile. Leasing companies usually charge fifteen cents a mile, more for luxury cars.

• Try not to accept a large disposition fee. A disposition fee is a fee to take the vehicle back into the dealership at the end of the lease. There is no logic for this cost; it is just a way to get more money from you, the consumer. This fee illustrates how sneaky leasing can be. In buying a new car, all the costs are up front. In leasing, many of the costs show up in the end, thereby making leasing appear cheaper initially.

Leasing Checklist

Interest rate: _____

Is it an APR or simple interest? _____

Length of the lease: _____

Interest rate for purchase of the car at
    the end of the lease: _____

Price guarantee of the car at the end
    of the lease: _____

Does the interest rate change if I lease
    or if I buy? _____

Does the price or financing change if
    I lease or if I buy? _____

Remember, negotiate the vehicle price first, then discuss leasing, then negotiate such items as interest rate, residual value of the vehicle, etc. Base your lease costs on that amount.

Leasing and the Internet

Leasing, the buying of a portion of the life of a car, is rendered a lot easier by access to the Internet. Using the Internet to lease a car (or to research leasing options for a car) has three distinct advantages over leasing through a traditional dealership:

1. It gives you a lot of sources from which to lease, other than through just the dealership. This directly affects price and the conditions you can extract from the car company.
2. If you can get the car price cheaper (capitalization cost), your leasing costs will be lower. So access to better car prices sets up a better lease.
3. A lot of literature exists on the Web that explains the whole process of leasing in detail. This makes a very complicated process a lot easier.

Web Sites of Interest

There are many automobile sites with leasing information; here are a few good sites worth visiting:

http://www.edmunds.com. Edmunds is *the* site of car sites.

http://www.kbb.com. Kelley *Blue Book.* This site not only lists values for used cars, but has information and advertisers who do leases.

http://www.aaa.com. American Automobile Association. Members and nonmembers can get good information on topics such as financing, insurance, auto buying and more.

http://www.leasesource.com. From leasing workshops to lease matchmaking, this site is a great resource.

http://www.carwizard.com. The Car Wizard site has its own program for buying versus leasing, as well as other leasing information.

CHAPTER 18

Financing

Once you've decided whether to buy or lease, you are ready to enter the last stage of the car buy, financing. (Remember the order of the buy?)

This is the place where you get everything together and see what it is you are going to pay and how you are going to pay it. This is the place where your power is the strongest. This is the place where you will be most aware of your power and the most careful not to blow the deal. The main difference between buying a car and financing it is that you will be dealing with a different specialist with different tricks.

Remember, have your homework done before you go to the showroom. This includes having your nondealer financing approved. You have gone to a bank, credit union or your favorite uncle and gotten the best loan for your vehicle. Know the dollar amount, the number of months and the APR.

By now, you have fought really hard and gotten a price approaching *Blue Book* wholesale for your trade-in. You have also gotten a price close to dealer's cost plus about $300 for that beautiful new car. Now is the time to make it happen, not to let anything slip away and not to get hit with any additional costs. Remember that there are four segments to a car transaction, and while you have just managed two of them (trade-in price and new-car price), you still have the financing and the purchasing of special items to go. Before we get into these two points, let's see some of the things the dealership may legitimately ask you to sign to expedite the transactions:

1. Power of attorney to allow the dealership to pay off your trade-in and/or register your new car for you. Sometimes, you will have to sign two of these forms so they can repossess your vehicle if necessary.

2. State law may mandate that you sign off that certain things have been explained to you. Beware that some dealerships try to use this signing off to pressure you into making a purchase.

3. You may have to authorize the dealership to look at your credit report if you finance through the dealership.

Options

In addition to signing off on the above items, you will be pressured by the finance person to buy certain extras and options. He certainly will not tell you which of these items are worth your money and which are not. Let's look at the options with your value in mind.

Extended Warranty

Never pay full price for the extended warranty. Warranty prices are highly negotiable. You found lots of places that sell extended warranties so you know what is available. I liked the set up at Warranty Gold (http://www.warrantygold.com). Dial in your car, and they give you a quote. There are lots of others. You may be willing to pay a few bucks more for the convenience of having it done and financed at the dealership. If you buy an extended warranty at the dealership you can probably finance it. If you buy it over the Internet it is cash. If you are the type of person who feels more secure with an extended warranty or have had good luck with them in the past, go for it. It may be worth your while to have this, if the price is right and you are worried about repairs. You may be able to get it for up to 50 percent off. Just keep asking, and watch the price drop. Dealerships will try for $150 plus per year of coverage. A six-year extended warranty could cost you $900. Dealerships will accept considerably less, but only if you push for it. Also, this is one item you do not have to buy now; you can buy it later if you want.

Life Insurance

Pass on this. This is a car dealership. Buy your life insurance from a reputable insurance agent.

Auto Insurance

Usually not an issue. Most people with cars already have insurance. However, you may have to show proof of auto insurance on a finance purchase before you leave the dealership with the new car.

Loans or Financing

Take dealership financing only if (1) you can get it for less than your financing from an outside source and (2) you expect to keep the car for the full term. You should get a discount on percentage rates of one half point (percent) in order to compensate for the Rule of 78 financing sold at dealerships. This financing is explained later in this chapter.

Antitheft Devices

No recommendations here either way. Only you will know if this is a necessary expense. Before you purchase the one offered by the dealership, see if you can get a markedly reduced price. Some of the cost may be partially compensated for by a reduced auto insurance rate. There are lots of systems on the market if you want one. You might want to shop around on the Net for some deals. The Edmunds site (http://www.edmunds.com) usually has everything related to antitheft options listed.

Rustproofing

The experts say this is probably not needed and is way too expensive. It's another clever way for the dealership to help you part with your money.

Outside Car Care Package

Nice as it makes the car look, this package has a high markup. See if you can get the price reduced by 50 to 66 percent. Better yet, see if you can avoid paying for it and still keep it on the car you are buying. Remember, at a low enough price, everything is an attractive purchase. (An alternative to the dealer's package is to buy the products and apply them yourself.)

Inside Car Care Package

If you really want it, get the price way down, same as the outside package.

Radios and Sound Systems

Outside sound systems from outside sources are very good and often less expensive. In addition, these sources install and warranty their products. If you know you want a good sound system, investigate before going to the dealership.

Performance Parts

The franchise dealerships are not really set up to customize a vehicle. Go online instead. Most of the big auto Web sites can't wait to send you a catalog. JC Whitney at http://www.edmunds.com/edweb/ JCWhitney/JCWhitney.html is a place to start.

Rule of 78

Throughout this book, I have referred to the most common financing done by car dealers as Rule of 78. Most people who have never worked in the car business have never heard of Rule of 78. Here is a review of this loan type, so you can be better informed of its details to decide what is the best option for you.

All loans are broken into two parts: principal (the amount borrowed) and interest (what it is costing you to borrow the principal). In the Rule of 78, the interest over the entire life of the loan is divided by seventy-eight. There are seventy-eight equal "pieces" of the interest on your loan. The first monthly payment made on a Rule of 78 loan consists of twelve of these pieces of interest with the remainder of the payment being principal repayment. The second monthly payment made on a Rule of 78 loan consists of eleven pieces of interest with the remainder of the payment being principal repayment. And so on until the twelfth monthly payment, which consists of one piece of this interest with the rest of the payment being principal repayment.

The total number of these pieces of interest paid in twelve months is seventy-eight $(12 + 11 + 10 + 9 + 8 + 7 + 6 + 5 + 4 + 3 + 2 + 1 = 78)$.

Hence, the Rule of 78. In the first year, all of the interest for the life of the loan has been paid. All future payments are principal only.

Rule of 78 is a financing gimmick set up to extract all the interest in a loan early in the loan payment period. You pay off all the interest and very little of the principal. It is true that if you keep your loan until its expiration date and nothing else happens, it doesn't matter if your loan package is Rule of 78 or simple interest. But what happens if you get in an accident and the insurance company pays off the car? You will have paid off all the interest, and the insurance will cover only a percentage of the remaining principal value of the car. You will be stuck with the difference.

Rule of 78 is great for the dealerships. They get their interest paid to them early in the financing contracts. More importantly, if you decide to refinance later to take advantage of a drop in interest rates, most of the interest has already been paid off, but you will be refinancing a large principal balance. Good for them, not good for you.

The Business of Financing

Now that you understand Rule of 78, let's look at what actually happens in the finance room. The first item on the agenda is to confirm that the finance person agrees with the prices you and the salesperson negotiated earlier. This must be done before you begin discussing the details such as length of financing, interest rate, lease or buy, etc. Let's look at the items to be discussed with the finance person.

Reaffirm the cost of the new car. Make sure he knows what you have agreed to pay for the new vehicle. Make sure you both agree on the items that will be on the vehicle. Don't negotiate. If he balks at the price, show him the figures you have written down, and call in the sales manager if necessary. There should be no surprises here.

Reaffirm the price given you on your trade-in. Go back to your notes, have him reaffirm that this price is fixed, firm and solid and that there will not be a sudden change in what you receive for that price.

Reaffirm the amount of down payment needed. Dealerships love cash; make sure the amount of down payment doesn't suddenly rise.

Recheck the amount of rebates, first-time buyer money, etc. This is all free cash to the dealership, but it is your free cash. If there is factory-to-consumer cash, it will be presented to you here. Make sure the price for the new car does not have this included in it already. It is important to have it made crystal clear that rebate money was not negotiated into the low price you got for the new car. Factory-to-dealer cash, on the other hand, is negotiated in the salesroom when getting the best price for your new vehicle. American car manufacturers typically give factory-to-consumer cash, while Japanese car companies provide more factory-to-dealer incentives.

Reaffirm the amount of package discounts. Make sure there is no mistake in this figure. If you have been promised power steering at no charge because you bought the air-conditioning system, make sure the finance person honors the commitment made to you earlier.

Ask about items such as alarm systems, extra pinstripes, extended warranty. Make a firm decision of yes or no on each one, then negotiate price. Review the "Options" list discussed earlier in this chapter. Remember the high markup, and try to cut price by at least half, or most items are not worth considering.

Ask how much time you have before your option to buy an extended warranty expires. Also ask if there is any other organization that will offer you an extended warranty on the car later. Don't expect a good answer from the dealership. Use the Net here. Warranty Gold at http://www.warrantygold.com is a good place to start.

Ask about the dealership's best financing package before stating that you have financing from an outside source. Once you have the information, compare it to the financing you have already obtained. Check for Rule of 78 financing. When you mention your outside financing, ask the dealer to beat your package. Tell him you would rather the finance money go to the dealership than to the bank. Make sure the finance person expresses the loan percentage in APR (Annual Percentage Rate), the loan amount in an actual dollar figure, the monthly payments and the number of months. Check your chart or calculator to make sure these figures make sense and are correct for the loan amount you are borrowing.

The dealership may offer you financing, but some of the terms of this financing will differ from those offered by your friendly local bank or credit union. Most dealerships offer interest rates that are based on the Rule of 78. Most outside lending institutions use a method with interest on the declining balance of the loan. Everything else being equal, take a declining balance loan over a Rule of 78 loan so that if you change your mind and get rid of your car early, you pay less interest. One-half percent is my rule of thumb for an "incentive" to take Rule of 78.

Financing Checklist

This list is meant to help you gather facts to show you how much your car purchase is really going to cost after everything has been added up. Make guesses for numbers 1 through 19 as sort of a practice run before going to the dealership so you have a rough idea of what the costs will be. Then fill the whole list during the financing part of the buy. Obviously, you will have items number 1 and number 2 before going to the showroom.

1. Lender _____

Interest rate _____

 % (APR) amount of loan _____

Type of loan _____

2. Lender _____

Interest rate _____

 % (APR) amount of loan _____

Type of loan _____

3. Dealership _____

Interest rate _____

 % (APR) amount of loan _____

Type of loan _____

4. Cost of new car (from your negotiations) _____

5. Trade-in value (from your negotiations) _____

6. Down payment (not including trade-in) _____

7. Amount of dealer rebate _____

8. Amount of package discounts (luxury package, etc.) _____

9. Amounts of other discounts and rebates (first-time buyer, promotional discounts, etc.) _____

10. Sales tax _____ % × (car price) = _____

11. Registration and licensing fees _____

12. Document fee _____

13. Insurance _____

14. Other items (extended warranty, etc.) _____

15. Transportation (freight) _____

16. Dealer's prep (usually included at no cost) _____

17. Initial gas and oil (should be included in price) _____

18. Dealer's advertising (negotiate for zero) _____

19. Figure the amount to be financed (4 minus 5, 6, 7, 8 and 9; plus 10, 11, 12, 13, 14, 15 and 16) _____

20. Monthly payments for _____ months at _____ %APR = _____

Leasing Financing Checklist

Remember, negotiate the vehicle price first, then discuss leasing. After you decide you are going to lease, you can negotiate such items as interest rate and residual value of the vehicle. Base your lease amount on those figures.

If you are considering leasing, here are some other important questions to ask in financing:

- What is the interest rate (APR)?
- What is the length of the lease?
- Is the lease figured simple interest?
- What is the interest rate for the purchase of the car at the end of the lease?
- What is the price guarantee of the car at the end of the lease?
- Is there a difference between the leasing and buying interest rates?
- Is there any difference between the leasing and buying prices or financing?

- What condition must the car be in when you return it to avoid a penalty?
- What is the maximum mileage per year? Are there penalties for exceeding this? Can I get a higher mileage figure without penalty?
- How much is the return fee?
- Are there any other fees on return of the car?

Items to Double-Check

- Have you been charged only for items you specifically wanted (no extras)?
- Did you get all factory cash, first-time buyer's discount, etc.?
- Was there anything else promised that the dealer conveniently forgot or nibbled away?
- Ask what else the dealership can do for you or give you to make the high cost of the car more palatable. Perhaps the dealer will throw in a cargo net, some sort of an upgrade or a free oil and lube on your first service visit.
- Have the finance person write up the contract and put figures on paper. Make sure each figure is explained.
- Ask the finance person if anything was added to the pricing of the car that you did not specifically request but that he thought you might need or want.
- Is the car a refugee from the lemon law? In California and other states with a lemon law, consumers are allowed to return a new car to the dealership if the car has an inordinate number of mechanical problems and/or need of repair. Carfax (http://www.carfax.com) has a free lemon-law checker.
- Is the car a flood car? A flood car is a new car that has been water damaged, rebuilt and offered for sale as a new car.
- Is the car damaged? Was it in an accident and fixed up? Occasionally, a brand-new car is stolen from a dealership, damaged, recovered and fixed up. This sort of trauma to a new car should be disclosed to the customer.
- Is there anything about the car I should know about in order

to make an informed decision?

- Have there been any recalls on this type of car? What type of recall?
- What is the length of guarantee on this car?
- Does the dealership provide loaner cars or transportation if the car needs covered repairs?
- Is the car really new? Has it ever been registered before?
- Did you get everything you asked for? Has anything been omitted or held back? (Check your list made during negotiations.)
- Double-check all the numbers used to price your car (in case of inadvertent substitution or error).
- If there are repairs or substitutions promised you, hold back a part of the money or refuse to sign until they are completed.
- Check to make sure no fees were tacked on after the final figure was decided upon (such as dealer's prep fee, which usually is included in the price of the car).
- Ask for the dealership to throw in some free floor mats when you sign.
- If the sales and finance people do a good job for you in all this, ask for a dealership rating form and give them good marks.

The Paperwork

Suddenly it is put-up-or-shut-up time and the paperwork comes out. What documents can you legitimately be expected to sign?

- **Power of Attorney.** To allow the dealership to pay off your trade-in and/or register your new car for you. Sometimes, you will have to sign two of these forms so they can sign your name if they repossess your vehicle.
- **Your Credit Report.** You may have to authorize the dealership to look at your credit report.
- **Buyer's Guide.** California has a buyer's guide that is put in the window of most cars and tells something about the car. You may have to sign off on it.
- **Report of Sale.** There may be one of these that goes to the

state's DMV to register the vehicle.

- **Bill of Sale.** Buyer and seller will have to sign this.
- **State Papers.** These list particulars that have been explained to you. State law may mandate that you sign off that certain things have been explained to you by the dealer.
- **Contract.** Contains all the particulars of your deal.

Special Tips for Buying a Used Car

CHAPTER 19

New Cars vs. Used Cars

Most of us would probably buy an expensive new car with all the extras if we had the money. We would all also like to live in a mansion, eat at the best restaurants, have the best of everything and not worry about spending at all. However, we are not able to do all that we want. If we go for a new car with all the trimmings, we may have to forgo eating and air-conditioning. That's why this chapter is devoted to comparing the differences between new and used cars. Let's look analytically at the reasons for choosing to buy each.

Common Reasons for Getting a New Car

Reason 1: I don't want to buy anybody else's trouble.

Response: Buying a used car does not necessarily mean buying another person's troubles any more than buying a new car is always a trouble-free experience. This reason is usually an excuse for being afraid to look for a great used car.

Reason 2: I have enough money. Cost isn't an issue, and I want a brand-new car.

Response: Can't argue with this one—buy that new car and enjoy it. The average person has to balance her spending. I personally prefer to spend less on cars and more on other items.

Reason 3: When I buy a new car, the dealer takes care of everything. I don't have to do a lot of extra legwork.

Response: True, but you pay an awful lot for that saved legwork.

Reason 4: I have such bad credit that if I have to buy a car, I need a dealer to take care of all the financial details and get me some credit.

Response: New-car dealers are not the only ones to supply credit; most used-car sellers have financing capabilities. If your credit is bad, why would you choose to pay more than necessary for a product and risk owing even more money?

Reason 5: I need long-term warranties to take care of any possible problems, and you can only get them with a new car.

Response: Not true. Warranties are also available at "after-market" places. Warranties are great for giving you peace of mind, but you do not need to pay dealer prices for that peace of mind. Take your newly purchased used car to the dealership, and see if there is an extended warranty that can be reactivated. If not, see if the dealership will sell you one at a reasonable price. Web sites such as http://www.warranty gold.com, http://www.warrantydirect.com and http://www .gmwarrantycentral.com (which sells GM after-market warranties) can help you.

Reason 6: It is very important to me that I get the exact color, style and options I want. It is possible to get exactly what I want only in a new car.

Response: If you can afford it, go for it. If money is a consideration and you feel you can compromise on some of these demands, consider a great used car. You might be pleasantly surprised.

Reason 7: I want the bragging rights that come with a new car.

Response: Bragging rights do come with a new car, and they are powerful bragging rights indeed. However, you can counter that brag with the information that your car cost 65 percent of the cost of the same car new. The really impressive bragging happens when you compare your monthly payments to that new-car owner's and indicate that you expect to spend Christmas in Hawaii with his car dealer.

Reason 8: New cars are better than used cars, and I deserve the best.

Response: New cars are better mechanically than old cars, but for the price, not all new cars are better than all used cars. For example, which is better, a brand-new $21,000 Chevy

Lumina with all the bells and whistles and no miles or a two-year old Cadillac Sedan DeVille with 15,000 miles obtained at auction for $21,000?

Reason 9: New cars have the most up-to-date technology and I want that.

Response: That is actually a good reason if you really want or need the latest technology. But most car changes are incremental, not revolutionary.

Reason 10: It's almost as cheap to buy this particular car new as it is to buy it used.

Response: Once in a while this is true. GM has come out with a credit card that garners the user rewards when using it. These rewards can be redeemed as cash toward a new-car purchase. If the rewards are sizeable, and they are coupled with rebates and a sale, it makes sense to buy a new car rather than a used car.

Reason 11: My financial situation is such that I need to lease or finance all car purchase costs. I need to finance all the extras I want. There is not much leasing available on used cars.

Response: This is true. If you buy at a dealership and get the right financing package you can finance your after-market warranties, high-end stereo and other extras. Unfortunately, you pay more for the privilege of financing all these items. And yes, it is easier to lease a new car than a used one.

Common Reasons for Getting a Used Car

Reason 1: The main reason for getting a used car is money. Used cars are cheap compared to new cars, and you do get more for your money.

Reason 2: A car loses as much as 50 percent of its value at the end of its first year. Look through any of Edmund's new-car price guides. You will quickly see that at the end of the first year, some cars sharply decrease in value. It takes only four more years (on average) to drop another 25 percent so that at the end of five years, many cars are down to 25 percent of their original prices.

If money is a factor, the best way to buy a car is to forgo the new-car smell and get a car at half price. I feel that the best bargains are used cars. The best bargains in used cars are one- to two-year-old off-lease vehicles with low mileage. These cars have already lost a large percentage of their original values but are still practically new.

Consider this: If you buy a $25,000 shiny leather-seated car, drive it off the lot and return in two months to trade it in, even if it only has five thousand miles on it, the trade-in value will be $17,000.

This is a substantial decrease in value. One of the main reasons is that a lot of the items you buy with a new car have absolutely no resale value.

These items include:

- Transportation. This fee varies from $200 to over $500. There is no way to get credit for this on trade-in.
- Ditto for taxes and registration.
- Document, insurance or title fees. There may be a whole host of little fees that your dealership tacks on (or must tack on by law). These also have no resale value.
- Leasing fees or penalties for early return of the vehicle.
- Dealer's advertising fee. I warned you earlier not to pay this one, but some car dealers break out an extra charge for this, even though it would seem to be part of their normal operating expenses.
- Special packages. Remember that special exterior finish and pinstripe combination for which you paid $350? The next buyer won't pay for your artistic taste and may even consider unusual exterior markings a deduction. There is no way you will get any credit for those items.
- Special interior treatments. Remember those marvelous floor mats and the rest of that stuff for which you paid an additional $500 when you found out it was already included on the car you wanted to buy? Well, you won't get any credit for that either.

- AMU or ADMU. You wanted a hot car and paid extra for it. The dealership won't pay extra to take it back unless it is still super hot as a used car.
- Dealer's profit over cost.
- Dealer's prep. Some dealerships will try to charge you for this as an extra even though it is and should be included in the cost of the car.

This list doesn't even include wear and tear and normal depreciation on the vehicle itself. It just points out items you paid for and won't recoup any money from. Again, these are costs you will never recover, costs that contribute to the car's phenomenal depreciation its first year. Just to let you know: For new cars, the big costs of owning a car are (1) depreciation, (2) interest on the loan, (3) insurance, (4) gas and (5) repairs.

Can you stand the uncertainty of buying a car that is not quite new if you can save a lot of money in the process? I hope so. A good used car is a great financial savings and should be considered for that reason alone. Most of the advantages of a new car can also be found in a nearly new car.

CHAPTER 20

Understanding Used Cars

This brief chapter is devoted strictly to providing you with definitions (and context) for commonly used terms you will encounter when buying a used car. These terms will also help you understand the used-car cycle. OK, let's go.

Used-Car Terminology

After-Market

A general term for car-related things that are sold after the car, new or used, leaves a retail dealership. After-market auto add-ons may not be cheap, but are usually cheaper than if sold through dealers while buying a car. The difference is the ability of the car buyer to shop around and do some comparison shopping when not under pressure at the dealership. The Internet is replete with after-market insurance, warranties, and high-performance products. Just type in the search words "auto insurance" or "auto warranties" and get buried in responses. A typical Web site is http://www.carprices.com for insurance or wholesale auto.

Broker

Someone who sells something he doesn't own (and makes money on it!). A broker has no inventory costs and no deterioration of his inventory. He has no service responsibilities or really any responsibilities at all after he hooks up a seller and a buyer. There are more brokers in the new-car field than the used-car field. Brokers are probably doing much better with the advent of the Internet. Typical Internet brokers would be Autobytel (http://www.autobytel.com) or Microsoft CarPoint (http://www.carpoint.msn.com) among others.

Draft

A promise by a dealer to pay for a vehicle usually when the title arrives sometime later. Typically the buyer signs a draft, takes the car and puts it on his lot—or wholesales it. Sometime later he gets a call that says his draft is due, and he is bound to come in to pay for it immediately. The time you get by "drafting" is called a "float." Drafting to get a float usually means a higher price to a dealer. Many times it is worth it.

Factory Credit Sources

> General Motors Acceptance Corp. (GMAC)—a source for auto loans
> Toyota Motor Credit (TMC)—a source for auto loans
> Ford Motor Credit (FMC)—a source for auto loans

Guarantees

A general term for assurances given by retail establishments. The dealerships themselves get them from services (insurance companies). They are certainly useful if you get them free or negotiate to have them included in the price of the car. They are probably useful if you get them at a good price. They are not so good if you pay too much for a guarantee. This term is used interchangeably with warranties.

Lease Terminations

Lease terminations might be the filet mignon of used cars. They are those two-year-old, just-off-the-lease, low-mileage, great-conditioned vehicles.

New-Car Dealer

This is a franchise dealership that sells new cars, typically by only one manufacturer.

Retail Customer

You, the person who picks up the car and pays all the bills.

Retail Dealer

Someone licensed by the DMV (or the state licensing agency) to sell used cars to retail customers. Usually a retail salesperson receives no formal training and the licensing, bonding and set-up processes are relatively easy and open.

Quick Turn

The ultimate high for car sellers, at least in a professional capacity. Lucky dealers contract to buy a vehicle (drafting), don't pay for the vehicle then, but take the vehicle and sell it at a profit. The selling step may involve turning the vehicle at a dealers-only auction, a new-car shop or a small lot. Later when the draft comes due, the seller pays for the vehicle with a business check and obtains the title. He then runs (not walks) to the place he sold the vehicle earlier and turns in the title. He gets a check for the car and title. He then quickly deposits the check in the bank at the same time his "buy" check hits. In essence, he has bought a car with no money or cash flow problems. The incoming and outgoing checks hit at the same time and the net effect is that no money comes out of his account.

Warranties

Given by Detroit, Berlin, Tokyo, Oslo or wherever new-car makers are headquartered. Warranties are free (at least the ones that come with the new cars) and great. They are usually scrupulously observed. You can buy extended warranties virtually anywhere, including the Internet at Warranty Direct (http://www.warrantydirect.com) and at all dealerships. For an Internet search type in the words "auto warranty" and see what comes up.

Wholesale Dealer

Someone who can only take vehicles from one dealer or source and sell them to another dealer. The process is called wholesaling. Wholesalers cannot directly sell vehicles to the public. While whole-salers usually occupy the lowest rung of the auto selling ladder, some make very good money.

CHAPTER 21

Evaluating a Used Car

Knowing the condition of a used car is key to knowing if it is a good deal. This chapter takes a close look at important aspects of a car that change during its lifetime and can influence price and suitability, and presents a four-prong attack for the actual evaluation process.

Important Used-Car Considerations
Engine and Drive Train

Without a doubt, the conditions of the engine and drive train are much more important than all other factors combined. They are the heart of the car (and thus its value). Unless you have very good mechanical advice, my general rule is that if either the transmission or the engine is not in great shape, you must walk away from the deal. Of course, dealers and professionals may buy a problem car at a very good price, fix it up and then sell it at a profit, but I do not advise the average consumer to do this.

Salvage Titled Vehicles

Salvage titles are given either for wrecks or theft recoveries. I am not a great believer in buying revamped wrecks, and I freely admit that I don't have enough experience to evaluate them properly. But I do know that if the price is right, it makes lots of sense to buy a salvaged vehicle, especially salvage titles from theft recoveries. What happens is that when stolen cars are recovered by the police (after the insurance company has paid off the vehicle), they are relicensed with a "salvage" designation on the title.

Salvage title vehicles are easy to buy at good prices and somewhat difficult to sell for the same reason. Salvage title cars sell cheaply because most financing companies will not finance them (many inexperienced credit union reps think all salvage titles are reconstituted wrecks). This means only people with cash can buy these vehicles, which is why the price is so low—it's more difficult to find cash buyers. On nearly new vehicles, I estimate that the salvage price can drop 25 percent or more for an essentially sound vehicle.

As vehicles get older and the value of a vehicle drops, the denigration in value caused by a salvage designation lessens. For a ten-year-old vehicle, for example, the salvage title has very little affect on price, whereas condition is paramount. Most ten-year-old vehicles are bought for cash anyway.

Frame-Damaged Vehicles

Yes, these are fine to buy, but make sure you get a good price and the damage is minimal or repaired. Horrible thoughts of twisted metal making your car unsafe race through your mind. "I *will not* put my family at risk by buying one of these," you say. As I have said, though, I have bought frame-repaired vehicles at a dealers-only auction and my mechanics have missed many problems until I alerted them. I really don't advocate buying vehicles with major front-end trauma unless you have a really good mechanic to make the decision with you.

To initially check for major structural damage, look for wavy body panels or mismatched colors of paint. Use a magnet (one of those soft refrigerator ones) and check to make sure all body parts are metal. Often accidents are repaired using a nonmetal called Bondo as fill material. The magnet will reveal its presence. Look in the trunk and under the pads in the back for indications of corrected rear-end damage. In conclusion, consider frame-damaged vehicles, but be careful and always get a good price.

High Mileage

High miles are not universally bad. The *Blue Book* has generally accepted tables for deterioration of vehicle value as mileage changes. A new-car warranty of three years or 36,000 miles means that manufacturers consider 12,000 miles per year average. We drive a lot more than that here in California; 12,000 miles a year is 1,000 miles a month, is 30 miles a day, is one 15-mile trip and back home. This is not a lot of driving. In fact, it is not unusual to see 50,000-mile, eighteen-month-old vehicles.

Mileage is certainly an accepted way of determining if a vehicle is suitable. According to the *Blue Book*, miles for a one-year-old car valued at $20,000 with 10,000 miles on the odometer depreciates at about 10 cents per mile. For a six-year-old car worth $9,000 with 40,000 on the odometer, it's about 2.5 cents per mile. So mileage reduces the price of a vehicle, and it reduces it much more for relatively newer vehicles.

Some vehicles, however, handle mileage better than others. Dealers, for example, are less concerned about the salability of high-end cars (BMWs, Mercedes, Volvos, Infinities) with high miles. The rational is that a high-mileage Ford 5-liter Mustang has been driven and beaten up by some kid who is street racing and couldn't afford the repairs. However, a ten-year-old, 160,000-mile Mercedes was probably driven by some older gentleman who had the cash to keep the car in good mechanical shape, fix all the seat rips, and not abuse the vehicle (even if he drove it a lot). The perception, and it may well be reality, is that luxury vehicles can take higher miles because they are built better and are pampered by their owners.

Passing Smog

One of the best indicators of a car's condition is whether it can pass a smog (emissions) test. Cars that can't are a major problem. In general, before you buy a car make sure the seller gets the car past emissions. Usually a good smog pass indicates that the engine and exhaust system are both operating well. Sometimes, however, passing smog testing is not the end of your problems.

Consider the following situation. A vehicle gets a preliminary nonpass on smog, because it is blowing a small amount of smoke, which should be handled by the catalytic converter. The ultimate cause is probably a bad set of rings or some valve trouble. The problem is masked, however, by buying a new but cheap catalytic converter—and the car then passes the smog test. The car is good for a while, but in two years when another smog test is due, the ring problem is still there (and may be worse). That means trouble.

So . . . a pass on smog is good and a fail on smog is bad, but a pass on smog may mean that a problem has been temporarily hidden. The latter happens more with older cars and is unusual for newer vehicles under warranty.

Air-Conditioning

Air-conditioning not working (or not working well) means serious dollars. When you check for working air-conditioning, turn on both car and the air-conditioning. It should run cold. If not, assume the worst; repairing a frozen compressor will cost at least $500. Make sure the fan runs. If you know what you are doing, check to see if the compressor is frozen or if it is something simple like a broken belt.

The Paint Job

A great paint job in a color you hate is a lot worse than a bad paint job on a car you love. In the latter case, you can hit the previous owner for enough bucks to get the vehicle painted the color you want, and you can get door dings and small body problems taken care of at the same time.

A perfect paint job on an older car can mean two things. First, it has a great original paint job. This is unlikely but wonderful, and probably means the vehicle was garaged and rarely taken to supermarkets or malls. The other—and more probable —reason is that the car was hit, repaired and repainted.

When you inspect a car, take someone with you who is meticulous and great at noticing small irregularities in car surfaces. And both of you should be on the lookout for repainted cars. On cars that have been partially repainted, you might notice differences in paint color or a slight misalignment of the hood, the trunk or the doors. Other signs include orange peel texture and overspray painting. Don't panic if you notice these things (after all, many vehicles have been hit during their lifetimes and only need cosmetic aid), because you can point them out to the seller and use them to your advantage when you negotiate. If, however, you find there's serious frame damage, you might question whether you should buy the car (see Frame Damage on page 184).

When it comes to assessing the paint job, it is best not to think any car that has been repaired and repainted is unsuitable. Rather, think *if the vehicle is suitable, and if it is a good deal at the price, we should consider it*. But don't forget that it's best to know a car's faults before you buy—instead of finding out six months after the purchase.

Sunroofs

Sunroofs that don't work cause my mechanic to swear more than any other type of repair, probably because they are so awkward to repair. Mostly they are jammed or the motors burn out, but they can be fixed. A sunroof that doesn't open and close is something you can tolerate; a leaking sunroof is another matter and should definitely cause concern.

Repair Records

Seeing repair records is important to some buyers. But do repair records have any real utility? It depends on the car. I, for example, have yet to meet a Mercedes buyer who didn't want all the papers and repair records to browse through. A complete record of all repairs almost surely guarantees a higher price for upscale cars. On the other hand, records have little or no meaning for the resale value of a Chevy Cavalier. As a person who appreciates a vehicle in good shape, I would pay more for a well-maintained vehicle than for a car with records. Repair records can always be fudged. Your best bet is to inspect the shape the car is in when you're ready to buy it, not to rely on its paperwork.

Cigarette Smoke

Nonsmokers understandably don't want a car that smells like smoke. Some buyers are so cautious they even pull out the ashtrays and smell them. As a nonsmoker I am sympathetic, but there are a few ways to handle deodorizing a smoking car (if the price is worth the effort). A good detailing might work, but what removes cigarette smoke smell best is a small ozone generator that plugs into the cigarette lighter. It gets rid of any kind of smell.

Ripped Leather and Upholstery

Ripped upholstery is for many a silent accusation that the former owner was mistreating his car. That's not always the case; used cars have imperfections. What I want to point out is that ripped upholstery is not a sign of an abused vehicle but an indicator that the former owner doesn't care about getting the best price for the vehicle. You should be the one to take advantage of his reluctance. It is relatively inexpensive (usually under $100) to fix leather and cloth rips, and there are auto upholstery places that handle it. A spot that usually "goes" first is the left side of the driver's seat where a man's wallet rubs as he gets in and out of the car.

Worn or Asymmetrically Worn Tires

Worn tires are cause for a price adjustment and a signal to look into alignment problems or frame damage. Bad tire wear should ring a bell about what caused the wear. Was it an accident? Does this correlate with a new paint job and some misaligned trunk or hood metal? I wouldn't eliminate a car from consideration because of tire wear, but I would work on an adjustment in price to compensate. Your cost could involve replacing the tires and fixing whatever is causing the tires to wear unevenly. Have your mechanic check the tires.

Missing Stereo Equipment

Missing stereo equipment should be a cause for rejoicing, not aggravation. I would guess that 35 percent of vehicles I buy have had the sound systems removed. Probably the original owner had a great Alpine system with a six-disc CD changer and wanted it for her next car. To make the most out of a missing stereo, all you need to do is decrease your offering price by more than enough to get the sound system you want, and then purchase that system (thanks to the previous owner).

Faulty Switches

Faulty switches are the usual cause for power windows not moving up and down. Sometimes in well-maintained, frequently detailed vehicles so much Armor All interior protectant is used that the switch contact points are covered with a film and electrical contact can't be made. A frequent cause is that the switch just breaks. This is not a major issue, usually it is not the window motor.

Quality of American vs. Foreign Cars

Foreign and domestic cars go for astronomically different prices on the resale market. Automatic newish Hondas and Toyotas get great retail prices (sometimes the prices are so high that it makes sense to buy new, not used).

I don't think there's a great discrepancy between the quality of foreign and American cars. Consider: Benz owns Chrysler, which had a big stake in Mitsubishi. Ford owns a big piece of Mazda and uses Mazda parts in its cars. Ford owns Jaguar, Volvo and Aston Martin. Will Lincoln be markedly different than Jaguar? Ford quality cannot be markedly different from Mazda or Volvo. GM and Toyota work together on Geo Prizms. They must have similar quality standards. In addition, the quality of parts is similar worldwide. The engineers have the same training. And all vehicles must meet the same safety, emission, lighting, braking and fuel economy standards. How different can they be? Today, you will be hard-pressed to find large quality differences between different car companies, foreign or domestic.

My suggestion is to buy the vehicle that suits your needs and that has a good "bang for the buck" ratio. When ten-year-old Caddies and ten-year-old Corollas approach each other in price, then its time to consider value and utility (not country of origin).

The Four-Prong Attack for Evaluating a Used Car

Evaluating a used car should be a four-prong attack:

1. You must assess the car's interior, exterior and mechanical condition.

2. You must scrutinize the title and other paperwork-related legalities.

3. You should get a professional mechanic's inspection.

4. You should check the car's history. Try Carfax at http://www.carfax.com to start.

Once you complete your four-prong evaluation of your potential car, you will know a lot about the car and its flaws. Then you can forge ahead and negotiate for a better price. We'll get into negotiating later, but now let's explore each evaluation prong in detail.

Prong One: Assessing the Car's Condition (Exterior, Interior and Mechanical)

Exterior

When inspecting the outside of a vehicle, I make a few circles around the car and answer these questions:

- Is there any broken or pitted glass?
- Is the paint in good condition?
- Are there any indications of a repaint job?
- Is there any major structural damage?
- Is there any minor structural damage? Look for loose trim, bent side mirrors, missing antenna, missing gas cap, broken door handles, loose bumpers, etc.
- Is there damage to the paint? Look for door dings, paint scratches and fading or peeling paint.
- Are the headlights and taillights intact? Do they work properly? What about the signals?
- Are the floor mats with the vehicle?
- Ask if the car has been garaged during its lifetime. See if the answer meshes with the condition of the paint.
- If the car is a four-wheel drive, ask if it has been offroaded. Look for evidence that it has been offroaded. Dings, especially roof damage, are strong evidence.
- How are the tires?
- Also note if the tire rims are upscale or base rims. If the car has base rims, ask if you can have the upscale rims if he has any.

Anybody with a good eye can check the exterior and thus get a good indication of the care and maintenance of the car. It should be relatively easy to spot evidence of prior neglect or an accident.

Interior

The goal of inspecting the interior is twofold: You want to see if the vehicle has been abused, and you also want to see if you feel comfortable inside the car.

- Are the seats in good shape? Look at the seat material.
- Sit in the seat and close the doors. Close your eyes and inhale. Do you get a good feeling, or do you feel uneasy?
- Sit in the backseats. Check the seating material and details in the back.
- How is the odor? Is there residual odor (vomit, beer, smoke, solvents, etc.)?
- Look for wear and tear that is not consistent with the mileage on the car. Torn seats or very worn pedals and armrests on a car that shows 32,000 miles is an indication that perhaps the mileage has been altered.
- Do the window cranks or power windows work?
- Check the lights and turn signals with someone on the outside. Also check the horn. If only you and the seller are present, ask him to try the signals while you check them from the outside.
- Do the window wipers and washers work? Check front and back.
- Do the seats move smoothly and easily?
- Does the radio work? Check all speakers. Note the stations that are fixed in memory. If it is, say, a Spanish station and the seller is not, ask (again) if he is a dealer and not the original owner.
- Start the engine, and turn on the air-conditioning. It should run ice-cold.
- Do all the interior panels light up? Do all the interior lights work? Are all the plastic covers in place?
- Is the dashboard in good condition?

- Is the steering wheel bent? This may indicate an accident.
- With the car in park (neutral for a stick shift), run the engine very high for five seconds and notice what comes out the tailpipe. Be ready to walk away if the smoke is heavy white or blue. An initial transient blue puff of smoke on a car that has been sitting for a long while may indicate a valve seal problem.
- Are there any missing small parts (such as knobs, window cranks, ashtray covers, etc.)?
- Ask about the mileage again. Is this the original mileage, or has the odometer been replaced or altered? If you have any doubts, have the seller guarantee the validity of the odometer reading in writing.
- Look in the glove box for the manual, recent repair bills, etc. Ask what has been done to the car recently.

This is the easy part for most buyers. Most of us feel competent to inspect the inside and the outside easily; there is no mystique here, no hidden frammis gauge or transverse Fitzwalter clutch assembly. What is required here is a good eye and an attention to detail, not sophisticated technical knowledge. Now for the hard part: evaluating the mechanical integrity of the vehicle.

Mechanical

These are things you can check even if you are not a professional mechanic. If you spot something that may be indicative of trouble, you will be able to ask your mechanic about it.

- Check the oil. If it is brand-new, you learn nothing except that the seller had the oil changed to enhance the selling chances.
- Look for a gelatinous goop around the inside of the oil fill cap or in the oil chamber. This may indicate a water leak. Be prepared to walk away at this point. Hard-caked muddy oil on a dipstick indicates that the oil in the past may not have been changed frequently. If the present oil is clean but the cap is muddy, the oil was recently changed. When inspecting the oil, look for metal flakes or grit in the oil. If any are observed, be concerned.

- Look for evidence of oil leakage on engine surfaces. Ask where the car is normally parked, and look for oil there. You will need a mechanic to evaluate if it is serious. With the car in park and the idle low, look at the pressure gauge. If the oil pressure is low, there may be an oil pump problem.
- Look for fluid leaking onto such items as brakes.
- Check the radiator water. See if the antifreeze is new or if it is rust colored.
- If the car has been sitting and is not hot, run your fingers around the inside of the tailpipe and see what comes out on them. If it is carbon and water, you are OK (maybe you need a tune-up). If it is oily, be careful. Do not put your fingers anywhere near the tailpipe if the car has been running; it gets hot.
- Check the belts and see if they are tight. If they look frayed or the edges are white, you may have some work to do.
- Listen for noises. The engine should start and run quietly. If there is too much engine vibration, there may be problems. A tapping or banging sound spells trouble. Any spraying of oil or water is bad news.
- Check out the gears. All of them (forward and reverse) should work, and they should shift quietly. Check for pickup and power.
- Check the transmission fluid. It should be pink. If it is yellow or brown and smells burnt, take it as evidence of major transmission problems.
- With the car in drive, use the lowest amount of gas and see if the transmission slips.
- At speed, slam on the brakes (warn your passenger first) and see how the car stops. There should be no squeaking, and the vehicle should stop quickly in a straight line. Any bumping indicates the brakes are about shot. If the vehicle pulls strongly to one side, a brake job will be necessary soon.

In your inspection of the car's exterior, interior and mechanical soundness, you should also be on the lookout for peripheral information that will help you negotiate for a better price. I suggest you review the chapter on the test-drive before going to look at a used car.

Also, be sure to consider the car's suitability for you. Do you really like the car? A vehicle you hate but buy because you can't resist the price is not a good deal.

Prong Two: Scrutinizing the Title and Other Paperwork

It would be nice to assume that every car is being sold by its real owner, but this is not always the case. When the seller shows you the title, check for the following:

- Is there a lien on the vehicle? Has the lien holder signed off claim to the vehicle? You may want to check with the lien holder to make sure it is really signed off.
- Does the VIN (vehicle identification number), the seventeen-digit number usually found on the dashboard looking in from the front windshield, on the title match the VIN on the car? Does the description also match?
- Does the car have a branded title, such as a salvage title?
- Make sure the registered owner is the one selling the car. Check with your local police department or the state DMV to make sure the car is not stolen or does not have title problems. You can check on Carfax (http://www.carfax.com), too.
- Get the name, address, phone number, driver's license number, social security number and place of business of the seller so you can track him down if you need to. If you know where he lives and who he really is, you have some way to rectify problems.

You can find additional standards for evaluating used cars from the Vinguard Web site (http://www.vinguard.com).

Prong Three: Getting a Professional Mechanic to Inspect the Car

You don't have to be a mechanic; you just have to use a mechanic. If at all possible, have the car evaluated by a competent mechanic. Have him check the compression, suspension, tires, percentage of the brakes remaining, etc. Open up the transmission and, if possible, do an electrical check on the vehicle. Remember to try to convince the seller to pay for the mechanic's inspection if you buy the car. This might be enough incentive to convince her to agree. What is a fair price to pay for a mechanic? Sorry, folks, I can't give you an answer; this is one thing you are going to have to negotiate all by yourself.

One note about mechanic's inspections: They sometimes go overboard, listing problems as small as a rusted battery pan. Look for the big items, like engine, transmission, indications of accidents, etc. Adjust the mechanic's report with the age and price of the vehicle. Don't dismiss a vehicle with a problem if the price is right. If you get the car cheaply enough, you can afford to take more risks in the purchase. In other words, most repairs are acceptable if the buying price is right.

Prong Four: Checking the Car's History

Along with the mechanical inspection, you should check the history of the vehicle. For about $20 Carfax (http://www.carfax.com) and Vinguard (http://www.vinguard.com) can help you do this. Also, try to get the owner to pay for a VIN check if you buy the car.

Taking What You've Learned to Negotiate a Better Price

The list below contains information you should collect to help you negotiate price:

- Repair work that must be done
- Tires that must be replaced
- Alignment or balancing that must be fixed
- Door dings or paint imperfections that must be corrected
- Seats that must be re-upholstered
- Carpeting rips that need mending
- Missing knobs, bulbs or other parts
- High mileage and perhaps mileage discrepancies
- Fender or frame damage
- Lack of maintenance on the car

It is certainly legitimate to ask for price reductions to compensate for defects. Make sure you compile a list during your inspection. It will prove invaluable when you begin negotiations with the seller. For more on negotiating, see chapters sixteen and twenty-seven.

✦ ✦ ✦

Finally, know that it's sometimes unwise to accept some types of problems, no matter what the price. A major frame bend can spell trouble and leave you with a car that never drives straight, never feels quite right, and could cause safety problems. Closely evaluate all the car's problems (at least all the ones you can detect) before you even consider making the purchase.

CHAPTER 22

Typical Options for Buying a Used Car

Everybody has heard some version of "The Wonderful Car Gift" story. It goes a little something like this: Uncle Albert dies at the age of seventy-eight, and Aunt Edith doesn't drive. You (little Al) were Uncle Al's favorite nephew, and rather than selling his car to a stranger whose very presence would defile the memory of her wonderful saintly husband of fifty-three years, Aunt Edith gives you the $8,000 Honda for only $500 because you are still in school and money isn't that important to her. Since it was only driven to church and back, it has only 30,000 miles. What a great way to get a used car!

Sorry, but the reality is that stories like this are few and far between, so don't wait for your favorite uncle to die. Instead use your brains and anticipate that you'll have to purchase a used car on your own. This chapter outlines the advantages and disadvantages to the three traditional options for buying a used car. Although most people get used cars in one of the three ways mentioned in this chapter, I want to tell you right now that there is a fourth—and, to me, the best—option for buying a used car: at a dealers-only auction. We'll cover that last option extensively in the next chapter (I love it so much I think it deserves its own chapter!). For now, let's go over the three typical ways most folks buy used.

Buying From a New-Car Dealership or Superstore
Advantages
- Selection. There is usually a good selection of nearly new used cars of the type the dealership sells.
- Accountability. These are licensed dealers. You may receive guarantees, and you know they will be there tomorrow. If they defraud you, you can go for a legal remedy or to the state boards

and get relief. This is your most reputable option.

- Financing. Longer-term financing is probably available.
- Condition. This is your best chance for the used cars to be in tip-top shape.
- Good title. The car should have a good title. (If not, you have legal recourse.)

Disadvantages

- Sales staff. The sales force is tough, hard and well-trained. (You can deal with them by following the guidelines listed in the first part of this book.)
- High financing. The financing is higher than you would pay at a bank. (You can beat this by obtaining outside financing as outlined earlier.)
- Limited choices. These places usually don't have older used cars. There are probably not more than 150 vehicles in each of their lots. They will have mostly their own type of cars/trucks.
- Cost. You will pay top dollar here.

Buying From a Nondealership Lot

Nondealership lots are run by licensed dealers, usually sole proprietors or a limited number of partners. These things spring open, run for a couple of years and go out of business without notice. These lots sometimes specialize, but usually they carry whatever the owner can get from a wholesaler, an auction or from a person who comes in trying to sell his old car and buy another old car. These small lots have a variety of service people who come to the lot—detail people, battery fixers, mechanics, parts deliverers, etc. The cars here may or may not be of the best quality. The place thrives on credit sales where the buyer of the vehicle puts out a high down payment, usually about equal to the lot owner's interest in the car, and pays off the loan monthly in less than two years. The lot owner sells cars quickly and repossesses them nearly as quickly.

Advantages

- Credit. Credit is available, but it is usually short term.

- The dealer is licensed and therefore accountable.
- The cars probably have good titles.

Disadvantages
- The sales force is tough and hard.
- The financing is higher than you would pay at a bank.
- If you miss a few payments, the car will be repossessed.
- These lots usually have older used cars.
- There are probably not more than fifty vehicles in the lot.
- Prices are high. You will pay top dollar here. The average profit margin per car is high.
- The businesses are here today, gone tomorrow.
- The vehicles may or may not be in great shape.

Buying From a Private Party

This is everybody's secret escape from having to deal with a hard, tough dealer. The buyer knows she will find a nice low-mileage car put up for sale by a refined old gentleman in a smoking jacket who will serve her lemonade while he cheerfully says, "I really don't know what my car is worth, but if you suggest a reasonable figure, I am sure I would agree to it." Of course, it is a one-owner car, has been garaged all its life, has all the service records and has had its oil changed religiously every 1,500 miles. The car is also mechanically perfect and is offered by the seller with a three-year unconditional warranty.

Unfortunately, buying through a private party doesn't usually work that way. From my experience in California, between one-third and one-half of the cars "privately" sold through the paper are really sold by dealers. These dealers buy cars from private parties or auctions, may fix them up and then resell them. These dealers disguise their identities and initially pose as private parties. Some individuals also make a living by buying low from one person and selling high to another. These people are not the original and only owner of the car for sale. They may well have owned it for only a few days before reselling it at a profit.

Advantages

- If everything goes right, this method of private party buying/ selling is the best. If it doesn't go well, it is the worst method.
- You may get an actual record of repair and maintenance.
- Most people don't know how to sell, so the price may be right.
- It may be your easiest buy. The transaction may be friendly, comfortable and convenient.

Disadvantages

- There is a possibility of a bad title. Many of these vehicles are of dubious title. Who really knows where the owner got the car or who the seller really is? The seller may have just bought the car from another party and gotten the other party to sign over the title. When you give him cash for the car, he will give you the signed title in exchange for cash. When the car is registered, this intermediate seller doesn't appear anywhere on the ownership chain. Trying to get back at him legally if you need to is almost impossible. This is called jumping title. Pay no attention to any promises or guarantees; you will have no way of holding him accountable.
- No guarantees. You are not dealing with a licensed dealer.
- No financing.
- Inconsistency. You can find all sorts of vehicles through the paper, and you cannot always trust the descriptions.
- You will have to ride all over town to see a small number of vehicles.
- Price will be highly variable. Most owners are not knowledge- able about the worth of their vehicles.
- The seller may really be a dealer disguised as a private party.
- You have no recourse if the vehicle turns out to be bad or immediately breaks down.

After comparing the advantages to the disadvantages, this doesn't look as safe and easy as you thought, does it? So now you say to yourself, "How can I get a used car with some guarantee against a bad title (at a reasonable price and from a reputable seller)?"

Believe it or not, there is a way, and we're going to cover it in detail in the next chapter. As I mentioned at the beginning of this chapter, it's my recommended method of buying a used car, as you'll soon see.

CHAPTER 23

The Best Option for Buying a Used Car

I have been attending dealers-only auction buying for over ten years, and both my customers and I really like the results. Obtaining a car this way combines all the good points of the methods mentioned in the last chapter, but it suffers from none of their drawbacks. Let's see why.

Why Go With a Dealer?

Auto dealers in Southern California get their inventories through five major dealers-only auctions, which run over ten thousand vehicles a week, fifty weeks a year. The vast majority of the vehicles are passenger cars and trucks. (The rest are limos, classic cars, kit cars, motorcycles, travel trailers, jet skis, boats and large trucks.) About one-third of the cars are three years old or less, and about 85 percent of the inventory is computerized and listed online to subscribing dealers. This means I can tap into inventory lists of most vehicles for sale at any given time and also find out what similar vehicles have cost in the recent past. Obviously a dealer looking for a vehicle (either for himself or for a customer) has a lot more choices than does the average retail buyer scanning the Sunday papers.

Why Go With an Auction?

The primary reason dealers-only auctions are so great is that they have more built-in safety (less risk of getting a lemon) than most retail sales. The key to my buying system, for example, is that if you buy correctly, you can get low auction prices *and* good guarantees. This is like getting a bond from your stockbroker that has high yields and safety. *That* is a difficult thing to find.

There are two types of guarantees usually available at the dealers-only auctions:

- The first and best applies to cars under three years old. You get the residual left on the original factory warranty. This is a bumper-to-bumper warranty, good for 36,000 miles, handled by the dealerships and paid for by the manufacturer. It is a great thing.
- The second applies to cars that have more than three years or more than 36,000 miles in them. It is a guarantee put forth by the seller through the auction, and it can be very useful. What happens is that you buy at a low auction price, drive the vehicle out of the auction, rush the car to a mechanic, get it smogged, test-driven, inspected and frame-checked. All uncertainty about the vehicle is alleviated. This is the heart of my buying system.

Why Not Just Buy From a Dealer's Lot?

Interestingly, one of the biggest costs for large lots and dealerships is called "inventory aging." This means that a car's value drops with the passage of time. So, if an expensive vehicle sits on a dealership lot for one or two *Blue Book* changes, it can drop $500 in book value. I never have to adjust my profit margins to cover this kind of loss because I sell my cars soon after I buy them. Therefore, no inventory costs, no aging costs and no major lot costs (or salesperson costs) accrue. These are the costs which you, the consumer, ultimately have to pay. A friend of mine once told me that if you have a business where you don't have to pay for inventory then you really have a business. He was right.

How the System Works

To let you see how auction-buying through a dealer really works, I will walk you through the steps of a typical dealers-only sale. This is the way this system works for me and my customers.

1. I will get a call, usually from a person referred to me by one of my former customers or other contacts. We chat for a while and discuss items like type of car preferred, costs, financing, etc.

2. I make an appointment and meet the individual at the auction

I think will be most likely to fit his needs.

3. We inspect hundreds of vehicles and pick out the ones that most interest him. We settle my commission and discuss prices for the vehicle. I help the individual clarify what it is he really wants and talk to him about possible bargains. If the individual is after reliability and price, we talk about stick shift American cars as the best current bargain.

4. I get a good-faith down payment, usually 20 percent of the expected price of the vehicle.

5. I buy the car or cars we agreed upon at the next auction if I can do so within the stated price range.

6. I have the car inspected, smogged and, if necessary, spruced up and repaired.

7. We complete the paperwork, and the car is transferred to the buyer. My fee and the costs for taxes, licensing, smogging, repairs, etc., are taken out of the down payment. Any funds owed to me are paid to me. Any funds owed to the customer are now returned to him.

Sounds pretty simple, doesn't it? Well, it often is, but I want to tell you what it's like to be at an actual auction.

Dealers-only auctions are crazier than a three-ring circus. Some have as many as thirteen lines running simultaneously, each with its own auctioneers and helpers. Some of the lines run at a rate of over one hundred cars per hour. The people and the cars coexist in the same crowded space. A panoramic view of the auction floor looks like cars driving on the sidewalk in Times Square on New Year's Eve. I personally love the place, except it is hot, smoky, noisy, tension-filled and full of obnoxious, hot, sweaty, noisy and tension-filled dealers.

Now let's look at the advantages and disadvantages of buying through a licensed dealer who goes to these crazy auctions.

Advantages

• You are buying through a licensed dealer. This is important because it gives you some legal recourse in case something goes wrong. You can always find a dealer. If he moves, the DMV can find him. He is usually bonded, and the threat of action against his license is strong enough to force him to back down if he is guilty of gross mischief. I know it is tough to think of car dealers as being reputable, but compared to the other possibilities, they are probably OK. My opinion is that all other things being equal, it is better to deal with a licensed and bonded person than just another pretty face. Legal recourse is one advantage that private party sales don't have.

• Titles are guaranteed. Membership to dealers-only auctions is limited to licensed dealers who are tied to the auctions through signed agreements which hold them accountable for delivering good titles before they get paid for their sold cars. In the ten years I have been dealing with dealers-only auctions, I have never gotten a title which had a problem which couldn't be easily resolved. This may not seem like much until you find out you have bought a car with a salvage title from a Mr. No-Name on a street corner. If you buy a car through a dealer at auction, you know you are getting a car that is not stolen and can be traced. This is another advantage that private party sales don't have.

• Reduced chances of fraud. In the buying and selling of property of any kind, especially expensive property, fraud is always a possibility. House sales, which are more highly regulated than auto sales and whose transfers take more time and are more painstakingly controlled, have their own set of problems. People even spend hundreds of dollars to get a company to guarantee title to a piece of property. No such option exists in the sales of used cars. Private party sales are inherently subject to this type of problem, especially misrepresentation of the physical condition of the vehicle.

• Dealers-only auction sales of cars have some built-in safeguards, which revolve around disclosure of mileage, mileage deficiencies, frame damage, fees owed and other such details.

• Security. The system is not perfect, and fraud undoubtedly occurs. Some of the most commonly attempted deceptions involve rolling back the mileage on the odometers of high-mileage vehicles and disguising engine or transmission problems. Auction rules requiring disclosure of items like frame damage, mileage, discrepancies of title, DMV fees, etc., are a strong factor in getting what you think you are getting. Most auctions also have some form of a drive train guarantee on certain makes and models.

• Low prices. This is where auction buying of vehicles really shines. There are two different types of automobile auctions: public auctions and dealers-only auctions. Auctions that are open to the public are usually advertised on the back pages of the classified section of the newspaper. These auctions are outlets for the sale of police vehicles, local government vehicles, etc. Sometimes these are represented as drug-seizure auctions. In an auction of seventy-three cars advertised in this way, you might find two that are from drug seizures and the newest of these might be a 1985 Chevy Camaro. But the public is caught up in the thought of buying a brand-new Porsche for $100. People will go to these auctions and end up paying over retail for vehicles they really don't like because they get caught up in the spirit of the auction. Public auctions can be dangerous to your financial health; I don't recommend them.

The better auctions to buy from are the dealers-only auctions. These are open only to licensed dealers who are registered. These are truly competitive auctions with vehicles supplied from lease terminations, repossessions, banks and dealer consignment. The buyers are true dealers who are buying seriously for retail resale from their lots. Retail customers are not allowed into these auctions, so you never see a bidding frenzy fueled by people who are used to buying at retail or higher prices.

Dealers will stop bidding long before a car reaches retail price. After all, how will they then sell those price-inflated vehicles? If they buy cars at auction at prices that are too high, how can they cover all the costs in a transaction, including the sales costs, and still make a profit? Dealers aren't even happy about buying a car for *Blue Book* wholesale; they prefer to get a vehicle for hundreds of dollars below that price. If the price of a car at a dealers-only auction goes too high, the dealers just stop bidding and walk away.

• Large selection. Typical used-car lots vary from the very small lots with only fifteen to twenty cars to the very large lots with several hundred cars. Typical dealers-only auctions have from one thousand to close to three thousand cars. These auctions are held weekly, giving the dealer quite a variety to choose from. You can find virtually anything you want in one of these auctions. The sheer volume seems overwhelming and you may wonder where they all come from. The number of cars for sale in just one auction dwarfs those listed for sale in the major southern California newspapers. The advantage for all of those people putting a car up for sale at a dealers-only auction is that the car will sell for immediate cash. These cars come from a number of sources.

• Repossessed cars, or repos (cars repossessed from people who have missed payments). Once these cars are repossessed, they belong to the institutions that financed them. Typical owners of repos are banks, GMAC Finance, etc. The quickest way for these owners to recoup some of their costs is to dispose of the cars at auction.

• Leased cars. 35 percent of the cars leaving new car lots in California are leased. When these cars come to the end of their leases, they can either be bought by the leasing party or returned to the leasing agency. Most of those returned eventually end up at auction.

• Factory demos, executive cars, etc. Most major manufacturers have "leftover" cars that are no longer new. These often are sold at auction.

• Theft recoveries and damaged vehicles. Insurance companies retrieve these vehicles and sell them at auction. These cars may have flawed titles. For example, recovered vehicles may have salvage titles rather than regular titles.

• Dealer overflow. Dealers will sometimes accept vehicles as trade-ins that don't fit on their lots. For example, a Cadillac dealership may take a Chevrolet on a trade-in, and it may be company policy not to sell any used vehicle other than a Cadillac. Vehicles like this are sent to the dealers-only auctions on consignment.

• In addition, if a car has been a particularly slow seller, a dealership may try to sell it at auction. It is possible that it will sell better in another neighborhood with a different clientele.

Disadvantages

All good things have downsides. Let's look at a few of them:

• Auction buys are cash buys. In order to buy a car at a dealers-only auction, you must be prepared to pay cash. If you arrange your financing beforehand so you can give cash to the dealer who is going to buy you a car at auction, you can pay for the car in cash and pay your bank back later. If you need somebody to hold your hand through the financing, a dealer might do it, but he sure will get paid more for it. That is the good and the bad with buying a car at auction; you have to have the money at the time of the purchase.

• Lack of adequate inspection. An auction buy does not lend itself easily to a full test-drive of the vehicle or a full mechanical inspection. It will be nearly impossible for you to know a lot about the car you are interested in, as you would if you were buying it on the street or from a dealer's lot. You may not be able to tell if the brakes need work or to check the compression or transmission. You can check most things and spot major problems, but not everything.

• You may get stuck with a bad car. This is a possibility, but every method of used-car buying runs some risk. There is no way to guarantee a perfect trouble-free used car. The rules that allow a retail customer to return a sale or change his mind do not always apply to auction buys. Once you have bought it, you cannot decide to buy a different car instead. You will have to figure out a way to sell it; you cannot return it. However, cars bought with auction guarantees can be returned or arbitrated for four reasons: major lower-engine problems, transition problems, bent frames and a bad title.

Dealers-only auctions offer the best balance for getting a good deal at a great price. If you decide to try to buy a car in this way, you need a good dealer you can trust to inspect your cars well and to represent you well at the auction. You also want one who is honest and has a reasonable commission structure. These car dealers do exist and word of mouth is usually the best recommendation. If someone you trust recommends a dealer to you, you have more information than you would if you were to walk into a dealership cold. People looking to tap into this market were those I wanted to service when I got my dealer's license. Let me tell you how I became convinced of the value of dealers-only auctions.

How I Came to Love Dealers-Only Auctions

In this book's introduction, I told you how I got into the auto business with my first buy of a Dodge Lancer. Learning how to buy the Lancer really taught me how to buy a new car. Let me tell you how I learned to buy used cars.

After I landed in California and bought my Lancer, which my wife loved, I changed jobs within my company and picked up a company car. Great inventions, these company cars: the boss paid for my gas, oil, repairs, tires, washes, etc., through his budget. When the car, a Ford LTD, reached either three years or 50,000 miles, it was scheduled to be turned in for a brand-new car.

When this time came, I was in need of another car at home. I thought this company car would be a natural if I could get it cheaply. So the first thing I did was to put in for new tires, a tune-up, new brakes, etc. I got the car fixed up nicely. It was absolutely immaculate. Then I went to see my boss and asked him if I could buy my company car when he replaced it and, if so, for how much. He got back to me a few days later with a figure that made me wince. He quoted me a figure close to $5,000. I gratefully declined to purchase it but asked him where the car was going. He said it would be returned to our rental agency, and from there it would be sold at auction. I called the rental agency and was told it would be sold at a dealers-only auction. I obtained the selling date from the rental agency.

It occurred to me that maybe I would get a dealer to buy my company car for me for a small fee. But I had no idea how to find that dealer. At a loss as to what to do, I went back to the dealership that had sold me my Lancer, half expecting to be thrown out or, at the least, ignored. What I found was that in the year or so since I bought that car, virtually the whole sales force had turned over (not so unusual an occurrence), and only one person, the sales manager, was left. He was also leaving the dealership, and it was his last day. He greeted me warmly. When I told him my idea, he promptly gave me the name of a dealer friend who could buy my company car at auction for a small fee.

Two weeks later, I was allowed into the dealers-only auction where I watched the dealer friend buy my company car for $2,500, well below the maximum bid I had budgeted. The person not only bought me my car but also did all the paperwork, registered the car and collected the taxes.

The following day I drove my old company car, now my own personal car, to work and left it in my boss's parking spot. Later in the day, I filled him in with the details of the transaction, including the fact that I had had it completely fixed up before I had turned it in. He laughed and said I had really caught on. He also asked me if I would do the same for him in the future if he wanted to buy back his company car.

That experience convinced me that the best way to buy a used vehicle, bar none, is to buy it at a dealers-only auction through a licensed dealer. As a matter of fact, I liked it so much I decided to go into business selling cars as soon as I found it existed. I still do this today in the Orange County area of California. If you are moving to the Los Angeles or Orange County area of California or if you live there, call me at (714) 996-9955 (my place of business) and let's see if I can fix you up with a used vehicle from an auction.

CHAPTER 24

Selling Your Car on Your Own

There is only one major advantage—and it is a big one—to bypassing a dealer and selling your car yourself: You will get more money. In fact, it's not inconceivable for you to make $1,000 more by selling your car on your own than you would trading it in. Sure, doing it on your own will take a little time, but it might take only ten hours or so. One hundred dollars per hour for selling your own wheels seems about right to me.

Now that we've gotten the primary advantage of selling your car out of the way, let's look at a host of concerns you should have.

• **Safety.** Most women sellers would not want to go for test-drives—a necessary part of the selling procedure—with strangers. If this is a concern for you, this can be easily remedied if you can enlist a friend (male or female) to join you. There is a certain safety in numbers. Choose a friend who is not going to be a liability—someone who can just be a silent presence and not become involved in the negotiations or small talk.

• **Time.** It takes a lot of time to sell a car. You have to place ads and then stay home and wait for phone calls. You have to show the car to people at their convenience, and you can kill a lot of weekends waiting for people to show up to view your vehicle. Many individuals work unusual hours and want to see the car at strange times.

• **Loss of privacy.** People will call at strange hours. Others who have seen the car may drop by unexpectedly to show it to someone else.

• **No-shows.** A lot of people will make appointments to see your vehicle and then not show up, and you will never know why.

• **General hassles.** A lot of people will pick the car to death for problems and then ask for a huge price reduction on the car. Some people will demand extensive repairs or require you to fix certain things (usually for free) before they will buy your car. Others will haggle endlessly to get what they want. People want guarantees, repair receipts, etc.

• **Dealers.** Dealers make ridiculous offers just to get the car cheaply.

• **Curiosity seekers.** You will get a lot of traffic from people who are just checking out the cars on sale or who are at the beginning of their car-buying process and are not really serious buyers.

• **Money.** This is always a problem, and some people may want or need you to help finance the car for them, take a trade-in or do a barter arrangement or some other deal that does not involve a cash transaction. These situations should be avoided. You want to receive the money from the buyer and not have to create a long relationship in order to get rid of your car.

• **Stress.** The selling experience may be stressful to you because selling does not come easily to you; you are just not a natural salesperson.

If you decide to sell your own car and the problems just outlined are not a major factor, go ahead and look at the process. You can, of course, just babble on and perhaps luck into an easy sale, but that doesn't always happen. In order to maximize your return from your vehicle, you need a strategy.

Four Steps to Selling Your Car

1. Your first step is to determine the dollar amount you need to part with the car. Here's how to check to see what your vehicle is really worth so that when you try to get maximum dollar for it, you are trying for a realistic figure.

Check the dealers' edition of the *Blue Book* or the NADA *Official Used Car Guide* (use a local bank or library), and evaluate the worth of the car. (Use the dealers' edition of the *Blue Book*, not the consumer edition. The consumer issue says "consumer issue" on the cover.) Include considerations for mileage and for extra features. If the vehicle has been damaged, factor that in also. Find a copy machine and copy both the base page and the mileage page for your records and calculations. Banks will be glad to give you this information and to show you how to read the figures. Make sure you receive a current reference book, not one that is months or years old.

You may find that different evaluations do not come out the same. This is to be expected, as these evaluations are approximate. Also, the evaluations do not take into account a variety of factors, including condition, color and whether the car is currently hot. Also, the *Blue Book* does not always reflect market changes in the value of a vehicle.

Remember, the *Blue Book* and others try to follow and report the market, not predict it. Naturally, they will deviate strongly from it in some circumstances. Use the *Blue Book* as a first look at a vehicle's worth. It is great for that.

2. The second step is to figure out where your car will sell best. If it is a high-end vehicle, pick a publication with a big presence in an upscale area. If it is a cheap car, find publications that do well in blue-collar areas.

3. The third step is to write a killer ad. There is a little bit of an art to writing an ad, tricks of the trade, so to speak. The sole purpose of the ad is to get a potential buyer to call you. Usually the papers or trade magazines have a format for you to follow, which basically lists the age, model, type of vehicle and features. There is sometimes other stuff that you legally have to include like license plate numbers or a private party or dealer designation. The price also gets listed.

For me, the best results always come from putting in some little personalized extras:

- One owner. This is the best thing you can say, even if it is not true. I usually prefer to think of it as one owner for the last two years. Hopefully the buyer won't use something like Carfax, at http://www.carfax.com
- Quality designators. I like to put down some grabber like "great condition," "must see," "garaged its lifetime," "leather seats," "ice-cold air" or "runs like new."
- Mention a color. A lot of people have strong color preferences. Include the interior and exterior color scheme.

- Mileage. If the miles are low, put down the number. If the miles are high, don't include the miles. Over the phone, my friend Stan always understates them, like saying the car has 120,000 miles if it has 150,000 miles. When the buyer arrives, he says he must have made a mistake and then hopes the price and the condition sell the car. For intermediate miles, advertise an indeterminate phrase like "good miles" or "freeway miles." When reading an ad in preparation for your own buy, realize anytime an ad does not include the mileage, it is probably very high.

4. The fourth step is to place your ad in the paper and wait for the calls to start coming in.

The Electronic Alternative

If you have Internet capability, you first want to go to the *Blue Book* site (http://www.kbb.com) and evaluate your vehicle. Remember that this site uses consumer figures.

The Internet provides you with a lot of easy alternatives besides the conventional ones to sell your own car. You can place your car on a cyberlot, thereby listing it for sale on the Net (for more on cyberlots, see chapter 2). You also can post your car for sale on a bulletin board, even if the bulletin board doesn't pertain to cars. People do this all the time; as I do. It's free advertising for my car-buying business. For fun you could auction it off at some Web auction site, like eBay (http://www.ebay.com), but car sales rarely go to completion on eBay. Or, you could put it in on one of the Web classifieds. Auto Trader is on the Net at http://www.autotrader.com as well as most newspaper classifieds.

Don't forget that the more places you can advertise your car, the better you can sell it. This is especially important if you live in a rural area where the selling options are limited.

Here are some good Web sites that can help you price and sell your car:

Autoweb, http://www.autoweb.com
Carlist, http://www.car-list.com

Car Prices, http://www.carprices.com
Excite classifieds, http://www.classifieds2000.com
Edmunds, http://www.edmunds.com
Kelley *Blue Book*, http://www.kbb.com
AutoTrader, http://www.autotrader.com

Here are some typical bulletin boards that contain discussions about particular types of cars. To access them, type one of the following into your browser.

alt.autos.bmw
alt.autos.ford
alt.autos.gm
alt.autos.mercedes
alt.autos.volvo
alt.autos.toyota

By checking out the above bulletin boards and looking at what other people want for their cars (private parties and dealers alike), you also get a good idea of what your vehicle is worth.

Fielding Phone Responses

The purpose of spending time on the phone with potential buyers is twofold: You want to weed out those people who are not serious buyers, and you want to get as many serious buyers as possible to see the car. There are several things you can do to assist yourself in this process. The first thing to do is to be comfortable with selling your car. To maximize the return from your vehicle, you need a script and a strategy for answering query calls (or even E-mails). Practice your sales pitch in front of a mirror, with another person or on a tape recorder until you feel comfortable with it.

Questions to Ask

• Get all callers' names, addresses and phone numbers. Don't go any further without this information. It protects you and screens out nonbuyers. It also allows you to call people back if they miss appointments or if you will be late.

• Don't allow yourself to be interrogated by the potential buyer. An interrogation is when they ask all the questions and you do nothing but answer. You want to ask questions as well as answer them.

• Always tell the other party that the car is great, shows well and has no problems. Save the problems for a face-to-face contact. Your telephone job is to get the customers down to see the car, not to describe the vehicle in detail.

• Say, "You will love the car. The paint [or something else] is really nice." Let the caller know it is a great car and that you hate to sell it.

• Have a viable reason for selling the car. Create one if necessary. Some good reasons are, "My son went to college and I am selling his car" or "We need a bigger car and I wanted to trade it in, but the new-car dealer wouldn't give me a fair price." Never indicate that you are selling the car because you are going bankrupt or because the car is giving you mechanical difficulties.

• Find out who the car is for and what he needs. Try to meet this need.

• Tell every caller that your car has gotten a lot of attention and is in great demand so he ought to see it right away. Talk about other people coming to see it. If this isn't happening the first time you say it, it will be by the second or third.

• Find out if the caller needs a car right away. In other words, ask callers if they are real buyers.

• Don't discuss price over the phone. Let the caller know that if he comes to see the car and is interested and wants to buy it, you are sure you can reach a mutually agreeable price.

• Schedule potential buyers close together in time so it looks as if the car is in great demand.

Questions to Expect

Have a sheet handy that lists and describes all the features of the auto. Be prepared to answer the following questions:

Q: How long have you owned the car?
A: The ideal answer is, of course, "I am the original owner."

Almost as good is "I have owned the car for most of its life" or "I have owned the car for the last three years." These are good strong answers and need no apology.

Q: How much are you asking for the car?

A: Do not answer this with a number. Instead, ask if the caller is prepared to make an offer. Ask if he will have a down payment with him. Ask if he is a serious buyer. Ask if he saw the ad in the paper. Get him to make a first bid.

Q: What's wrong with the car?

A: Don't disclose everything immediately. You can build confidence by indicating something small, like the radio has a loose wire. Don't get caught in a fit of excessive honesty; don't answer questions that aren't asked, and don't volunteer more than required. Once the caller sees the car and becomes attached to the idea of buying it, you can answer more directly while pointing out assets to counter the faults.

Q: How long has the car been for sale?

A: Don't answer with a number of days or weeks. Indicate that it hasn't been for sale too long and that you have been getting a lot of action on the ad. Remember to tell the caller that it looks like your car is pretty hot.

Q: Don't these cars have a lot of problems?

A: This car has had only the normal sorts of problems and repairs. Don't volunteer information on major problems over the phone. You may scare away potential buyers.

Q: Has the car ever been in an accident?

A: If the answer is yes, minimize the impact by answering indirectly. Say, "The bumper and fender have been replaced, and the car now looks immaculate and drives perfectly."

Q: Is this the original mileage, or has the odometer ever been turned back?

A: "Yes, this is the original mileage," is the only correct answer. You should never tamper with the odometer.

Face-to-Face with a Potential Buyer

Selling your trade-in to a professional as part of a new-car buy presents one series of problems (see chapter eleven), but selling your car to a private party presents quite another. You are the true salesperson in the latter case and have the salesperson's advantages. Here are some tips to use as a salesperson to help you sell your car.

• One of your key responsibilities as a salesperson is to qualify the potential buyer. Ask if he has a down payment with him. Look to see if he can afford the car. See if he is serious before you spend a lot of time and energy negotiating. If the buyer is not serious, doesn't have the money or is just trying to grind you down, decide if you want to string him along, get rid of him or if you really need his business.

• Be pleasant, yet a little reserved.

• Have records handy. Be prepared to show your title, repair bills and any other documentation that will help convince a potential buyer that this is the car for him.

• Remain in control of the situation. Remember to ask questions rather than just being interrogated.

• If forced, give a price that is realistic but that will give you $200 to $300 bargaining room.

• Give way grudgingly on price or other details. When making concessions, make smaller ones than he does and act as if you are nearing the end of the line.

• When you feel he has been given enough information to make a decision, ask directly if he is interested and what he needs to make a decision to buy the car TODAY.

Negotiating Tactics

Negotiating is tough, especially if you are not used to negotiating, not strong enough to stand up to forceful personalities or intimidated by the whole process of selling a car for the first time. When you are trying to settle a price with a serious buyer, several of the sales techniques I warned you about earlier can be used to your advantage here.

• First, ask the buyer, "Are you prepared to buy now?" That will indicate if the other party is a real buyer. Then ask follow-up questions, including: "What is important to you in the purchase of a used car?" and "What do you need to buy now?" When you find out what he needs, try to supply it. Find his hot button.

• Tell the buyer only what he needs to know, no more, no less, and slant it to your best advantage. Answer only the questions that are asked, and do not volunteer information—especially harmful information.

• Play dumb if it helps you. Responding with, "I'm not sure," or "I just don't understand," can put off a major question and answer session.

• If your original asking price is $4,900, indicate to the buyer that you have already turned down $4,200—even if you haven't. This will prevent his making a ridiculously low offer.

• When tempted to accept an offer, compare it to the offer given to you by the dealership. Don't panic into an acceptance. If it is considerably above the dealership offer, consider taking it rather than haggling endlessly and risking letting the sale slip away.

• If the buyer wants to have his mechanic inspect the car, offer to pay for it *if* he buys the car. If the inspection is good, you will pay for it, but he must put down money and commit. Indicate that if the inspection is not satisfactory, you will not pay for it, but that you are confident the car will pass. This usually prevents a person from demanding a mechanical inspection unless he is serious about buying the car.

• If more than one person comes to inspect the car, find out who will use the car, who has the money and who is making the final decision. Your job is to make the person who will drive the vehicle love it, to show the money person that everything is legit and that the price is right and to convince the decision maker to say yes. Compartmentalize your discussion. Discuss color and other features with the one who will drive the car. If one of the people is a pain, ignore him if you can. They may be playing a game with you.

Parting Thoughts

Before I close this chapter I just want to remind you of two things.

1. Clean the car. Make sure the car is as tidy as possible inside and out. Also have it warmed up before the potential buyers come

to visit. Nothing is more embarrassing than a dirty car that won't start immediately, even if it's never happened before.

2. Off brands are sometimes hard to sell. People might buy them if they see them on a lot or sitting in front of a house with a sign on it, but no one goes to look for them. A typical example is selling a four-door sedan. A Ford Taurus will sell from the paper a lot easier than a Mercury Sable, even though they are essentially the same car. I think the reason is that people will go into the auto trader or the classified section of the local paper and look for a Taurus, which they know about, and not even look for the equivalent Mercury Sable. For the same reason, Ford Probes sell easier than Mazda MX-6s.

Armed with these techniques, you should do well against all but the most experienced car buyers.

Web Sites of Interest

You can place an ad to sell your car on the following Web sites:

CarPoint, http://www.carpoint.msn.com
AutoTrader, http://www.autotrader.com
Edmunds, http://www.edmunds.com
Worldwide Classified's Auto Stop, http://www.theautostop
.com/wwc.htm

CHAPTER 25

Buying a Car From a Used-Car Lot

Buying a used car from a lot is similar to buying a new car from a dealer. The salespeople pretty much use the same techniques, but the used-car salesperson's pitch is a little less "slick" than a new-car salesperson's. The smaller the lot (say twenty cars), the better chance you'll get an honest salesperson. Going to a big lot is like going to a new-car establishment, with all the same pressures. The one small difference is that with a used lot there's less chance a salesperson will try to sell you undercoating or an upgraded sound system. But used-car lots, like new-car dealers, will try to get your trade-in at a good price (for them). Used-car lots also will help you get the car financed. For more, see the section on new-car buying.

Sticker Prices

In the early years of car selling there were no window stickers on any cars, not even new cars. A salesperson could quote any price for a vehicle and perhaps even get it. He could quote different prices for different buyers. Many times, the salesperson himself didn't know what price to ask and just pushed for what he could get. This is because there were no public listings of manufacturers or dealer costs for vehicles. The negotiation advantage was solidly in the court of the dealer. Does this sound like used cars today?

Sometime in the late 1950s or early 1960s, however, federal regulations came out mandating that new cars display a window sticker with the MSRP (among other things such as year, mileage, etc.). This was good news for consumers looking for a new car, because the balance of power started to swing to their side.

Unfortunately for buyers, no such sticker mandate occurred in the used-car business. Mandated sticker prices have never to this day existed on used cars and probably never will. Sure, you can go to almost any used-car lot and see a few numbers written on the windshield, like "$4,995," or a few words, like "Best Deal," "One Owner," or "I Need a Home," but that's about it. And such information is entirely voluntary on the seller's part."

The used-car buyer simply has little knowledge or control over used-car prices. Nobody quite knows what a used car costs a dealer, and thus nobody knows precisely what a good deal is. The "used-car acquisition" process is designed to keep the consumer in the dark. That's just the way the business is. And nobody knows what used cars sell for either. With this in mind let's explore factors that will help you approximately determine what a car costs a used-car dealer.

Market Forces
Dealer Expenses

The biggest expenses on used-car lots, both big and small, involve carrying costs (interest), aging costs (depreciation) and employee costs (salaries). There are usually no offsetting income sources such as factory-sponsored repair work or customer repair work. The money to be made comes from the sale of the used vehicle, a profit on a trade-in and maybe financing.

Behind the Scenes: Figuring a Car's Worth

The worth of a used car varies from place to place throughout the country. There is an active vehicle interstate trade. We'll take California as an example to show what happens.

In the California dealers-only auctions, a lot of western state dealers pay over book (*Blue Book* wholesale—dealers' edition) for hot vehicles such as trucks and jeeps. They sometimes pay almost as much at California wholesale auctions as California dealers' can retail the vehicles for locally. Years ago, my son Andrew first noticed this trend, and we bought Wranglers on the streets of Orange County and sold them at the auction. This is the direct opposite of what we normally do. We normally buy at auction and sell retail. The reason we reversed the process this time is that during spring and summer, out-of-state dealers buy large quantities of open-top jeeps at premium prices for their customers in rural areas. When the mercury plummeted, the auction prices for open-top jeeps plummeted.

Out-of-state dealers also have an edge buying cars that carry costly late-registration penalties for California registration (imposed by the California DMV). Such dealers buy cars with big California late-registration penalties and ship them back home. The vehicles are then registered penalty-free in their new home states.

California dealers-only auctions also get their share of cars imported from other states. Obviously shipping cars across the country costs money, and those who do the shipping want to make money. The prices at auctions are relatively stable, but sometimes a car costs more than it should; other times you can get a bargain. As you can see, it's often confusing to figure out what a car costs a dealer, and by extension it is difficult to determine a dealer's selling price.

The Financing Factor

The vast majority of used vehicles are financed, often at a higher percentage than more expensive new cars. People who buy used cars, especially older used cars, tend to have less money than new car buyers, and they also have poorer credit histories. Less money translates into less down payment money. Poor credit translates to high interest rates on loans. Put these together and you see that the used-car buyer (the poor buyer) pays more for credit and more for the car. The result is being forced to pay high prices for a vehicle that's actually worth much less.

A lot of older used cars are sold at high interest rates, and those who buy them do often have only marginal credit. It has been my observation that if you are poor, you pay more for everything. The reason is that people with low incomes are more likely to default on payments and are not able to afford maintenance. Nobody is going to professionally detail a 1982 Corolla, or spend $112 at an auto upholsterer to fix a small rip in a seat. If an older car is repossessed, lawsuits are less likely to get some of that finance money back.

Three Rules About Dealer's Cost for a Used Car

1. There is no way you can get an absolute fix on the dealer acquisition cost of a particular used car unless you sneak a look at his books.

2. If a dealer's cost is too high, he will eventually eat the losses and bail out of the vehicle with a loss. There is no other way out for the dealer, short of getting just the right customer (a magic event that doesn't happen often). Eventually the vehicle will be unloaded at a price related more to market forces than acquisition cost.

3. A competent dealer knows, at least roughly, what a vehicle can be bought or sold for at a dealers-only auction. The reason that other sources of vehicles don't become the benchmarks of vehicle value is that most other sources don't list what vehicles are sold for. Dealerships, for example, don't tell other wholesalers what they get for their trade-ins, and no one tells anybody the value for his inventory stock. These figures cannot be found anywhere, not even on the Internet or in the library.

Used-Car Data Sources

There are only two sources for used-car data. The first are price guides like the *Blue Book* or the NADA handbook. Although these guides are the most reliable sources available, they're not entirely accurate. Plus the *Blue Book* comes in both a consumer edition and dealer edition. No dealer uses the consumer edition. The data compiled in these guides are largely culled from dealers-only auction sales figures.

The second source for used-car prices are the actual dealers-only auction reports, which list the prices for vehicles sold in past auctions. You need to beware, though, that the data is abbreviated and it doesn't include important factors like salvage titles, TMU announcements, frame damage, bad paint, accidents, extra equipment and other things that affect vehicle price. Recently, many auctions have formed online subscription services, which give subscribing dealers the data over the Net. The average consumer has virtually no access to auction prices.

Dealers estimate what a car is worth (or at least what it is selling for) by "booking it out" with a guide like the *Blue Book* and then checking the auction reports. If most cars of a particular type sell for $1,000 below the "book" value, a dealer will feel that the worth of the car is $1,000 "back of book." He may pay a little more for a clean car or less for a rough car, but that will be his comfort range. If he can pick up that car at $2,000 back of book, he will make some serious money on the car.

Where to Start the Negotiation

You now know how difficult it is for you to determine the used-car dealer's bottom line price. So what can you do? How will you know if you're getting a good deal? The following steps are the best you can take to get a decent buy from a used-car lot. Make sure you follow them.

- Look up the car in the current dealers' edition of *Blue Book* or NADA handbook.
- Check out your local used-car guides to see what the car is going for in your area. Knowing such figures will put you in the ball park.
- See what similar vehicles are selling for in your local newspaper. This will tell you the price for which comparable vehicles are retailing.
- Try to find out (even pay a dealer) what similar vehicles are selling for at a dealers-only auction. This lets you get an idea of the used-car dealer's acquisition cost.
- Start your negotiation at $500 over the auction price.

How to Handle Fixed-Price, No-Haggle Megastores

Despite their large size and benevolent appearance, large megastores (like AutoNation) are just used-car stores. Don't be too impressed or intimidated by them. They can be easily handled. Megastores are also despised by other auto sellers. In fact, every small dealer, even franchise stores, love to kick megastore butt. Dealers will always undercut megastores on price to get your business. With that in mind, here's how you can use megastores to your advantage:

1. Go in, use their resources, find a vehicle or vehicle type you want.

2. Note the condition, miles, equipment and all the other vital points.

3. Get a fixed no-haggle price from these nice people. And get it in writing!

4. Leave the megastore.

5. Go to a comparable, yet smaller, we love-to-haggle dealership, and find a similar car.

6. Drop the quote from "no haggle city" on the dealer's desk and ask him to beat it by $300. People do this every day —why shouldn't you?

Whether you purchase a used car from a small or large dealership, a megastore or even an arena tent sale, the mechanics of researching and negotiation are essentially similar to buying a new car. The primary difference is the challenge of finding out what to pay for the used car you want to buy.

CHAPTER 26

Buying From a Private Party

For some people who have always bought new, or whose parents always bought new, buying a used car is a foray into the uncertain and the dreadful. Such buyers wish circumstances were such that they could just buy new and forget about the demands of buying used. "It's so dangerous to buy a used car," they say. "I wish I could just buy new and not worry." Sometimes poverty is a bummer.

For those of us who have been buying used cars successfully most of our lives, used-car buying is the method of getting good, reliable transportation. And finding that gem of a used car at a good price can be a great (and even fun!) adventure.

Know the Seller

Once you know you want to buy a used car, you'll probably turn to the newspapers or automobile trader magazines. Doing so is a good idea because you can get some great deals. But you need to know what you're buying and whom you're buying from.

If you've selected a potential vehicle you're interested in, the very first thing you want to do is find out whether the vehicle is being sold through a private party or a commercial car lot that's using classified advertising. The best deals are often found through private party sales, because you are not dealing with a professional car salesperson. You're just dealing with somebody who wants to get rid of his car.

A dealer advertising in the classifieds should be treated differently than an individual selling his personal prized vehicle. If you find out you are dealing with a dealer (and you should ask, see below for more on this), make sure you read the first part of this book carefully. All the information about dealing with a new-car salesperson is applicable to dealing with a used-car salesperson as well.

Many people selling a car have done some research and figured out approximately what their car is worth. They typically try to get somewhere between low and high *Blue Book* (wholesale and retail) price. But either out of ignorance of the current market or because they must get a certain number of dollars for the car (in order to pay it off) before a sale is possible, some private parties price a car far higher than its market value. Such folks are invariably surprised and depressed when they get no phone calls. (They feel even worse when they resort to going to a dealer and the first words out of the dealer's mouth are "give me your bottom-line price right now." Then no matter what price they quote, the dealer will follow with "that is way too high," and before long, seller and dealer come to a compromise price of 35 percent of the original listing price. The seller walks away wondering what happened.)

Private party sellers, nice as they may be, shudder at the thought of giving any sort of guarantee to the buyer of the vehicle.

Telephone Contact

When you answer an ad—even if the ad specifies the car is being sold by a private party—the first question to ask is, "Are you a dealer or a private party?" There is a lot of deception practiced by dealers posing as private parties. Why? Three reasons:

1. People treat a private party better than they treat a dealer. Buyers are less suspicious of private parties and are thus basically polite to Mr. and Mrs. Jones, and less polite to a salesperson (because their guard is up for sneaky dealer tricks).

2. Some people will buy only from a private party, never from a dealer —no matter how good the deal. So dealers think: *Why miss a potential sale?*

3. Newspapers charge considerably more for a dealer classified ad than for a private party ad. In Orange County, California, for example, private parties get a week-long ad plus a free renewal week for about $22. The same ad would cost a dealer about $100. So if you're a dealer, why not tell the *Orange County Register* classifieds that you are a private party?

To find out if the particular ad you're interested in comes from a private party or from a dealer, call and frankly ask, "Are you a private party?" Then try to analyze the answer. If there's hesitation and then a "yes" you know the seller is a dealer. If there's slight hesitation and the words "Well, I am selling it for my cousin who is a dealer," you also know it's a dealer. If the response to your inquiry is a quick "of course" or a similar positive answer, you are probably dealing with an honest private party.

You can get good deals from both a private party and a dealer. You just need to make sure you know who you're buying from, because it affects later negotiations and tactics. And it certainly will affect price. If you catch the seller in a lie, use it against him later in negotiating.

Used-Car Phone Query Checklist

Once you have established whether you are on the phone with a dealer or a private party, you can go on to the business of inquiring about the car. To save yourself a lot of work and to preserve some sense of control over the negotiation, first ask the other party to describe the car. Then ask for specifics. Here is a checklist to help you out.

Query Checklist

- car type _____
- Does the car have a salvage or lemon law title? _____
- mileage _____
- Is the mileage real? _____
- Is the car True Miles Unknown (TMU), as in has the odometer been replaced or stopped? _____
- engine size _____
- number of doors _____
- type of transmission—stick or automatic _____
- special model or style _____
- color _____
- interior condition _____
- exterior condition _____

- asking price _____
- Is this price negotiable? _____
- power steering _____
- power brakes _____
- cruise control _____
- tilt steering _____
- power seats _____
- leather seats _____
- safety equipment _____
- air bags _____
- antilock brakes _____
- sound system _____
- regular AM/FM _____
- cassette deck _____
- compact disc _____
- other premium sound items _____
- special light group _____
- special luxury group _____
- special wheels _____
- special tires _____
- floor pads _____
- Are the service records available? _____
- Is the car title on hand? _____
- Is there any lienholder on the vehicle? _____
- Can I get the VIN so I can check the car's history with Carfax (http://www.carfax.com)? _____
- Has the car ever been in an accident? _____
- Are there any surprises for me on the car? _____
- other questions or comments: _____

The best phone advice I can give is to keep the interview focused on your questions so you do not get bamboozled with lots of statements about how nice the car is. Your job is to find out as much as you can without having to actually go see every car you call about. The seller's job is to make his car sound fantastic. Let your fingers do the walking by filling out the above chart rather than spending your day driving all over town. Remember, the seller's goal is to get you to go see his car. Yours is to get the most information in the most time-efficient manner, which means not wasting your time and gas going to see unsuitable cars. In small towns, this may not be a major problem, but in larger suburban areas, it can be a tremendous waste of time and energy.

Additional Questions

In addition to the telephone query checklist, there are several strategic negotiating questions that will help you determine more about the car. Don't be shy about asking lots of questions. The seller should want to spend the time with you, as this indicates your interest. Also, the more questions you ask before seeing the car, the easier it will be to formulate your buying strategy. Furthermore, as you ask each question, the seller is apt to feel less secure each time he has to admit the car's faults or lack of features you may want. Astute questioning is a precursor to an eventual push on price, so feel free to ask the following:

- Why are you selling the car? (You may or may not get a real answer, but you won't get anything if you don't ask.)
- Are you the original owner? (Do not automatically accept "yes" as the truth.) A follow up question is "Are you selling this for someone else?" Posing this question may help you to determine if the seller is jumping title or is not a private party. Check to see if the selling party's name is on the title and that he is the registered owner. If not, you should hear an interesting story. Asking "How long have you had the car?" may get you a different answer from "Are you the original owner?"
- What is wrong with the car? (Never ask what condition the car is in. Everybody always says "excellent.")
- If this is a recreational vehicle, has it ever been taken off-road or rolled?
- Is the price negotiable? (Almost everyone will say yes—especially to someone perceived as a serious buyer.)

- What is the bottom-line price?
- Where exactly are you located? (See if there is any way the seller will give concessions to entice you to go see the car. Also, ask if the seller will bring the car to you. The answer is almost always no, but if it is yes, the seller may be desperate.)
- How is the body's condition? Has the car been in any accidents? Is there any rust?
- How new are the tires? Do you still have the receipts and warranty?
- Will you guarantee the car?
- How long has the car been on the market? (The longer it has been for sale, the more likely the price is negotiable.)
- Has the car had any recent repairs? Do you still have the service records?
- (Ask again) What price do you need for the car? Would you consider $500 below that price?
- Do you own the car outright, or is there still money owed on it? (This is a key question. If there is money owed on the car, it may be difficult to get the lien removed.)
- Are you in a hurry to sell the car? (If he has to sell the car fast, he may accept less money.)
- Have you had a mechanic look at your car since you put it on the market? Is it a problem if I have my mechanic look it over? (See if the seller will take the car to your mechanic. See if the seller will pay for the inspection if you do end up buying the car.)
- How good is the paint?
- What is the *Blue Book* retail and wholesale for the car? (Even if you know, ask.)
- Will you pay for the smogging or smog inspection and any work necessary to pass the testing if the car fails the inspection?
- When was the last tune-up? If it has been a while, ask, "Will you pay for a tune-up? If not, will you pay half the cost of a tune-up?"
- Is the car registered in your state? (Out-of-state registrations may be difficult to transfer, and out-of-state cars may not pass an incoming state inspection—mechanical or smog.)

Ask anything else that interests you. Remember, you don't know what you will find out or what he may give away. Also try to get the seller to talk price concessions over the phone. If he does, he is desperate or naive. Both are desirable characteristics in a seller.

One final tip for your telephone calls: If you don't like or don't want the vehicle, or you get a bad feeling when talking to the seller, cut the conversation off quickly and get on to the next call. Don't get sucked into staying on the phone listening to the sales pitch.

When You See the Car

When you actually see the car, be reserved but not negative or stand-offish. A neutral stance is always the best negotiating stance, because you neither commit yourself by your enthusiasm nor poison the seller by your negativity.

If you do want to look more closely at a car you have explored over the phone, take it for a test-drive and have a mechanic look at it. Remember that you asked the seller to pay for this inspection if you buy the car. If the test-drive and the inspection are both satisfactory, you might want to think seriously about buying the car.

Questions That Must Be Answered By the Seller

Here are some questions to ask and some items to watch for. Many of these questions were explored in your initial telephone query, but you cannot really get the answers until you are looking at the car and talking face-to-face with the seller. You must find out the following information. If you do not, you may be unpleasantly surprised when you try to register the car you just paid for.

- Has the car ever been in an accident?
- Does the car need major or minor body or mechanical work?
- Was the car every physically or mechanically abused?
- Is there any guarantee at all?
- What is the car really worth? (Compare records, appearance, etc., with your research, as there is no published MSRP.)
- What does your mechanic say about the vehicle?
- Do you have a legal title? Is it a salvage title?

- Do you owe money on the car?
- Has the vehicle failed a smog test? (It may be worth your while to check up on the vehicle through the local DMV.)

Negotiating Tips

The very first thing you should do is make a low offer. If the seller is eager to get rid of the car, he may take a low offer from a serious buyer if the car has been on the market for a long time.

Always bring along the money to pay for the car. If you really like it, cash will allow you to demand and get major reductions in the vehicle's price. Cash up front is a rare sight to those living on weekly or monthly salary checks. As suggested earlier, if you live a long distance from the other party, have him come to you. He will command a much lower price in your backyard if he feels he may have to go all the way home empty-handed.

I know it is difficult to haggle or to try to get a better price (especially if the seller seems really nice, or reminds you of your Aunt Mary). But look at it from a practical viewpoint: Would you rather avoid all the hassles and aggravation and pay this private party her price and drive off in a glow of friendship and good fellowship, then have to work three extra weeks at a job you don't really like to make up the $1,500 you gave away by not negotiating hard? Or would you rather prepare well, go in smoothly and efficiently, get that car at your price, come out a winner, have a great feeling of accomplishment, and develop a life skill that will earn you money for years to come? You can also think about that vacation you might take with the money you just saved!

Web Site of Interest

http://www.specialinterest.com. This is a Web site for antique cars, and it seems to be a good place to look if you want to buy an old, old used car from a private party.

CHAPTER 27

Negotiating With a Private Party

There are three primary reasons negotiating for a used car from a private party is different than negotiating for a new car.

1. You must figure out who you're dealing with. When you buy a new car, you know the staff are trained salespeople who are eager to make a sale. There are no other issues —you know the playing field. When you buy from a private party, however, other concerns arise: Is this really a private party? Why does the seller want to get rid of the car? Is he really the original owner? Is this guy honest or just trying to make a fast buck? Is the seller demanding a high price to pay off a lien?

2. You must determine the car's condition. New cars do not have condition problems, high mileage, accident or repair histories, or shoddy maintenance. Used cars definitely can. Some used cars may have safety- or smog-related problems, which certainly affects the condition (and thus the sale).

3. You must realize the car has no fixed value. No one really knows what any used car is precisely worth, so there is what's called a "variable value" to used cars. Each car is different and has its unique history. Unlike with new cars, in which every dealer pays a certain fixed amount, with a used car there is no fixed buying price and thus the value—and selling price—is difficult to gauge accurately.

Prenegotiation Pointers
Evaluate the Seller

To negotiate well you must understand the seller. In addition, you need to have the answers to some of the key questions mentioned in the previous chapter. One of the least painful ways to gain information is by making small talk. Make sure you determine the following during your chat:

- Is he the real seller?
- Why is he selling the vehicle?
- Is he comfortable selling the vehicle?
- What does he need from this transaction?
- How long has he been trying to sell this vehicle?
- What is his real bottom line?
- What can you trade off to get a better price?
- Does he own the car, or does a bank or finance company?
- Does he need to sell the car quickly to get money for a new vehicle?
- Is he the type who can handle the sale and continually negotiate without getting his feelings bent out of shape?

There are ways to tell if you are dealing with an experienced seller. If the seller does any of these things, you can bet this is not his first sale:

- Uses techniques mentioned throughout the rest of this book (flinching, etc.)
- Has a dealer's plate on one of his other cars
- Is a dealer
- Has more than one car for sale
- Asks a lot of questions of you
- Is constantly trying to build rapport with you
- Is constantly closing in on you for a commitment to buy
- Somehow or other makes you feel he is in control

On the other hand, the following are indicative of an inexperienced salesperson. If the seller does these things, you can be pretty sure he is inexperienced:

- Keeps saying "honestly" or "truthfully"
- Doesn't seem to know how to ask for the sale
- Doesn't use any of the tactics you saw earlier
- Talks all the time rather than asking you what you need or what

is important
- Gives way on price easily when you voice an objection
- Looks embarrassed when negotiating

Please keep in mind that selling is always tough, but selling is hardest for an untrained person who doesn't like to sell (and who is uncomfortable selling a car with faults). When you buy a car from an untrained private party, not only is he uncomfortable selling his vehicle, he most likely doesn't have the stomach for negotiation, much less a confrontation.

Unlike seasoned used-car salespeople (or new car salespeople for that matter) who tend to know why a car isn't selling, the amateur seller is often confused about why his car won't sell. So he interrogates himself with all sorts of worries: Is it the price? Are the people detecting the flaws he tried so hard to hide? Is it the mileage? The color?

Over time the amateur, who doesn't feel comfortable talking money to begin with, becomes upset because customers make appointments and don't show up. Even when buyers do show up, it doesn't take long before the amateur seller grows tired of showing the car to people, tired of being insulted and tired of being hassled. It sometimes gets to the point where he just wants to get the whole deal over with as soon as possible and so he'll lower the price and settle. What usually happens, though, is that the frustrated seller holds to his price, loses customer after customer and eventually—when the tension level gets too high—just gives the car away for a great price to the first good negotiator. And that person could be you.

Discuss the Vehicle

Once you size up and know who you're dealing with, your next step is to shift the discussion to the vehicle itself. It's your goal to lead the seller into talking in detail about the car, such as how it performs mechanically, what works and what doesn't, etc. Here's some helpful information to request:

- Ask if the car has ever been in an accident and fixed up.
- Ask to see repair records.

- Ask about gas mileage.
- If you have looked up this car in *Consumer Reports* and know what types of defects are typical for this type of car, ask specifically if these repairs have ever been necessary.
- Ask when the brakes were last done.
- Ask when the oil and filter were last changed.
- Ask when the car was last lubed.

Every negative response further decreases the value of the car in the seller's own estimation.

Looking Like A Real Buyer

Although you are not buying a car from a professional car dealer, it is still crucial that you establish yourself as a real honest-to-goodness buyer. If you are perceived as a real buyer with real money, the seller will put up with a lot of aggravation to make the sale, unload his beloved car and get back to a normal life.

We have already covered how to appear like a real buyer to a professional salesperson. The key points include saying, "I really want to buy a car today," appearing solvent, having a trade-in ready and spending time with the salesperson.

Obviously, the professional salesperson is trained to pick up on all these cues. How do you impress on a private party that you are a serious buyer for his car?

Let's look at some cues that he will easily understand:

- Flash some cash. Let the seller see that you have enough cash on your person for a down payment. The visual presence of cold cash is a strong sign that you are serious about making a purchase immediately. My son Andrew and I do this easily because we are both 6 feet, 2 inches and 230-plus pounds. Make sure you use common sense. Don't flash cash in bad neighborhoods or potentially dangerous situations. (In fact, don't even go alone to bad neighborhoods or potentially dangerous situations.) Women will have to be especially careful regarding the safety of such a move.
- Indicate that you have been shopping a long time. Tell him about other vehicles you have seen and their faults. Create examples

if necessary. Tell him that you really want to buy a vehicle soon—if you can get the right car at the right price.

• Inspect the vehicle carefully. Don't talk money until you have seen the vehicle, carefully inspected it and gone for a test-drive. If the vehicle is obviously not what you want, walk away. If the vehicle is suitable, take the time for a careful inspection as outlined in the previous chapter.

• Establish the seller's ownership of the car. Although we discussed this earlier, it cannot be overemphasized. Remember, when you are buying from a private party, you don't have the same guarantees of ownership you have when buying from a licensed dealership. When responding to an ad by a private party, you have to be sure you are not buying a stolen car, a car that has had its miles turned back or a car that has been wrecked and then fixed up. Ask to see the title, and inspect it carefully. Look for erasures or additions of data. Look for branding on the title. A later KSR (a way of finding ownership details at the California DMV offices) is helpful, as is a later check by Carfax at http://www.carfax.com over the Internet. Also question it if something just doesn't make sense.

• Ask the seller for his address, phone number and driver's license number. If he gets upset about these requests, be cautious. You are about to spend money on something that you assume you will own. Make sure the person selling the car has the legal right to sell it. You are entitled to request and receive any information necessary to make sure the seller is the current owner. If he won't supply that information, assume the worst and walk away.

• Make sure the VIN on the title matches the VIN on the vehicle. Make sure the vehicle description on the title matches the car. In short, make sure you are buying what you think you are buying.

• Inquire if any liens on the car have been signed off. If necessary, get a verification from the lienholder that the loan has been paid off. A call to the party listed as lienholder will provide you with sufficient verification.

• Either bring a mechanic with you or take the car to a mechanic. Nothing makes you look as serious as having a mechanic with you.

• Ask questions. Ask lots of questions. Find out why he is selling the car, how long it has been for sale, what works and what doesn't, if he has had a lot of interest, etc. When asking questions, see what the other party doesn't respond to comfortably. Take notes; nothing makes a person trying to hide a problem squirm like a notetaker. If you are writing down information, you must be a serious buyer.

OK, now you have inspected the car and established to the owner's satisfaction that you are his white knight, a real buyer. Now what do you do?

Negotiation Tactics
Create Tension

This is difficult for most of us. We are nice people who spend our lives smoothing ruffled feathers, not intentionally ruffling them. But here, your prime objective is to get the best price possible. In order to do this, you must create tension that he will want to relieve, hopefully by lowering the price. Your job is to create tension and make the seller relieve it by giving in to you on price or some other issue.

You don't create tension by agreeing, by being empathetic or by giving the other person an easy reason to dismiss you. Make it an easy decision for the seller to do what you need him to do and difficult for him to do otherwise.

The essence of good negotiation is finding common ground and negotiating a win-win solution, developing a relationship wherein you and the person from whom you bought the car will live happily ever after in mutual love, respect, harmony, peace and tranquility. However, to gain that love, respect, harmony, peace and tranquility, you will have to give up some money. With that money, you can buy a vacation in the Bahamas and for a week or two find tranquility, peace, harmony, respect and, if you are really lucky, love.

The point here is to try to get the very best deal you can. I call this type of car-buying transaction a "commando raid." This is my name for a one-time transaction after which neither party will ever meet with the other again and in which cutthroat tactics are appropriate. This is not the time to build up trust for future transactions. You won't see or negotiate with the other party again, and a typical win-win transaction doesn't really make sense because there is only one issue to be decided: price. You want the most you can possibly get for your money.

When you deal with your spouse, interact with your boss or trade favors with your neighbors, you know you will see or work with these people again. You will probably never see this stranger again after you buy his car. Even if you are a nice person who treats everybody fairly, how do you know that this stranger will treat you fairly or that his car is really as good as he says? I am not suggesting that you cheat the seller, only that you get the best possible deal for yourself and make sure he doesn't cheat you.

Now with the morality of creating tension out of the way, let's see how to create tension in the other party that you can then help relieve to your advantage.

Don't Be the First to Mention Money

As a buyer of a vehicle, the longer you can delay mentioning what you want to pay for the vehicle, the better your chances of getting a lower price from the seller. Get the other party to talk money before he fully talks about the virtues of his vehicle. If he mentions a price and you ignore his offer and go on to other details, he may cut his own price, trying to get an offer or some expression of interest from you. He is lowering his own tension level. Create tension for him to relieve.

Learn to Flinch on Command

I know this sounds strange, but when somebody mentions money to you, it is to your advantage to flinch. Practice it so that when somebody mentions a price you will twitch or jerk—seemingly spontaneously—and say something like, "Really, that doesn't seem like such a good price." The person mentioning price will question the validity of his statement. He may think, *Wow, this price must be way off.* He then feels he must do something so as not to lose this valuable customer. He may immediately say something like, "Oh, excuse me, did I say the car cost $4,900? I meant to say $4,650, no wonder you jumped." At least give him a chance to change his own bid before you mention a price.

If a flinch means, "I don't like the figure," then the lack of a flinch when somebody mentions price is a tacit acceptance of a figure. The person who gives you the figure thinks to himself, *That price must be close; he didn't even bat an eyelash.* Always flinch. It won't ruin your dignity, and it may help you keep a bit more wealth.

Responding to an Offer

To review this point, let's look at how you can mentally rephrase the seller's first offer so that you do not hear it as a take-it-or-leave-it offer. (We covered this in the section on new cars.) If the seller says, "I will sell you my beautiful Ford Taurus for $4,900," mentally rephrase it to sound like, "My initial price is no more than $4,900, and you can probably talk me down." If you rephrase his offer in these terms, it is less difficult to counter his bid.

Remember, each time you are given a price, flinch and then rephrase the offer in your own mind so you can respond to it better.

Also, don't feel it is necessary to answer a person's offer directly. Many times it is to your advantage to skirt the issue of price rather than going head-to-head with the seller. For instance, if the seller says, "I will sell you my beautiful Ford Taurus for $4,900," you could respond directly by saying, "I don't want to pay any more than $3,850 for it." This will create a reaction of dismay and a lowering of goals (both good for you) in the seller. In addition, he may possibly show irritation because you seem to be playing with his mind (not so great). This is one way to start a catfight over price.

A more productive response to his initial offer of $4,900 would be to flinch, then respond indirectly by saying, "It is a nice vehicle, but before we discuss price, let's discuss how much it will cost to fix the knock in the engine." The seller is going to feel an increase in pressure because he mentioned price and you did not respond directly. He wants you to counteroffer so he can settle the matter. He also intuitively knows that a detailed discussion of the car's faults is going to lower the price.

The indirect response changes the subject and subtly indicates that $4,900 is unacceptable without offering an alternative. This increases the tension for the seller. He knows he will have to compromise on the price since his $4,900 is marred by a mechanical problem. What will happen next is that the knocking problem will be solved by the seller indicating that he doesn't think it is serious. He will probably offer to give you a couple of hundred dollars off for mechanical repairs—if you settle for $4,700.

He wants to settle right away. Your best response to this second offer is another indirect response. Say something like, "Great, that takes care of the knocking problem. Now, what are you going to do about this broken power window? Will you pay to have it fixed?" Your best response is to tacitly accept his concession and move on to other problems on the vehicle without giving any concessions of your own. Do this as long as you can.

Don't Give the Seller an Easy Out

The easiest way to end a commando raid is for the raided party to find some easy way not to deal with you. For instance, if you insult the other party, he can easily—and rightly—ask you to leave. Thus he relieves the immediate stress, but of course it doesn't settle his long-term stress of having to sell his car. Always be polite, forceful and aware of the fact that you are the customer and you have the money so you can call some of the shots.

Don't Be Too Friendly or Too Nice

This is not a social event, and people tend to push really nice people around. Your attitude should make him just a little uneasy. He should know that if he tries to jerk you around, he will lose the sale. Take command, act offended if it helps your cause, be a little flaky and excitable. Good acting skills are a big plus.

Control the Agenda

Make him stick to your important points. Many people don't like to dwell on the difficult points immediately. The seller will try to build the car up in your eyes so that any potential problems seem minor in comparison to the great car there in front of you. Sellers will circle around the bad points and will get to the vital issues only if forced.

Your job is to focus your attention and questions on the things he avoids. This helps you in several ways: It begins to devalue the car in his eyes, thus making a price reduction more likely; it keeps his tension level high, thus making him want to relieve it; and it keeps the conversation going where you want it to, not where he wants it to.

The following scenario puts this together in an easy-to-emulate example.

Seller: Nice car, huh? I am only asking $5,950 for it.

You: The car is certainly usable. But what are you going to do about allowing a mechanic's inspection and giving me a fifteen-day guarantee on the car?

Seller: I hadn't really thought about a fifteen-day guarantee. I've never heard of anyone doing that before. Why don't I just drop the price to $5,750?

You: A price of $5,750 is certainly more realistic, but let's concentrate on the mechanic's inspection and the guarantee, shall we?

Note: You have accepted his price reduction without giving anything in exchange and now are focusing on the two issues you want to discuss. If this discussion goes on long enough, say ten minutes or more, the seller will forget he asked $5,950, will accept the $5,750 price and may be amenable to another price reduction if you drop the guarantee issue.

Seller: OK, if you give up the guarantee issue, I will let you take the car to your mechanic and I will lower the price by $250 to $5,700. OK?

You (flinching): I will accept a $250 price reduction for dropping the guarantee requirement, even though I am worried about the drive train, but we had been talking about a $250 reduction from the last price of $5,750, right? We haven't discussed the $5,950 price since I first got here.

Seller (possibly confused, afraid he will lose the sale and noting that the amount is not huge): I was talking about the original figure, but it is obvious you weren't. If we can settle on this number and do it now, I will settle for $5,500.

You: OK then, that solves the guarantee issue. Just one more small thing and then we can settle the price.

Remember, nothing gets resolved. The tension on the seller is not relieved until you, the buyer, resolve it.

Give Him a Take-It-Or-Leave-It Offer

As mentioned before, this is the way we have been trained to think about financial transactions. This is the main negotiating philosophy in the good old U.S.A. It is promulgated by the way we automatically buy things without negotiating. Apples are 59 cents a pound; if you don't want to pay the price, go somewhere else. However, you usually have more options than to take it or leave it. If an offer is halfway decent, the average American feels he has to react—to either take or leave the offer. As I've said before, try to hear offers as a starting point and resist a take-it-or-leave-it offer when given to you. In addition, you should try experimenting with giving a take-it-or-leave-it offer to the selling party. Who knows, he may just take it.

◆◆◆

If you have decided you want the car at the right price, now is the time to do something about it. I guarantee that if as a buyer you are a little uneasy and uncertain about how to jump into it, then the seller, especially if he is a first-time seller, is feeling even worse.

As mentioned above, you want the seller to be the first to tell you how much money he wants. This is even better if he has given way on some issues before the first price is mentioned.

If you are ready to make an offer, a good lead-in based on the above scenario would be: "I would now like to talk seriously about buying your car. It seems that we have resolved the knock in the engine and the power window problems, and that was after you gave me your bottom price of $5,500. I must tell you that I like the vehicle, and I like you personally and feel you are a fair and honorable person, and I want to buy the car today. However, I feel the price is too high.

Can you help me on that some more? What is your best price for the vehicle if I buy it right now?"

Make sure you are very nice at this point. Prior to starting a serious negotiation, it is useful to compliment the person you are dealing with so as not to give him a reason for dismissing your low bid (and it will be low) and relieving the tension on him because he thinks you are insulting him or playing with his mind.

By mentioning the defects in the car and the resolution of issues after a bottom-line price was mentioned, the stage is set for the seller to drop the price and to accept this lower price as his initial price in a negotiation.

As the negotiation proceeds, pick out some tactics that might work and try them. For instance, try the broken record and "yes, but . . . " tactics and see how he handles them.

Seller: I really think the car is worth $5,500.

You: Yes, I know you like your vehicle and think it is a good price, but I think the car has some problems, and I have to fix them.

Seller: The repairs are minor and won't cost more than $50. If we settle now, I will drop to $5,450.

You: Yes, I am glad you will pay for the repairs, and I thank you for it, but $5,450 is still very high.

You can also try the "you have to do better than that" tactic:

Seller: I really think the car is worth $5,500.

You: I would like to drive home in this vehicle today, but you really have to do better than that.

Seller: What? How much better?

You: You have to do considerably better than that.

If the seller doesn't react well to a particular tactic, try another one. One of them is bound to work. Eventually you will agree on a price. Make sure the car has a valid title and an acceptable price. Confirm that all the conditions have been agreed upon.

Final Transaction Points

After a price has been agreed upon and all the terms have been settled, three final steps must be taken—rather simultaneously—to complete the deal.

1. You, the buyer, will pay the purchase price with either cash or a cashiers' check; occasionally a personal check will suffice. If you do write a personal check, however, it's possible—and entirely acceptable—for the seller either to hold the car until the check clears or go to the bank with you and cash the check in your presence.

2. The seller will give you the car, the title and all keys, and also typically provides manuals, repair logs and smog or emissions inspection reports. The seller signs off at the appropriate place(s) on the title and may provide an additional bill of sale or other necessary paperwork. If the lienholder has not signed off but the seller has a lien release, the seller should provide it. If the lienholder still has to be contacted and the car still needs to be paid off, both parties can go to the bank or the finance company and take care of it. This is usually done before any money changes hands.

3. You must go to the local DMV and have the car put into your name. The seller usually sends in a form to the DMV stating the facts about the transfer. This may vary somewhat from state to state.

Additional
Buying Tips

CHAPTER 28

Buying Cars
Over the Internet

The Internet is changing the way people buy and sell cars (for more on what the Internet can and can't do for you, see chapter two). It's that simple. Consider some recent figures from J.D. Power and Associates: In 1998, Internet car sales accounted for about 1 percent of all auto sales, and in 1999 that number was 2 percent, and for 2000 it is projected to be 4 percent.

Although the above figures might seem small, they are an indicator that car purchases over the Internet are on the rise. What's more, even if people are just beginning to buy through the Internet, they are certainly using it for research purposes, collecting lots of information before they purchase a vehicle (again, see chapter two for more). In 1998, an estimated two million new-car buyers tapped the Net for information.

What's exciting is that Internet buying is new to us all, so there are no seasoned experts. No doubt changes will keep taking place at a fast pace, which will create more confusion (and minimize the number of experts with an upper hand). Right now, both new- and used-car sellers are looking for the best way to market their wares over the Net, and the "players" (the online dealers) are testing how to best sell new and used cars (and also trying to determine which of the two types of sales is more profitable). Recently, for example, AutoNation (http://www.autonation.com) began redirecting itself from being a traditional used-car superstore to concentrating on selling both new and used cars over the Net. More recently it went out of the used-car business entirely. The methods of selling are also being tested and changing. Autobytel (http://www.autobytel.com) is now trying to auction off new and used cars, and in the process is challenging Amazon.com and eBay, both of which have been unsuccessful in their car auctioning attempts. Will Autobytel fare any better?

The Buying and Selling Process

Car buying over the Internet generally doesn't begin until you've selected the car you'd like to purchase, including its color, trim level, engine size, etc. This means you must do a lot of research by yourself (see chapter two), either traditionally (visiting dealerships) or through the Net. Those of you who are stout of heart will go to your local dealer, physically look at the stock, perhaps take a test-drive and then slip away when the salesperson tries to secure a sale. In addition to knowing the car you want, before shopping on the Net, you should also have researched details like insurance, warranties and after-market additions. And you should know the value of your trade-in, or that you will sell your old car yourself.

Lets look at how Internet buying takes place. There are currently two different types of car-buying exchanges operating over the Web.

Buying Services

Buying services are the first type of exchange. What happens is that you contact the site and the site sends you (and other inquiring customers) to subscribing dealers, who will handle the sale, promising to give you a no-haggle, low-priced deal. The dealers pay a referral fee to the referring agency.

The larger buying services are essentially nationwide networks of dealers. Such services claim to have franchise dealerships in every part of the country. Their power is to reduce sales costs by gaining qualified leads through the Internet. They should also be able to streamline the process of buying a car and to pass the cost savings on to you. If you've done your research (you know what a good price is and know what you'd like to buy), you can get a quote at a market price very quickly, with no haggling and no obligation to buy. The paperwork and delivery processes are typically streamlined, too, since more contact time with the customer does not result in the additional profits.

The Internet-buying process begins with you logging on and filling out a purchase request form. You'll need to include information about you and the car you intend to purchase. You E-mail the form to a car-buying service. After the form is received and processed, hopefully within twenty-four hours, the car-buying service attempts to locate a dealer in your area. It then forwards your information to a dealer. The local car dealer contacts you by telephone or by E-mail and hopefully helps you fine-tune your vehicle selection. Then he quotes you a price without haggling.

One potential problem you might encounter at this stage of the game is that the chosen dealer might try to coerce you into buying another car he has on hand instead of your selected car. This is similar to you walking on a lot looking for a blue Sentra and getting a price on a green one, which is in stock now and has a bigger engine and leather seats. Be aware that this can happen. And remember that if you're not comfortable with any aspect of the transaction, you are free to look elsewhere. If you're happy with the deal, the dealer processes the paperwork and you own a car—all without going to the dealership. Sometimes, however, you might actually have to (or even elect to) go to the dealership to take care of the appropriate paperwork, but that's all after the deal is done.

The ultimate drawback to Internet-buying services is that they eventually must make a substantial profit, and to do this they must raise their referral rates. But the rates should always be competitive, because there are so many competing brokers on the Net.

Buying service sites are typified by the likes of Autobytel (http://www.autobytel.com), CarPoint (http://www.carpoint.msn.com), AutoWeb (http://www.autoweb.com), and AutoVantage (http://www.autovantage.com). Of course there are many others, but these are good places to start.

Bidding Brokers (Backward Auctions)

The second way to buy a car is using "bidding brokers," or what I call a "backward auction." What happens here is that the company you select will put your name out to many dealers and have them bid on a car that has your chosen specifications. So instead of being fixed up with one local dealer who will make you a price on a car you request, your specs are distributed to many local dealers who submit bids. The "bidding brokers" indicate they will get you five quotes.

Good "bidding broker" sites to begin with are AutoAdvisor (http://autoadvisor.com) and CarBargains (http://www.carbargains .com).

Here's an example of how a "bidding broker" site works:

CarBargains, an auction-type broker, has a four-step process. You contact them through their Web site, mentioned above, and fill out a form.

1. You tell them the make, model and style of the car you want to buy.
2. They say they will get at least five local dealers to bid against each other for this car.
3. CarBargains.com will send you some items including:
   - dealer quote sheets
   - invoices showing the dealer cost
   - used-car pricing
   - financing options
   - extended service contracts
   - other useful information
4. You contact a dealership (presumably the lowest bidder).
5. You identify yourself as a CarBargains client, select the car, confirm the bid and drive off into the sunset.

As for fees, CarBargains currently charges you about $165; AutoAdvisor charges about $350.

Nonbrokers

Remember that a broker is a person who sells what he doesn't own (see chapter two). What is emerging right now as a third new-car buying option is essentially a nonbroker model, in which companies buy vehicles directly from a local dealer and deliver it to you. And they give you a great guaranteed price. These nonbrokers quote you a price, and then try to get it from a local dealer at a better price. If they can't do this, they eat the difference. Most demand a nominal deposit of $500 or less.

Two good nonbroker sites (there are more, so research on your own) are CarsDirect (http://www.carsdirect.com) and carOrder (http://www.carorder.com).

Buying Directly From the Manufacturer

If consumers can buy through a broker, it seems to be a short step to buy directly from GM or any other manufacturer. It will happen. What this will mean is the unraveling of the traditional franchise dealership. Right now it's not yet legal but you can see signs of it beginning. GM, for example, tried to do this in Texas with its DriverSite project, but the local Department of Transportation nixed the idea. NADA, a trade organization of auto dealers, is fighting GM's effort to directly sell new and used cars to retail customers in the Houston area. Not surprisingly, NADA is opposed to anything that circumvents the dealer.

My guess is that GM and others will be remarketing (a fancy term for selling) its used cars directly to the public in the next two years, using its Web site (http://www.gmbuypower.com). Already, the site enables consumers to select a vehicle for a road test. Consumers can complete the sales transaction at the site's store, where sales consultants assist in "no-haggle transactions."

Final Thoughts

It can be difficult buying used cars with confidence over the Net. I must say, however, that I do particularly like the AutoTrader site. Registering your own cars for sale is easy. It took me less than five minutes to put my vehicle in this cyberlot. When looking for a car to buy, I was also able to get phone numbers and E-mail addresses for most of the sellers. After you find the vehicle you are looking for, the process is very much like going through the classifieds, except you have more options. The prices asked were nothing great; however, they were pretty much retail prices. The only problem is the difficulty of negotiating for price with someone you can't see for a vehicle you haven't seen.

Although the Net is still in its infancy, you can expect more opportunities to buy through Web sites in the future. Heck, it's possible you'll be lucky enough never to step foot into another dealership.

Web Sites of Interest

These sites will help you with buying cars over the Internet:

AutoAdvisor, http://www.autoadvisor.com. This site provides consulting services.

Autobytel, http://www.autobytel.com. The Autobytel site works by first having you submit a purchase request. It takes about five minutes and includes your personal information, info about your trade-in and rough information about what you want to buy. The site promises your local Autobytel.com accredited dealer will contact you by phone or E-mail within twenty-four hours to provide vehicle pricing and delivery. Autobytel also indicates that after the dealer contacts you, you can accept the dealer's offer or walk away. There is no risk, no obligation, no haggle and no hassle. And—best of all—it's free!

AutoTrader, http://www.autotrader.com. There are a lot of vehicles here.

Autovantage, http://www.autovantage.com. This is a good starting place for new or used cars. It also provides a 360 degree-look at various vehicles. What a neat toy!

Autoweb, http://www.autoweb.com. You'll find interesting information on maintenance, financing and research.

CarBargains, http://www.carbargains.com. Their motto is "Make dealers bid for your business," and their services cost $165.

carOrder, http://www.carorder.com. This is a good place to start to find a car or build a car.

CarPoint, http://www.carpoint.msn.com. Prices, quotes, *Blue Book*—it's all there.

CarsDirect, http://www.carsdirect.com. This is a good site to start looking.

Edmunds, http://www.edmunds.com. This is a great general Web site.

FightingChance, *http://www.fightingchance.com.* James Bragg, author of *The Car Buyer's and Leaser's Negotiating Bible* (Random House) and operator of the Fighting Chance Web site thinks the best way for anyone to negotiate for price is to avoid the showroom. I recommend you check out this site. Bragg also sells an information package that might make sense for some of you. He suggests using your fax machine as your primary tool. I think E-mail would work as well. Fax or E-mail your new-car request to as many local dealers as you can and ask them to quote on a vehicle. Bang one against the other until you get where you want to go. [Jim (Spike) Bragg and I met for lunch awhile ago. New cars are his real forte.]

GoTo at *http://www.goto.com.* This site impresses me with its ability to point you to lots of good car information.

CHAPTER 29

Special Concerns for Women Buyers

Deborah Tannen's landmark book, *You Just Don't Understand* (Morrow, 1990), provided me with great insights into the differences between the thinking processes and communication styles of men and women. While *The Insider's Guide to Buying a New or Used Car* is not a psychology book, I do think the following information will help women understand why negotiation has not been easy for them and will teach them a new style that is more appropriate for car buying.

Tannen focuses on the impact that same-sex communication in the formative years has on the style of interaction we carry with us into our adult years. As a generalization, males tend to play hard and to compete in groups, while females tend to be more cooperative. The groups negotiate differently—males to win, females to cooperate. These different negotiating methods present different problems for each gender. Unfortunately for the women, the male style of negotiation is the one most frequently encountered. Buying a car or a house requires the competitive, male style of negotiation.

Earlier, I talked about the commando raid (a one-time transaction after which neither party will meet the other again, and in which cutthroat tactics are appropriate). According to both Tannen's definition and my conversations with women, this type of negotiation is particularly difficult for most women. It just goes against their grain. Obviously, there are some women for whom hard negotiation is easy and some males for whom it seems impossible. This information is by necessity a generalization.

One of the key ingredients in successful negotiating to create tension. As a rule, this is difficult for women to do. They are trained to ease tension, not to create it. I illustrate this in the classes I teach on how to buy a car. I try to help students hone their negotiating skills, including their ability to create tension. As a preliminary exercise, I choose a male from the audience and strongly criticize his appearance and apparel. I make terrible comments about his clothes, his fashion sense and, finally, his posture. Then I invite any woman in the class to do the same thing to any other woman in the class. I explain that everyone knows that it is just an exercise and that the volunteer can apologize in advance. I even tell her to explain that she is just doing the exercise to show up a chauvinistic, egoistic, obnoxious male. I have never had a taker. This is just the type of attack necessary for a commando raid.

In addition to the difficulty women have in creating tension, there are six primary trouble spots for women in using a commando raid. These are physical safety, win-lose situations, product knowledge, victim status, required forcefulness and direct confrontation.

Physical Safety

PROBLEM. In some car-buying situations, fear for physical safety is a factor. As mentioned elsewhere, I often shop for cars with my son Andrew. Both of us are 6 feet, 2 inches and over 230 pounds. We do not feel threatened carrying cash and going into a stranger's house to negotiate over price. I also don't feel threatened when going for test-drives with people I don't know. I will often get calls from female acquaintances asking me to accompany her and a male customer who is inquiring about her used car. Unfortunately, security has to be a priority for women.

As a result, it is more threatening and difficult for women to sell their cars themselves. Test-drives are not the only discomforting possibility; many women are understandably reluctant to give out their names and addresses to people they do not know. Women's safety concerns are realistic in the world as we know it.

SOLUTION. Those women who do decide to sell their cars themselves are already at a disadvantage if they are physically intimidated by male customers. While it makes the process a bit more cumbersome, I suggest that single women who choose to sell their used cars arrange to have friends go with them on test-drives and to be in their houses when potential buyers arrive.

Win-Lose Situations

PROBLEM. It is particularly difficult for women to negotiate in a way that isn't "nice" to the opposing negotiator. In car buying, there is no long-term friendship to cement, no reason to make the car seller like you. Once the transaction is over, you will, in all likelihood, never see this person again. As Tannen stresses, women work to create connection. This is in direct opposition to the tactics required to win in a car negotiation.

SOLUTION. Mental preparation is the key here. You must be prepared to drive a killer deal. This is done by collecting information during the negotiation. This is actually easier for women than for men. According to Tannen, women are better at opening conversations and asking questions. One key to getting a big win is to ask for it. Ask, ask, ask. Don't be shy or beat around the bush.

Product Knowledge

PROBLEM. As a rule, many women are at a great disadvantage in car transactions because of their lack of auto knowledge. Many men don't know a fuel injector from a valve lifter any more than do most women. Yet, in order to evaluate a new or used vehicle, you must be able to put a value on the vehicle. This presents a problem to all buyers, but it is more of a problem for women than it is for men. Most men have had more conversations about car value, etc., than have most women.

SOLUTION. Remember the section on homework? This section is of paramount importance to women looking for a car. The more research you have done into your particular automobile, the less easily you will be confused or intimidated—or dismissed—by a professional car salesperson.

Having said that, let me stress that it isn't enough. You must at least appear marginally knowledgeable on the mechanics of the car as well—especially for used-car purchases. There is a lot more negotiating power available to you if you have checked the exhaust for black soot and checked the condition of the oil and can combine that information with the research you have done. To tell a seller that his car is not only rated poorly, but has obvious mechanical problems beyond those concerns is going to devalue his car in his eyes.

If you do not possess enough product knowledge by the time you go to look for a car, take along someone who can help you. It is to your advantage to pay a mechanic to look at a vehicle. Not only can the mechanic locate any problems and put your mind at ease, the threat of a real expert examining the car is sometimes enough to intimidate a seller into coming down on price. If you are selling your car, pay a garage to inspect your car carefully and provide an itemized checklist to present to potential buyers. Get any help you can. Remember that you can compensate for any deficiencies you have by utilizing the expertise of those around you. It is not important that you know everything, just that you know how to find the answers to any questions you might have.

Victim Status

PROBLEM. Claiming victim status has become a great negotiating ploy of the 1980s and 90s. The car salesperson knows this and will try to use it on you ("I have to sell a certain number of cars this week or I may lose my job because my boss is so unfair"), but it will not work on him. If you appear weaker, you will not get a better or fairer deal; you will lose the respect of the dealer and he may well treat you like a victim.

SOLUTION. There is no way that you can "guilt" a car salesperson into giving you a better deal. It just doesn't work that way. You must negotiate strongly and take charge. Otherwise, you will not get the deal you deserve.

Required Forcefulness

PROBLEM. In order to win in negotiating the best price for a car, you must be forceful and direct. One of the best tactics is to force or browbeat the other party into submission. Wear him out, beat him down, make him want to give in just to end the confrontation. These are not elegant tactics, but they work amazingly well.

SOLUTION. These tactics only work if you can be convincing. If this makes you so uncomfortable that you cannot possibly pull it off, remember the other tactics covered in the book. Also, there are some people against whom they won't work at all. See what response you get from the opposing negotiator. Does he get defensive and hostile, or does he seem intimidated? If the tactics work, keep them up. If they don't, try the other tactics covered in the book.

Direct Confrontation

PROBLEM. Expect commando raids to be characterized by direct confrontation. Expect this from the other party, and do not allow yourself to become intimidated. Money is at stake here for both the buyer and the seller. Be prepared to stand tough in the face of harsh directness on the part of the salesperson. Pay special attention to the advice on negotiating that's offered in this book. By being a strong force and resisting the temptation to give in to the pressure of the salesperson, you can get more car for your money.

SOLUTION. You can counter the intimidating tactics of others in several ways. If they try to intimidate you by crowding your physical space, ask if there is a place you can sit down to negotiate. Then put some distance between you and the other party. Counter his fast-driving, intimidating forcefulness by slowing down the negotiations and going over things more slowly and thoroughly. Remember, stay in charge. If the salesperson is rude, remind him that it is your money, that you really want to buy a car today and that you will take your money and your business elsewhere if he insists on being rude to you. Do not allow him to treat you like an inferior being—you are not. You are the customer, and you are in charge, whether he likes it or not.

Web Sites of Interest

The following Web sites are geared toward women in the market for a car:

http://www.womanmotorist.com. Woman Motorist features articles, classifieds and more—all targeted to women drivers.

http://www.caranddriver.com. The Web version of *Car and*

Driver magazine reviews new cars each month. Check the extensive buying guide.

http://www.cartalk.com. Car Talk is recommended by celebrity surfer Heloise. Radio personalities Click and Clack share their advice on car maintenance and everything else.

http://www.womensautohelp.com. The Women's Auto Help Center has good articles on negotiation and the like. It also has good links. Get the latest info on automotive technology like airbags and global positioning satellite systems, reviews of new models and info on your car's impact on your health and your family. And don't miss the Q&A department.

http://www.thunval.com/racing. This is the Thunder Valley Racing site. If car racing fires up your engines, then head to this site, which is dedicated to providing opportunities and encouragement to women race car drivers.

CHAPTER 30

Handling Trouble Legally

In all auto transactions, even the best of them, things go wrong. Things are rarely perfect in the world of automobile sales. It could be anything from a rattle in the front to a transmission that suddenly goes south. In car sales, where the stakes are large, customer dissatisfaction becomes a serious issue. It seems that everyone who has ever driven has an auto horror story.

Let me give you some advice on what will work and what will not in situations where, as the Rolling Stones would say, you "can't get no satisfaction." The other party may not give you what you want, but you will be treated seriously and have a better chance to get redress for your grievance if you tell him that before you see anybody else (a regulatory agency lawyer, etc.), you want to talk in hopes of resolving the issue peacefully and without rancor.

The following examples show how I work with extremely irate people. I often feel that no one is more irate than a person whose car has just been repossessed because he hasn't made his payments. These are emotional exchanges, but they can be handled relatively smoothly and settled without reference to litigation. Whether you are the customer or the dealer, you have a problem you want to resolve and turn into a win-win situation.

Usually, before I go to the extreme action of getting my repo guy (actually it is a man and his mother—yes, you heard me right—who do the dirty work of physically repossessing my vehicles), I make five to ten calls, leaving messages on answering machines or pagers, exhorting the person, his relative or whoever picks up the phone to get in here and pay. In spite of my most above-and-beyond-the-call-of-duty efforts, I still find myself repossessing a percentage of my customers' vehicles.

Initially, assume that the customer wants to please you and right the situation. Try not to say or do anything that will produce a negative reaction. In the following exchange involving the customer after his car has been repossessed, you will notice the employment of some of the negotiating techniques mentioned earlier.

> **Customer** (storming into my office): Awe, man, why did you get my car?
>
> **Me:** Tom, I can't believe you made me do it.
>
> **Customer:** What the hell are you talking about? Give me back my car.
>
> **Me:** Tom, I must have called you twenty-five times trying to get you to come in and pay. What's wrong with you?
>
> **Customer:** I don't know, man. Money has been real short recently, and I meant to call you.
>
> **Me:** Look, Tom, I know times are tough. Sit down and let's see what it will take for you to get your car back today. Is that OK? Oh, do you want a cup of coffee before we start? Tell me what is going on in your life.

Then I prepare to sympathetically listen to some really long, sad stories. I get him to vent his anger. I get in close, hit him with guilt, find out what kind of terms he needs to continue to make payments and then make a settlement he can live with.

I routinely deal with another kind of "mad bull," a person who has fallen behind in her payments and is experiencing car repair problems and doesn't want to pay because her car is not working. Here is a typical scenario.

> **Customer:** This damn car is not worth a #@!*!, and it hasn't run well for three months, and I'm not going to pay for a car that doesn't work well. (etc.)
>
> **Me** (after listening for a while until she has made her point): Sue, if you lose this car, how are you going to get to work?
>
> **Customer:** It's a problem.
>
> **Me:** Tell you what, I guess you can't afford to pay for the car

and get it fixed. Am I right?

Customer: Yes, and the car is a piece of junk.

Me: Tell you what, suppose I fix the car at a dealer's price, you cover the cost of the parts, which won't be too bad, I finance you for the labor and you can pay for this over the next four weeks. Would that be OK? We can have it done by tomorrow if you want.

Customer (usually): Yeah, I guess that would work.

In this kind of emotionally charged situation, both parties should avoid escalation by not mentioning certain fighting words.

Words to Avoid
No-No Number One

Mentioning the words, "I am going to talk to a lawyer," is not a negotiating tactic but a useless, belligerent way of turning the very person who can do you the most good into an angry, uncooperative opponent. It also marks you as a neophyte of the "argue with me and I will kick your butt" variety. That's because every dealer knows that the most a lawyer will do is give the customer advice at $250 an hour or write the dealer a threatening letter. Most dealers, because the auto business is highly regulated and monitored, have their paperwork in order and will fend off a lawyer easily. So after your lawyer threat, most dealers will not give you the time of day.

No-No Number Two

Uttering the phrase, "I am going to take you to small-claims court" is another nonviable threat that dealers are not afraid of. Never threaten them with court action, especially if you don't have the resolution to go through with it. Most people don't know what to do and eventually lose and are embarrassed in small-claims court even though the small-claims courts generally favor the little guy. Most people don't have the knowledge or the endurance to win.

If you decide to try it anyway, there are many good books available on the subject. One pretty good one is called *Everybody's Guide to Small Claims Court*, by Ralph Warner, and is put out by Nolo Press of Berkeley, California. There is also a national guide by Warner. Call (510) 549-1976 and request a catalog; it has great stuff in it. You might also call your local small-claims court system for more information.

To Sue or Not to Sue, That is the Question

Usually, in the small-claims court arena, where most of your cases are going to end up, cases are argued without the help of lawyers; people represent themselves. Their presentations (both sides) are usually emotional, disjointed and focused on why they are mad rather than strictly on the issues.

In a typical auto court case, the average guy goes to the judge and claims, for instance, that he stopped his payments because the dealer misrepresented the car, and as a result, he had to put lots of money into fixing it up instead of into his car payments.

> **Dealer** (merely producing all the signed documents and paperwork): Here is his deficiency balance.
>
> **Judge:** Sir, did you take your car to a mechanic before you bought it?
>
> **Customer:** No, sir, the dealer said the car was OK, and it looked OK, so I went along with it.
>
> **Judge:** Did you realize that the contract said "as is"?
>
> **Customer:** Well, I saw that, but I didn't really know what it meant.
>
> **Judge:** How long before the vehicle broke down?
>
> **Customer:** About two weeks.
>
> **Judge:** Decision for the dealer.

The case is over.
Similar scenarios go as follows:

> **Customer:** I stopped paying because the car broke down one month after I bought it and required $1,250 to fix the engine.
>
> **Judge:** So why did you stop paying?
>
> **Customer:** Why should I pay for a car that doesn't run?
>
> **Judge:** Does this mean you don't pay for clothes you don't wear

or jewelry you don't have on at the moment?

Customer: Uh, well. . . .

Judge: Decision for the dealer.

The case is over.

Perhaps the customer says, "I live in this country expecting to find freedom and justice," or something emotionally charged and irrelevant like that. Invariably the judge will say, "Decision for the dealer," and the case is over.

Here Comes the Judge

I recently interviewed a judge in the San Bernardino, California, court system and got some interesting feedback. Here's how a small-claims court judge who handles a lot of automobile-related cases sees the battlefield from his bench.

Of the court cases he hears that involve vehicles, this judge feels that about 80 percent of them involve repair problems and only about 20 percent involve buying and selling of cars.

Most repair issues involve:

- mechanics cutting corners in repairs, leading to long-term problems
- repair shops neglecting to provide itemized bills and/or other agreements in writing
- repair shops charging for unauthorized repairs
- repair shops charging for unnecessary parts
- miscommunication or lack of communication as to what should be done

A typical repair problem case might be summed up as, "He fixed my car, charged me $825 and it still doesn't work."

Cases involving the buying and selling of vehicles center on two issues:

1. Buyer's remorse—"I don't know why I bought that lemon."
2. Lack of money—"The car is broken, and I can't afford to fix it and make my payments."

A typical buy or sell problem might be stated as follows: "He repossessed my car, and now he wants me to pay the balance of the loan."

Your Worst Arguments

These usually don't work at all:

Reason 1: "I was lied to, and the situation was misrepresented to me, so I shouldn't have to pay." (No substantiation of any of the charges is provided, just heated jawing.)

Reason 2: "The car is broken, and therefore I shouldn't have to pay for it."

Reason 3: "I can't afford to pay for it now."

Reason 4: "I paid too much for the car/repair/service contract, and it wasn't worth it."

Reason 5: "I didn't know what I was doing, and I signed the contracts because the salesperson was so nice [or whatever reason you give].

Your Best Arguments

These usually have a good chance of working:

Reason 1: "I was lied to, and the situation was misrepresented to me, so I shouldn't have to pay." (This is substantiated with bills, witnesses, documents, etc.)

Reason 2: "There are technical problems with the contract itself, such as lines not filled in, missing signatures or the wrong vehicle is described."

Reason 3: "The financing fell apart, so I should be able to unwind the deal." (This is called failure of consideration.)

Reason 4: "There are some serious safety issues that are not trivial, and the vehicle is now unsafe to drive."

Homework Again

It is amazing that the number one complaint that works, claiming misrepresentation, is also the number one complaint that doesn't work, if done poorly and without substantiation. The difference here is that claiming fraud and misrepresentation works when you have a case and when you do your homework.

Winning in Court

According to the judge, claiming misrepresentation and fraud can work if you do the following:

- Research the issue and the law. Understand what is possible and what is not. Get a working background of what is possible.
- Decide what you want to accomplish and pursue that. Don't try to sue for everything, including a flat tax system and saving the whales.
- Organize the case so you can describe it easily. It works best if you can outline your case and put it on paper for the judge to read.
- Be calm and concise during your presentation. Don't ineptly ramble during a presentation and get emotional.
- Establish your credibility by bringing in supporting evidence like a certified mechanic (this is better than just a letter from him); competent, to-the-point witnesses; hard facts; pictures.
- Take the initiative to have the vehicle checked out by a competent mechanic before you take possession of the vehicle. If you don't care enough or are too cheap to have the car inspected, you will have to bear the burden of having it fixed later.

The Judge's Pet Peeves

It is interesting here to see what the person on the bench needs to make a decision in your favor.

The key element here is to establish your credibility as a petitioner or defendant. A bad presentation can severely undermine your credibility and also annoy any judge. It is important not to prejudice your case by doing any of the following, which just happen to be the judge's pet peeves:

- lying or severely bending the truth
- arguing with the judge when she is explaining her rationale for

doing what she is doing
- showing disrespect for anyone—the judge, the other party or her witnesses, etc.
- sarcasm
- not listening to what is being said

A bad attitude can destroy your credibility more easily than anything. Judges really want to decide the case on the facts, but if you irritate them, they give your views less credence, and you will be penalized accordingly. Both parties initially start off with the same credibility, but one side or the other has the capability to destroy his believability.

Alternatives to Small-Claims Court

The best way to get satisfaction from a dealer is through his paperwork and through any gross malfeasance he has performed, not by claiming to have hurt feelings because the car doesn't run well.

Let's say you and the dealer have varying opinions of who should pay for after-sales repairs on your newly bought used 1994 Ford T-Bird. Here are some things you might say to a dealer that will get him to give you his full attention:

Tactic 1: "I want to unwind the deal right now, and you will do it because there is a mistake in the paperwork that misled me into thinking we had another kind of deal." (Actually, this is only a starting negotiating position. What you may want to do is to keep the car and have him pay for part of the repairs.)

Car dealers, like everybody else, are constrained to do their paperwork correctly. Many of them will do it flawlessly, but there are a lot of little details that must be done correctly. There are forms they should fill out and give to you, there are spaces on the contract that must be filled out and there are places that must be signed.

Have a lawyer check the filling out of the contract, and if there is a problem, act on it to get what you feel is just. This is not trivial, and it will require a firm resolve and some determination to see the problem to the end. It will not be a quick-and-dirty, in-and-out, hit-and-run, but it is a possible course of action.

Tactic 2: "If I cannot get this issue resolved, I am going to DMV investigations."

This is a serious, serious threat to any legally registered dealer but not much of a threat to a civilian selling his own car or jumping title on an occasional vehicle. (A lot of people buy cars by having the sellers sign off on the titles. The buyers then fix up the vehicles and sell them at a profit. They just pass along the fixed-up cars and paperwork without putting their names on the titles. This is called "jumping title.")

For a dealer, being "introduced" to DMV investigations is a serious matter. If a dissatisfied customer threatens this action, it is tantamount to a declaration of war. This threat is not the first thing you do, but it is the last. The DMV people usually answer all complaints, but if the complaint seems frivolous, they will initiate a discourse with the dealer as follows (I know—it has happened to me):

DMV person: We have received a complaint about you, but I think it is frivolous.

Dealer: Who is the person?

DMV person: Here is her name, and here is her complaint. Does it have merit?

Dealer: She is a flake, and here is what happened. . . .

DMV person: Can I see the file? (He inspects the file for a while.) Just as I thought, there is no cause for action. Thank you. Oh, by the way, I am writing you up for a few minor violations because there are no buyers' guides on two cars and you didn't have your new salesperson's license displayed on the wall.

The dealer knows that if he gets a visit from the DMV, he probably will not get away unscathed even though he may very well beat the charges against him. Your threat is a concern to the dealer because he wants to remain invisible to the agency that regulates him, and that he and many other people describe as a "group of storm troopers." Give him an out that he can live with and that makes sense for you. If you do this, you probably can reach some agreement. Make the demands reasonable. Wait three days for him to consider this threat. Check back with him, and then, if necessary, complain to the DMV.

Tactic 3: You could threaten to go to an organization like the Better Business Bureau, but my personal feeling is that this is not much of a threat and should be avoided unless your only goal is to just "spit in his soup."

Tactic 4: The threat that you will paint lemons on your car and hire picketers to stand outside the dealership is a real one, but unless you convince the dealer you are serious, he might not take it seriously. Also what do you do if he threatens to counterpicket you at your office, house or business? This should be a last, last resort used only if you lose your court case and are temperamentally suited to be a public spectacle.

In Sum

This section on how to handle trouble should really be called "How to Avoid Trouble." That's where the bullfighter approach and the psychology of negotiation come in. There are alternative paths that often can provide redress to your auto transaction problems. Try them first. Hopefully your efforts and expertise will lead to a win-win situation for the buyer and the seller. But if you are determined to seek legal recourse, be sure to do your homework, prepare your case well and present it in the best way you can. Equally important is determination to see the whole long and often aggravating legal process to the end. Remember the old adage: The wheels of justice grind slowly. But the process does work for those with the knowledge, patience and perseverance to pursue their goals.

Web Sites of Interest

Check out these sites for more legal information:

http://www.nolo.com. The Nolo Web site offers lots of free legal advice in plain English.

http://www.kingfeatures.com/features/cclack/index.htm. Where would we be without "Click and Clack Talk Cars," by Tom and Ray Magliozzi, to tell us how to get out of auto trouble?

Index